Prisoners of Their Premises

Prisoners of Their Premises

How Unexamined Assumptions Lead to War and Other Policy Debacles

GEORGE C. EDWARDS III

THE UNIVERSITY OF CHICAGO PRESS   CHICAGO AND LONDON

The University of Chicago Press, Chicago 60637
The University of Chicago Press, Ltd., London
© 2022 by George C. Edwards III.
All rights reserved. No part of this book may be used or reproduced in any manner whatsoever without written permission, except in the case of brief quotations in critical articles and reviews. For more information, contact the University of Chicago Press, 1427 E. 60th St., Chicago, IL 60637.
Published 2022
Printed in the United States of America

31 30 29 28 27 26 25 24 23 22   1 2 3 4 5

ISBN-13: 978-0-226-82280-8 (cloth)
ISBN-13: 978-0-226-82282-2 (paper)
ISBN-13: 978-0-226-82281-5 (e-book)
DOI: https://doi.org/10.7208/chicago/9780226822815.001.0001

Library of Congress Cataloging-in-Publication Data

Names: Edwards, George C., author.
Title: Prisoners of their premises : how unexamined assumptions lead to war and other policy debacles / George C. Edwards III.
Other titles: How unexamined assumptions lead to war and other policy debacles
Description: Chicago ; London : The University of Chicago Press, 2022. | Includes bibliographical references and index.
Identifiers: LCCN 2022007568 | ISBN 9780226822808 (cloth) | ISBN 9780226822822 (paperback) | ISBN 9780226822815 (ebook)
Subjects: LCSH: Political science—Decision making. | Political science—Decision making—Case studies. | International relations—Decision making. | International relations—Decision making—Case studies. | Politics and war—United States. | United States—Foreign relations.
Classification: LCC JF1525.D4 E39 2022 | DDC 352.3/3—dc23/eng/20220325
LC record available at https://lccn.loc.gov/2022007568

TO BARRY
WHO PERSISTED IN ENCOURAGING THIS PROJECT AS ONLY A BELOVED
YOUNGER BROTHER CAN

v

Contents

Preface   ix

CHAPTER 1.   The Power of Premises   1

CHAPTER 2.   Assuming Problems: The War in Vietnam   10

CHAPTER 3.   Ignoring and Underestimating Problems   36

CHAPTER 4.   Ignoring and Underestimating Problems:
             The Chinese Intervention in Korea in 1950   55

CHAPTER 5.   Assuming *and* Ignoring Problems:
             The Invasion of Iraq   78

CHAPTER 6.   No Silver Bullet   101

Notes   109

Index   147

Preface

At the core of public policy are decisions. The most important of these, such as preparing for an enemy attack or going to war, are made by chief executives and other high-level officials. History shows that when faced with such choices, leaders frequently make calamitous decisions with devastating consequences for their country—and other nations as well. Moreover, these same officials often persist in failed policies, resulting in yet more death and destruction.

How can we explain this pattern of self-destructive behavior? Are decision makers simply incompetent, irresponsible, or psychologically flawed? There are exceptions, of course, but typically those who make decisions regarding war and peace are accomplished, diligent, stable, and patriotic men and women.

Perhaps leaders' advisory systems or their styles of decision making have been dysfunctional. There is no doubt that there has been plenty of room for improvement, but can we really conclude that better-organized advisory systems would have caused leaders to anticipate the attack on Pearl Harbor or the Chinese intervention in Korea in 1950? Would they have prevented the war in Vietnam, the invasion of Iraq, or the protracted conflicts in those countries?

I have puzzled over these questions for half a century. I begin with a paradox. Decision making, the most important function of the president, is the one we understand the least. The reason is simple: it is difficult to study decisions. Obtaining timely access to policymakers and extensive information on their thoughts and deliberations is problematic.

Fortunately, scholars of international relations have written innumerable case studies of foreign policy decisions, many of which are of high quality. These scholars have also produced more general treatises on decision making, which are invaluable to anyone seeking to understand the subject. All this work provides a wealth of information as to the participants in decision making and the information and options they considered. What it has not done is attempt to isolate the role of officials' premises in their decisions.

I am hardly the first author to think about the impact of premises. Useful insights are scattered throughout the literature on international relations. My point of departure is to focus explicitly on the foundation of all decisions: identifying problems. Before officials gather information and consider options, and before they make choices among alternatives, no matter what the decision-making process, they must implicitly or explicitly decide whether there is a problem to solve and, if there is, what their goals are in dealing with it. I explore the impact of the premises already in decision makers' heads before they begin considering their options and making choices.

Two well-understood aspects of the human psyche, limits on rationality and motivated reasoning, provide the potential for premises to exercise a powerful influence on policymaking. It is not surprising that they often distort leaders' processing of information and bias them against changing their minds. If decision makers' premises lead them to assume erroneously the existence of a problem, the rest of the decision-making process will be fatally flawed. Premises may also blind policymakers to problems that require their attention or cause them to underestimate the likelihood of problems arising. Similarly, premises about the efficacy of a policy may distort their evaluations of its success and discourage their consideration of changes to it.

I engage in a thought experiment. Focusing specifically on policymakers' premises, I ask, "What if we knew little else about the influences on decision makers aside from their core premises regarding a policy?" I then examine some of the most important foreign policy decisions of American history and find that in cases such as Vietnam in 1964–1965 and Iraq in 2002–2003, policymakers mistakenly assumed that problems existed and required forceful action by the United States. Similarly, leaders often overlooked looming problems, ranging from the attack on Pearl Harbor to the Chinese intervention in Korea and the aftermath of the invasion of Iraq, that required their urgent attention but did not receive it. They also ignored fundamental problems with the options they chose, such as Jefferson's embargo or Kennedy's Bay of Pigs invasion. To round out the picture, I also address similar problems among allied leaders dealing with the

German invasions of France in 1914 and the Soviet Union in 1941. In all these cases, the decisions of capable, hardworking, and well-intentioned officials ended in disaster.

Leaders are not the only ones who may become prisoners of their premises. In 2002–2003, I supported the invasion of Iraq. I remember attending a Council on Foreign Relations meeting where a former CIA director detailed the reasons that such a policy was necessary and would result in a relatively costless success. I had been offering the same litany to others. I spent most of 2002 at the School of Advanced Study at the University of London and was ready to confront those protesting a possible war. Their arguments were generally uninformed. (Saddam Hussein was not a satisfactory leader and the invasion was not all about oil.) I even made sure to wear an American flag lapel pin when I attended the ballet at Covent Garden on the evening of the largest antiwar protest, in case anyone wished to engage in political discussion. It is just as well that no one did, because I was wrong. I had failed to rigorously evaluate my premises.

Unexamined premises plague public policy. I have no simple solution to the problem, but we can be certain that the first step in ameliorating it is understanding the power of premises.

George C. Edwards III

CHAPTER ONE

The Power of Premises

"We are never deceived; we deceive ourselves."—Johann Wolfgang von Goethe

The specter of catastrophe haunts the history of public policy. Capable, dedicated, and patriotic men and women frequently make disastrous decisions that squander the lives, fortunes, and goodwill of their fellow citizens. Why do such debacles occur when the incentives are so strong to make good decisions and there is every reason to believe that leaders strive to do so? Why is it so difficult to for decision makers to deal with facts that challenge their understanding of events and issues? Moreover, why are they often slow to adjust their policies in the face of failure?

Premises

Leaders and their aides bring to office sets of beliefs about politics, policy, human nature, and social causality—in other words, beliefs about how the world works as it does and why it does so.[1] Decision makers have in their heads dozens of policy-related premises, such as the intentions and capabilities of other nations, the predilections of other leaders and their responsiveness to a variety of incentives, the capacity of their own governments to produce results, and the consequences of their current policies.

These beliefs provide a frame of reference for identifying problems, evaluating policy options, filtering information and giving it meaning, and establishing boundaries of action.[2] Most important, premises predispose leaders to make certain decisions.[3]

One explanation for ruinous policies is that decision makers are often *prisoners of their premises*. This captivity discourages them from questioning the fundamental assumptions underlying a policy and leads them to ignore or dismiss facts and arguments pointing toward a different decision. Historian Barbara Tuchman termed assessing a situation in terms of preconceived, fixed notions while ignoring or rejecting contrary evidence as "wooden-headedness." In Tuchman's view, acting according to one's predispositions and refusing to be influenced by facts is a form of self-deception, epitomized by her summary of Philip II of Spain: "No experience of the failure of his policy could shake his belief in its essential excellence."[4]

Unfortunately, the incidence of such dysfunctional behavior is not limited to inbred hereditary monarchs and plays a significant role in more contemporary government decision making.[5] Two core traits of human beings assure that premises will play a prominent role in decision making.

Limits on Rationality

There is widespread understanding that there are important limits on the possibility of rational decision making in politics as in other areas of life. Sometimes we refer to these limits as "bounded rationality."[6] There are cognitive limits to the ability of the human mind to process and analyze information. There are also limits on the time a person can devote to any decision. Finally, decision makers, particularly public officials, face intractable difficulties in choosing policies, including:

- Identifying problems
- Selecting goals for policies
- Prioritizing among goals
- Choosing among a restricted range of options and incomplete information on them
- Predicting and measuring the consequences of policy alternatives
- Applying alternative criteria, such as efficiency and equity, to evaluating predicted consequences

Decision makers cope with these decision-making challenges by simplifying and organizing their world. They are "cognitive misers" who take shortcuts whenever they can.[7] One broad strategy is satisficing, which entails seeking a satisfactory solution rather than an optimal one by searching through the available alternatives until an acceptable threshold is met.[8] Thus, humans prefer to think efficiently rather than analytically. They do so by applying a number of heuristics or mental shortcuts in their decision making.[9] Although more efficient than systematic analysis, reliance on heuristics increases the probability of biased information processing because cognitive misers ignore much of the relevant information to reduce the demands on their minds or they overuse some kinds of information to avoid searching for more information.

Beliefs or premises fulfill a need for cognitive simplicity by making our complex and contradictory world comprehensible. They also help busy people cope with complex decisions to which they can devote limited time. Despite the utility of beliefs in facilitating efficiency in decision making, they provide their holders a simplified and thus inaccurate representation of reality. Sometimes these inevitable distortions are severe and lead to disastrous policies. Nevertheless, because they are useful for coming to grips with the complexity of the world, basic beliefs about politics and policy are resistant to change.

Motivated Reasoning

Cognitive limits explain why we hold premises and why there is a strong potential for them to be faulty. In addition, people simplify reality not only to deal with the world's complexities but also to meet their psychological and social needs related to decision making. Meeting these requisites sustains the power of premises.

The physiology of human cognitive processes, the way we think, produces a psychological bias toward continuity. Human beings share a need for consistent thoughts, beliefs, and attitudes.[10] Thinking about something in a certain way reinforces this pattern, making it difficult to reorganize or adjust or our views. As a result, there is an unconscious tendency to view persons and events in the world in a way that is compatible with how we previously viewed them. In other words, we process information in a way that buttresses our existing beliefs.

This human propensity distorts our analytical handling of evidence and produces a number of related biases.

- The *confirmation bias* refers to searching for, interpreting, favoring, and recalling information that confirms prior beliefs.
- The *prior attitude effect* involves viewing evidence consistent with prior opinions as more compelling than evidence that is inconsistent with them.
- The *disconfirmation bias* entails challenging and dismissing evidence inconsistent with prior opinions, regardless of their objective accuracy.

These biases may distort a person's exposure to and perception of new information and the conclusions reached about it. Most people seek out information confirming their preexisting opinions and ignore or reject arguments contrary to their predispositions. When exposed to competing arguments, they typically accept the confirming ones and dismiss or argue against the opposing ones. People also tend to interpret ambiguous evidence as supporting their existing position. Moreover, they are unlikely to search for information that challenges their views, or for options contrary to those they advocate. Instead, they tend to incorporate new information in ways that render it comprehensible within their existing frames of reference. In other words, they rationalize information to support their previously held beliefs.[11]

Another cognitive strategy that can sustain premises and distort analysis is defensive avoidance, in which decision makers attempt to avoid or postpone the stress of making a decision. Irving Janis and Leon Mann argue that defensive avoidance can take three forms: procrastination, shifting responsibility of decision to others, and bolstering. Bolstering occurs when decision makers cannot identify an altogether satisfactory option, so they choose the least objectionable alternative and exaggerate its positive consequences and minimize its costs. A more systematic appraisal would force them to acknowledge the high costs and risks of their policy. Moreover, they try to keep from being exposed to communications that might reveal the shortcomings of the action they have chosen. When they do encounter contrary information, such as warnings of impending problems such as an enemy attack, they downplay it through wishful thinking.[12]

Both dissonance reduction and stress avoidance can be institutionalized if leaders encourage their subordinates to report or emphasize information that support their premises, as we will see below. In extreme cases, decision makers may simply cut off dissident information. For example, the U.S. Forest Service was committed to preventing forest fires, and it disbanded its research arm when the unit showed that healthy forests required periodic burning.[13] In such cases, premises are constantly reinforced and become even more resistant to change.

In addition to being motivated by cognitive consistency and stress reduction, people also unconsciously strive to maintain their positive or negative feelings, generally referred to as "affect," toward political actors and issues. When called on to make an evaluation, people instantly and unconsciously draw on their prior attitudes. A heuristic mechanism for evaluating new information triggers a reflection on "How do I feel?" about the topic. This drive for affective consistency results in a bias toward maintaining existing affect, even in the face of disconfirming information. Moreover, the effects are strongest for those with strong attitudes and knowledge because they have repeatedly connected their beliefs to feelings, and they have the information to rationalize away disconfirming evidence and better defend their prior attitudes.[14] People do not reason to find the right answer; they reason to arrive at the answer they want to be right.

To be clear, people are generally not closed-minded, consciously deceiving themselves to preserve their prior beliefs. Indeed, cognitive biases are powerful because they are not volitional, occurring unconsciously and automatically.[15]

Scholars have long known that beliefs are resistant to change. Francis Bacon, often credited with developing the scientific method, summarized them exactly four centuries ago.

> The human understanding when it has once adopted an opinion . . . draws all things else to support and agree with it. And though there be a greater number and weight of instances to be found on the other side, yet these it either neglects and despises, or else by some distinction sets aside and rejects, in order that by this great and pernicious predetermination the authority of its former conclusions may remain inviolate.[16]

In essence, we tend to see what we expect to see on the basis of our prior beliefs. Moreover, we seek and are more receptive to information that supports our views, and we resist information that is contrary to them.[17] There is a related tendency toward premature cognitive closure, terminating a search for information when we get enough information to support our existing views. Sometimes this tendency is aggravated by time pressures or the desire to finish an unpleasant decision task.[18]

Thus, we are reluctant to revise or update our beliefs.[19] As a result of biased reasoning, most people remain unreceptive to major revisions of their beliefs in response to new information unless extraordinary circumstances force them to do so. Instead, we focus on what we know and neglect what we do not know, which makes us overly confident in our beliefs and our intuitions. As Nobel Prize winner Daniel Kahneman put it, we have an "almost unlimited ability to ignore our ignorance."[20]

We know, then, that individuals have cognitive biases that strongly influence their decisions. But what about high-level officials? The fact that leaders occupy positions of power is evidence that they are in at least some ways exceptional. Moreover, the stakes for making the right decision about, say, war and peace are infinitely greater than the decision to buy an automobile or choosing for whom to vote. Thus, political leaders have incentives to invest more fully in challenging their assumptions. Are public officials able to overcome the biases of ordinary citizens and carefully and dispassionately consider at least the most important options for a policy?

Joshua Kertzer has found that although elites and masses may differ in their traits, this does not necessarily mean they will significantly differ in their decision making.[21] Some systematic research has concluded that officials, like the rest of us, engage in motivated reasoning and biased decision making, even during critical times of international crisis.[22] As Philip Tetlock puts it, "experts neutralize dissonant data and preserve confidence in their prior assessments by resorting to a complex battery of belief-system defenses that, epistemologically defensible or not, make learning from history a slow process and defections from theoretical camps a rarity."[23] Moreover, subordinates learn and adopt the policy biases of their superiors and may focus on identifying and reporting information supporting such beliefs while diluting data that challenges them.[24] Leaders are especially likely to resist change if they have had success in the past with their views, if their beliefs are deeply entrenched, if the stakes—and thus, the related emotions—of decisions are highly consequential, and the relevant information on alternatives is ambiguous.[25]

The Role of Premises

Limits on human rationality and motivated reasoning inevitably distort leaders' processing information and bias them against changing their minds. These characteristics of individuals can affect any stage of decision making, and they explain why premises are often faulty and resistant to change. However, cognitive limitations and motivated reasoning do not explain the impact of premises on policy choices. To answer this question, we must turn to leaders in action.

Studying the Power of Premises

To investigate the impact of premises in the most rigorous fashion would require isolating their influence. However, there are many other factors in addition to the limits of human rationality and motivated reasoning that can influence decisions, including personality characteristics such as personal insecurity, distortions in the information and options presented to decision makers resulting from bureaucratic politics and bureaucratic structure, the organization and management of advisory processes, interactions among advisors and between them and the principal decision maker, an official's personal style of decision making,[26] and decision makers' ethical and normative beliefs. There is no doubt that each may influence decision making at one time or another.

Studies of decision making tend to focus on the consequences of one of these variables such as psychopathologies, "groupthink," the organization of advisory processes, or bureaucratic politics. Lacking measures of the various influences on decisions, we are not well-positioned to rigorously control for their impact while focusing on the significance of a particular component of decision making. It is not surprising, then, that although decision making is the most important role of political leaders, it is the one we understand the least.[27]

It may always be thus. As John F. Kennedy wrote, "The essence of ultimate decision remains impenetrable to the observer—often, indeed, to the decider himself.... There will always be the dark and tangled stretches in the decision-making process—mysterious even to those who may be most intimately involved."[28] Nevertheless, there is a path forward, and following it allows us to advance our understanding.

Nathan Leites developed the concept of the "operational code" of leaders in his masterful work, *Study of Bolshevism*.[29] Nearly a generation later, Alexander George structured the concept and argued it was important for understanding political decision making, particularly in conflict situations.[30] An operational code in Leites's and George's terms is a set of general philosophical beliefs about fundamental issues of history and central questions about the nature of politics and conflict, as well as instrumental beliefs about the efficacy of various strategies for advancing their interests. Perceptions of the enemy are particularly important components of an operational code. These beliefs influence decision makers' understanding and diagnoses of political events and influence their choice of strategy and tactics.

Although some work was done applying the concept of operational code,[31] the complexity of the concept has limited its utility in explaining decisions.[32] To Leites and George, an operational code begins with a set of master beliefs at a high level of abstraction. My focus is on premises more directly related to specific policies. Tying premises to policy choices is more useful for explaining decisions than applying an operational code for each participant. In addition, these premises are more easily observed. We know, for example, what French planners thought about a possible German invasion in 1914. We know what U.S. decision makers thought about Iraq's possessing weapons of mass destruction in 2002.

Inspired by David Mayhew's classic work, *Congress: The Electoral Connection*,[33] I engage in a thought experiment. Focusing specifically on premises, I ask, *What if we knew little else about the influences on decision makers aside from their core premises regarding a policy?* If their premises predict their decisions, then we have a basis for concluding that leaders were indeed their prisoners. If, on the other hand, decision makers routinely challenged their core assumptions and adjusted their decisions accordingly, we may infer that the analytical biases represented by premises were one of many influences on decisions, the effects of which sophisticated leaders can reliably overcome.

Where should we look to determine if decision makers are often prisoners of their premises? To examine the power of premises, I focus on major decisions in both the U.S. and other nations. These are the policies that are most consequential. The choice to go to war, for example, is different in kind than decisions regarding military strategy, economic mobilization, logistics, or peace negotiations. All these matters are important, but I am particularly interested in the decisions that set the general course of a nation's policy or a leader's mindset that prevented a recognition of significant developments in other nations such as surprise attacks.

On what aspect of decision making are premises likely to have their greatest impact? My point of departure is the foundation, explicit or merely implicit, of all decisions: identifying problems. Before policymakers can focus on developing and evaluating policy options, they must have an idea of the goal or goals the options are supposed to achieve. Policy goals usually focus on solving a problem such as a threat to national security, a stagnant economy, polluted air, or inadequate access to health care. Thus, most decision processes begin with identifying a problem to be solved, and decision makers need a clear and accurate understanding of the nature of a problem to best evaluate options for ameliorating it.

Problems, then, are the base of decision making. They do not come defined, however. Officials must delineate them. If decision makers share premises that lead them to assume the presence of a problem that actually does not exist, the rest of the decision-making process will be fatally flawed. You cannot solve a problem that does not exist. Moreover, you are likely to waste time, resources, and even lives, and pay substantial opportunity costs, in attempting to do so.

Premises may also blind policymakers to problems that require their attention or cause them to underestimate the likelihood of problems arising. Presuming away problems may give policymakers undue confidence in their favorite options, whether they are designed to maintain the peace or prepare for war, and thus cause them to evaluate certain options more positively than is appropriate. Similarly, policymakers need to carefully and dispassionately evaluate feedback on the consequences of policies they or their predecessors have put into place. However, premises about the efficacy of a policy may distort their evaluations of its success and discourage their consideration of changes to it.

In my thought experiment, I examine some of the most important foreign policy decisions of American history, with a special emphasis on the major wars since World War II—Korea, Vietnam, and Iraq. These were the most consequential national security policies of their times, and it is here that premises could have had the most influence on the nation's well-being. I begin with an analysis of the war in Vietnam in chapter 2, where policymakers fought a costly war on the basis of false assumptions about the existence of a problem. In chapter 3, I turn to officials ignoring or underestimating problems that *do* exist and discuss prominent foreign policy disasters in U.S. history, including Jefferson's embargo, the attacks on Pearl Harbor and the Philippines in 1941, and the Bay of Pigs invasion. I also address similar behavior among allied leaders as they prepared for the German invasions of France in 1914 and of the Soviet Union in 1941. Chapter 4 examines the same issue of ignoring and underestimating problems with a detailed examination of the Korean War, in which the United States endured costly surprise attacks twice in one year. In chapter 5, I focus on the war in Iraq, which illustrates decision makers going to war on the basis of a faulty premise about the existence of a problem *and* then ignoring or underestimating the challenges of the war's aftermath. In chapter 6, I address the inevitable question of constraining the power of premises.

CHAPTER TWO

Assuming Problems

The War in Vietnam

"It is difficult to explain why I, and others, did not force the key issues to the surface, debate them fully, then proceed on the basis of our conclusions."—Secretary of Defense Robert McNamara[1]

We saw in chapter 1 that premises are especially likely to influence officials in the identification of problems, the first stage of decision making. Premises may blind leaders to the existence of a threat to the nation or cause them to underestimate the extent of it. On the other hand, premises may also lead officials to conclude that there is a threat when there actually is not. In this chapter, I focus on the latter problem. In chapters 3 and 4, I address ignoring or underestimating problems. In chapter 5, I analyze the war in Iraq, which illustrates both consequences of premises.

Not all problems are as clear an enemy attack, a recession, or a pandemic. Especially in the realm of national security, enemies or potential adversaries often attempt to conceal their behavior. Because threats, especially those that may be particularly detrimental to a nation, may be ambiguous, and because leaders are naturally concerned with protecting a nation's interests, there is the potential for leaders to see what they want or expect to see.

Decision makers who *assume* a problem exists are less likely to devote attention to the collection and evaluation of evidence regarding the problem. Indeed, gathering evidence may be more for selling their policy than for illuminating a problem. Even more significantly, officials may fail to evaluate the basic premises of their policies. Bypassing a rigorous assessment of the nature of a problem and attempting to solve one that does not exist or that exists in a different form than decision makers envision may result in a costly waste of resources and a myriad of unintended, negative consequences. Often such policies end in tragedy.

Vietnam haunts Americans. The United States fought its longest and least successful war in its jungles and rice paddies, at the cost of more than 58,000 U.S lives and 150,000 seriously wounded. The Vietnamese, North and South, suffered millions of casualties among both the military and civilian populations, and Vietnam was left in ruins, as were large parts of Laos and Cambodia. The war caused deep social divisions and intense conflict in American society and fostered cynicism about government. Financing the conflict triggered severe inflation and diverted resources from pressing domestic needs. In the end, the United States failed to achieve its goals of preserving an independent, non-Communist South Vietnam. What set us on the path to war in the faraway jungles of Southeast Asia?

The story is a long one, but here I focus primarily on the critical period from the fall of 1964 to the summer of 1965. In this period, President Lyndon Johnson made the most fateful decisions of the war. Facing a deteriorating situation in South Vietnam, the commander in chief decided in December 1964 to approve strategic bombing of North Vietnam and launched Operation Rolling Thunder, the beginning of a graduated war against the North Vietnamese. In July 1965, with the collapse of South Vietnam imminent, the president agreed to the deployment of 125,000 American ground troops there, ensuring that the United States would take the major responsibility for conducting a ground war.[2]

In this period, the president transformed a limited commitment to assist South Vietnam in putting down an insurgency into an open-ended commitment to use American military power to maintain an independent, non-Communist South Vietnam. The U.S. objective changed from convincing North Vietnam it could not take over the South to defeating it on the ground.[3] As the president wrote in his memoirs, "Now we were committed to major combat in Vietnam."[4] As we will see, policymakers' premises drove the country to war, kept it fighting for a decade, and shaped the nation's military strategy.

Premises about Vietnam

In the period prior to the major U.S. commitment to fighting a war in Vietnam, high-level U.S. officials shared a consensus that:

- It was essential for the U.S. to resist aggression.
- North Vietnam was an aggressor backed by an international Communist conspiracy.

- The conflict in Vietnam was not a civil war but rather that of an aggressor nation, North Vietnam, attacking South Vietnam.
- If South Vietnam did fall to the Communists, the rest of Southeast Asia would follow.
- It was essential to aid South Vietnam to maintain U.S. credibility.
- The U.S. must not "lose" a country to communism.
- South Vietnam would fall to North Vietnam without American aid.
- It was important not to provoke a major intervention by China or the Soviet Union into the war.
- Controlled escalation of coercion would end North Vietnam's efforts to unify the country.

Each of the first seven premises reinforced the others and propelled the United States toward war. The final two premises determined the strategy leaders chose to wage the conflict. Decision makers were correct that South Vietnam would fall if the United States withdrew its support. Each of the other premises deserve more attention.

Resisting Aggression

American officials saw North Vietnam's effort to unify the country as aggression against South Vietnam.[5] Just as importantly, most high-level officials firmly believed that it was necessary to counter aggression. Lyndon Johnson reflected in his memoirs, "when a President faces a decision involving war or peace, he draws back and thinks of the past and of the future in the widest possible terms."[6] High-level policymakers commonly—and unquestioningly—looked back at their formative years in the 1930s and employed the analogy of the Western European nations trying to appease Hitler's aggression with the 1938 Munich agreement.[7]

Memories of World War II magnified the stakes of Vietnam, and the Munich analogy predisposed decision makers toward intervention.[8] When President Johnson announced that he was sending U.S. combat troops to Vietnam in August 1965, he invoked Munich: "we learned from Hitler at Munich that success only feeds the appetite of aggression."[9] Thus, if he pulled out of Vietnam, he would be doing "exactly what Chamberlain did in World War II."[10] According to the president, "I deeply believe we are quarantining the aggressors over there ... just like FDR and Hitler."[11]

There was a more immediate historical example at hand, however, one that was perhaps even stronger in inclining policymakers toward war in

Vietnam. Korea was the historical analogy most widely invoked by U.S. officials in their deliberations and public statements. It preoccupied President Johnson and was also central for Secretary of State Dean Rusk and other of the president's closest advisors.[12] Johnson admired Truman's decisiveness in responding to the North Korean invasion in 1950, so much so that he wrote President Truman a letter at the time and chose to reprint it in his memoirs.[13] Even twenty years after the war ended, decision makers still found the Korea analogy compelling.[14] Thus, Korea reinforced memories of Munich and predisposed decision makers to intervene in Vietnam; as we will see, it also reinforced the form the intervention took.[15]

Although it may make sense to resist aggression in many circumstances, it does not follow that a nation must do so in *all* instances. Would the United States feel it necessary to resist aggression between, say, Bolivia and Paraguay? Probably not. The fundamental lessons of Korea were more than the need to resist aggression. More important was that international communism was the aggressor, making the political stakes very high and necessitating military action by the United States to counter such aggression.

Communism as an International Conspiracy

The overarching national security policy of the United States from the late 1940s until the 1990s was containment of communism. Containment was widely accepted and central to decision making about Vietnam.[16] The need to counter aggression was magnified by the fact that officials saw North Vietnam not simply as an aggressor nation, but rather as a Communist one supported by an international Communist conspiracy.[17]

On January 6, 1961, Soviet premier Nikita Khrushchev delivered a speech promising aid for "wars of national liberation," and policymakers took notice.[18] When they perceived aggression against South Vietnam, it became a battlefront in the Cold War.[19]

After writing a history of the war in Vietnam, George Herring concluded

> U.S. involvement in Vietnam was not primarily a result of errors of judgment or the personality quirks of policymakers, although these things existed in abundance. It was a logical, if not inevitable outgrowth of a world view and a policy—the policy of containment—which Americans in and out of government accepted without serious question for more than two decades.[20]

The fact that the Korea analogy included the dangers of an international Communist conspiracy strengthened predispositions toward resisting aggression. Officials were concerned that failing to counter aggression would encourage aggressors—Communist aggressors—to continue their expansionist efforts. President Johnson remembered,

> knowing what I did of the policies and actions of Moscow and Peking, I was as sure as a man could be that if we did not live up to our commitment in Southeast Asia and elsewhere, they would move to exploit the disarray in the United States and in the alliances of the Free World. . . . As nearly as one man can be certain of anything, I knew they could not resist the opportunity to expand their control into the vacuum of power we would leave behind us.[21]

Similarly, he told his national security assistant, "If you start running from the Communists, they may just chase you right into your own kitchen."[22]

An underlying assumption of the view that communism was an international conspiracy was that the leading Communist countries, the Soviet Union and China, were acting in a coordinated fashion and were directing the war in Vietnam. Many policymakers believed they were,[23] but they were wrong.

These officials were slow to accept the growing estrangement between the Soviet Union and China, which began in the late 1950s.[24] The CIA reported on this split,[25] but policymakers sometimes ignored its evaluations. By the mid-1960s, officials recognized that there was a rift within the Communist world,[26] although they did not necessarily accept its implications.

More important, decision makers could not grasp the possibility of North Vietnam acting on its own initiative. In 1948 and 1949, U.S. officials admitted they could not find hard evidence that North Vietnam took its orders from Moscow. When the Communists took power in China in 1949, however, the American focus became blocking further Communist expansion in Asia.[27] Anticommunism and a belief in a worldwide Communist conspiracy blinded policymakers to nationalism as the source of conflict in Vietnam.[28] Dwight Eisenhower dismissed the power of nationalism because he thought it was incompatible with communism. In his view, Communists would always bow to Moscow.[29]

To avoid confrontation with the United States, both the Soviet Union and China pressured North Vietnam to accept the 1954 Geneva Accords that partitioned Vietnam at the 17th parallel. The North saw the agreement as a tragic loss and would never again defer to its Communist brethren.[30]

Remarkably, policymakers overlooked centuries of animosity and distrust between Vietnam and China,[31] antipathies that continue in the twenty-first century. The North Vietnamese hated the thought that the Chinese might intervene in the war with ground troops.[32] More than a generation after the war ended, former Vietnamese diplomat and leading scholar of the war Luu Doan Huynh commented on the U.S. belief that North Vietnam was directed by China:

> If I may say so, you were not only wrong, but you had, so to speak, lost your minds. Vietnam a part of the Chinese expansionist game in Asia? For anyone who knows the history of Indochina, this is incomprehensible.[33]

It is not surprising, then, that in 1979, just four years after the fall of Saigon, China launched an offensive against Vietnam in response to Vietnam's invasion and occupation of Cambodia in 1978, which ended the rule of the Chinese-backed Khmer Rouge and stopped the genocide by the Khmer Rouge that was in some ways directed toward the Vietnamese. Vietnamese maps today do not include the designation of the South China Sea. Instead, they label that area of the ocean the "East Sea."

Neither China nor the Soviet Union controlled North Vietnam,[34] as the CIA routinely reported.[35] Indeed, China did not want to intervene in the war[36] and was not particularly eager for a united Vietnam.[37] The Soviet Union's support for North Vietnam was more about its rivalry with the United States than about spreading communism.[38] It was not especially enthusiastic to aid Hanoi. On the one hand, such support might undermine the emerging détente with the United States. On the other hand, not providing aid would leave it open to charges from Peking that it was abandoning a sister Communist country.[39] Given their allies' mixed motivations, North Vietnam effectively played China and the Soviet Union against each other.[40]

Secretary of Defense Robert McNamara later lamented the failure to understand Vietnamese autonomy, concluding that officials such as himself underestimated the power of nationalism and made the mistake of viewing the conflict primarily as a unified Communist drive rather than a nationalistic civil war. Thus, they misjudged the intentions of the North Vietnamese and the threat they posed to the U.S.[41] As George Herring put it,

> By wrongly attributing the Vietnamese conflict to external sources, the United States drastically misjudged its internal dynamics. By intervening in what was

essentially a local struggle, it placed itself at the mercy of local forces, a weak client, and a determined adversary.[42]

Civil War or International Aggression?

Herring raises a key issue in the decision to intervene militarily in Vietnam. If North Vietnam's forceful efforts to unify with South Vietnam represented a civil war rather than the aggression of one nation against another, much less an onslaught controlled by an international Communist conspiracy, U.S. intervention in the war would be much less compelling. Both the Korea and Munich analogies magnified the stakes for Vietnam, blowing a civil war into international significance, indicating that the stakes for aiding South Vietnam were high and that it was necessary and morally correct to do so.[43]

As I have noted, throughout history, the Vietnamese have at great cost resisted encroachments on their territory by major powers, including the Chinese, the French, and the Japanese. North Vietnam anticipated unifying the country in elections the 1954 Geneva Accords promised would be held in 1956. However, at least some U.S. officials saw Munich as an appropriate analogy for the accords,[44] and the Eisenhower administration was not prepared to have a country vote freely to be under Communist control. It is not surprising that the North Vietnamese saw the Americans as the colonial successors to the French.[45] The United States was just the latest foreign power that they needed to resist.[46]

Most analysts have concluded that the conflict between North and South Vietnam was a civil war,[47] not an example of Communist expansion directed from Moscow and Beijing. Nationalism rather than the dispersion of an ideology as part of an international Communist conspiracy was the basis of the North Vietnamese cause. By assuming that the North Vietnamese were pawns of the Communist giants Russia and China, American policymakers failed to understand that the North's goal was Vietnamese independence, not the spread of communism.

Nevertheless, U.S. officials' premises biased them to see Communist expansionism, not a civil war. As President Johnson told a biographer, "It's just perverted history to claim that it's a civil war, just pure bad history."[48] Secretary of Defense McNamara later admitted that he and his colleagues failed to probe the nationalist roots of the Vietnamese struggle or understand the history of the Vietnamese fighting China hegemony.[49]

They saw North Vietnamese leader Ho Chi Minh first as a Communist and only secondarily as a nationalist. Thus, they misunderstood that the North's goal was unification rather than conquest and that a unified Vietnam was not a threat to the West's security.[50]

In the case of Vietnam, policymakers relied heavily on the analogies of Munich and Korea, but there was an alternative analogy that might seem appropriate: the French experience in Indochina. This analogy defined the problem as one of the Vietnamese fighting colonial domination, an untenable moral position for a Western power. Moreover, the analogy pointed to France's ultimate defeat.

In a memo to the president on June 18, 1965, Undersecretary of State George Ball reviewed the French experience to argue against expanding the conflict into a U.S. ground war with the Viet Cong.[51] On June 29, he reiterated his doubts in a nineteen-page memo to the principal policymakers, with a seven-page summary to the president the day before. Once again, he raised the French experience to argue that the United States should not escalate the war.[52]

On June 30, the president received a memo from his national security assistant, McGeorge Bundy, challenging the viability of the analogy.[53] In the end, none of the top officials found the French comparison compelling. The notion of repeating the French failure was at too much variance with the national self-perception of most officials.[54]

Falling Dominos

The West took action to counter the invasion of South Korea but took no effective action to protect Czechoslovakia. The Munich analogy suggested that Vietnam was the first victim in the expansion of communism, just as Czechoslovakia was the first victim of the Nazis.[55] Officials commonly employed the domino theory—which held that the United States must prevent countries from falling to the Communists because a chain reaction would occur and countries would fall one after another, like dominos—as a simile to justify U.S. intervention in Vietnam. They reasoned that if South Vietnam fell to communism, other nations would soon follow.[56] Clark Clifford remembered "the unanimous sentiment among his [Johnson's] senior advisors that the domino theory was unquestionably so."[57] Because of its significance in the debates about the war and because its evolution illustrates how premises may develop, the domino theory deserves detailed attention.

In February 1947, the British informed the U.S. State Department that Great Britain could no longer provide financial aid to the governments of Greece, which was trying to combat a Communist-led insurgency known as the National Liberation Front, and Turkey, which faced Soviet pressure to share control of the strategic Dardanelles Strait. In a meeting with key congressional leaders shortly afterward, Undersecretary of State Dean Acheson articulated what would later become known as the domino theory. He told the leaders that there was more at stake than Greece and Turkey, for if those two key states should fall, communism would likely spread south to Iran and as far east as India.[58] President Harry Truman addressed a joint session of Congress on March 12 and asked for $400 million in military and economic assistance for Greece and Turkey—the first installment in what became known as the Truman Doctrine. The president argued that if Greece and Turkey did not receive the aid, they would inevitably fall to Communists, with grave consequences for the spread of communism throughout the region.

In September 1945, the Vietnamese nationalist leader Ho Chi Minh proclaimed Vietnam's independence from France, beginning a war that pitted Ho's Communist-led Viet Minh regime in Hanoi (North Vietnam) against a French-backed regime in Saigon (South Vietnam). Under President Truman, the U.S. government provided covert military and financial aid to the French. The rationale was that of the domino theory: a Communist victory in Indochina would precipitate the spread of communism throughout Southeast Asia. By 1950, makers of U.S. foreign policy had firmly embraced the idea that the fall of Indochina to communism would lead rapidly to the collapse of other nations in Southeast Asia. Secretary of State Dean Acheson wrote President Truman on February 16 that he had the choice of supporting South Vietnam and other non-Communist governments or facing the extension of communism over the rest of Southeast Asia and perhaps even more territory.[59] In a report to the National Security Council (NSC) on February 27, 1950, the State Department concluded, "The neighboring countries of Thailand and Burma could be expected to fall under Communist domination if Indochina were controlled by a Communist-dominated government."[60]

In a memorandum on January 31, 1951, advocating military aid to Indochina, then Assistant Secretary of State Dean Rusk (later to be secretary of State for Presidents John F. Kennedy and Lyndon Johnson) wrote "It is generally acknowledged that if Indochina were to fall under control of the Communists, Burma and Thailand would follow suit almost imme-

ASSUMING PROBLEMS: THE WAR IN VIETNAM

diately. Thereafter, it would be difficult, if not impossible for Indonesia, India and the others to remain outside the Soviet-dominated Asian Bloc."[61] The National Security Council included the theory in a 1952 statement of policy on Indochina.[62]

Dwight Eisenhower became president in 1953, and the domino theory retained its power. A National Security Council paper approved by the president in January 1954 predicted the "loss of any single country" in Southeast Asia would ultimately lead to the loss of all Southeast Asia and then India and Japan, and finally "endanger the stability and security of Europe."[63] On March 12, 1954, Admiral Arthur Radford, chairman of the Joint Chiefs of Staff, wrote to the secretary of defense,

> Should Indochina be lost to the Communists, and in the absence of immediate and effective counteraction on the part of the Western Powers which would of necessity be on a much greater scale than that which could be decisive in Indochina, the conquest of the remainder of Southeast Asia would inevitably follow. . . .
>
> Orientation of Japan toward the West is the keystone of United States policy in the Far East. In the judgment of the Joint Chiefs of Staff, the loss of Southeast Asia to Communism would, through economic and political pressures, drive Japan into an accommodation with the Communist Bloc. The communization of Japan would be the predictable result.[64]

Ultimately it was the president who propelled the domino analogy into the public consciousness. On April 6, 1954, during the decisive battle between Viet Minh and French forces at Dien Bien Phu, President Dwight Eisenhower told the National Security Council that "Indochina was the first in a row of dominoes. If it fell its neighbors would shortly thereafter fall with it."[65] (He had held such views at least since 1951.)[66] The next day, in a press conference, he articulated what he termed the "'falling domino' principle" for the whole nation.

> You have a row of dominoes set up, you knock over the first one, and what will happen to the last one is the certainty that it will go over very quickly. So you could have a beginning of a disintegration that would have the most profound influences.[67]

The former supreme allied commander's sanction lent the theory extra weight and wide visibility. It became common for officials to employ the phrase "domino theory" as a shorthand expression of the strategic importance of South Vietnam to the United States, as well as the need to contain the spread of communism throughout the world.[68]

Eisenhower continued to express the domino theory throughout his tenure and after leaving the White House.[69] On his last full day in office, he warned his successor, John F. Kennedy, and the incoming secretaries of state and defense that if Laos should fall to the Communists, it would be just a question of time until South Vietnam, Cambodia, Thailand, and Burma would collapse.[70]

Kennedy increased the commitment of U.S. resources in support of the regime in South Vietnam and of non-Communist forces fighting a civil war in Laos. He publicly reaffirmed belief in the domino theory and the importance of containing communism in Southeast Asia. For example, on September 9, 1963, when asked by journalist Chet Huntley whether he believed in the domino theory, the president responded, "I believe it. I believe it."[71]

So did his advisors. On November 8, 1961, a memorandum for President Kennedy summarized their views: "The fall of South Viet-Nam to Communism would lead to the fairly rapid extension of Communist control, or complete accommodation to Communism, in the rest of mainland Southeast Asia and in Indonesia. The strategic implications, world-wide, particularly in the Orient, would be extremely serious."[72] On January 13, 1962, the chairman of the Joint Chiefs of Staff, General Lyman Lemnitzer, wrote the secretary of defense (who forwarded the memo to the president) on behalf of the joint chiefs,

> It must be recognized that the fall of South Vietnam to Communist control would mean the eventual Communist domination of all of the Southeast Asian mainland.... Of equal importance to the immediate losses are the eventualities which could follow the loss of the Southeast Asian mainland. All of the Indonesian archipelago could come under the domination and control of the USSR and would become a Communist base posing a threat against Australia and New Zealand. The Sino-Soviet Bloc would have control of the eastern access to the Indian Ocean. The Philippines and Japan could be pressured to assume, at best, a neutralist role, thus eliminating two of our major bases of defense in the Western Pacific. Our lines of defense then would be pulled north to Korea, Okinawa and Taiwan resulting in the subsequent overtaxing of our lines of communications in a limited war. India's ability to remain neutral would be jeopardized and, as the Bloc meets success, its concurrent stepped-up activities

to move into and control Africa can be expected.... It is, in fact, a planned phase in the Communist timetable for world domination."[73]

Lyndon Johnson also bought into the domino theory, using it to justify the escalation of the U.S. military presence in Vietnam from a few thousand soldiers to more than 500,000 during his tenure. In his memoirs, he explains that if South Vietnam were to fall to the North, he expected "all of Southeast Asia would pass under Communist control ... at least down to Singapore but almost certainly to Djakarta."[74] Johnson reported that early in the war all his senior civilian and military advisors agreed with the domino theory.[75]

In early June 1964, President Johnson submitted a formal question to the CIA: "Would the rest of Southeast Asia necessarily fall if Laos and South Vietnam came under North Vietnamese control?" The agency's reply on June 9, 1964, was prepared by the Office of National Estimates and challenged the domino theory. "With the possible exception of Cambodia," the CIA memorandum said, "it is likely that no nation in the area would quickly succumb to Communism as a result of the fall of Laos and Vietnam. Furthermore, a continuation of the spread of Communism in the area would not be inexorable, and any spread which did occur would take time—time in which the total situation might change in any number of ways unfavorable to the Communist cause."[76]

The CIA's analysis seemed to fall on deaf ears. Decision makers' premises were too set. Indeed, Johnson's request came about eleven weeks after he had already made the domino thesis a part of formal U.S. policy in a National Security Action Memorandum (NSAM 288) on March 17, 1964. The memorandum asserted that unless South Vietnam became a viable, non-Communist state, all of Southeast Asia would probably fall under Communist dominance or accommodate to Communist influence.[77] The day before the NSAM was issued, Secretary of Defense Robert McNamara sent the president a memorandum declaring that unless the United States succeeded in preserving an independent, non-Communist South Vietnam, "almost all of Southeast Asia will probably fall under communist dominance."[78]

Many years later, McNamara wrote about the June 9, 1964, CIA study but omitted the language cited above, drawing the conclusion that it supported current policy.[79] In September 1964, General Maxwell Taylor, the ambassador to South Vietnam, testified to Congress that if the United States withdrew from South Vietnam, America "would be pushed out of the Western Pacific, back to Honolulu."[80] Secretary of State Dean Rusk also held to the domino theory,[81] as did McGeorge Bundy. It is significant that Bundy later concluded that the domino theory "was an extraordinarily unfitting simile, a preventor of discourse."[82]

In a November 1964 paper by the National Security Council Working Group on Vietnam, some officials argued that the domino theory was "oversimplified," but they still concluded there was a good chance of Southeast Asia going Communist if South Vietnam did so. The Joint Chiefs of Staff dissented from this view, arguing that "the domino theory was perfectly appropriate to the South Vietnamese situation."[83] When the principals met to discuss the paper, they leaned toward the military's view of the domino theory.[84]

In September 1967, the CIA again questioned the domino theory,[85] but the U.S. was too committed to the war for any clear-headed evaluation of the premises of its leading policymakers. As Robert McNamara put it directly, "Our mindset was indeed on of the fear of 'falling dominos' ":

> Throughout the Kennedy and Johnson administrations, we operated on the premise that the loss of South Vietnam to North Vietnam would result in all of Southeast Asia being overrun by communism and that this would threaten the security of both the United States and the entire noncommunist world.[86]

He and his fellow decision makers "believed that the Soviets and the Chinese were cooperating and trying to extend their hegemony": "That was the foundation of our decisions about national security." Thus, they inferred that they needed to contain Communist expansion and fight in Vietnam because it was the first domino in Southeast Asia.[87]

After the war, some key U.S. policymakers, including McNamara, concluded they were wrong about Vietnam as a domino. They also recognized that communism was not monolithic after the Sino-Soviet split in the late 1950s.[88] Most tellingly, the former defense secretary lamented that he and his colleagues had failed to question their premise by asking, "Was it true that the fall of South Vietnam would trigger the fall of all Southeast Asia?"[89]

The simplistic nature of the simile of falling dominos indicates how much room existed for differences between that view and reality.[90] The analogy failed to account for the character of the North Vietnamese and Viet Cong struggle in the Vietnam War. Communist forces in Laos and Cambodia were victorious at the same time that North Vietnamese forces occupied Saigon in 1975, but communism did not spread throughout the rest of Southeast Asia. Moreover, Vietnam attacked Cambodia in 1978, hardly evidence of a coordinated Communist conspiracy.

Maintaining Credibility

The premises of the necessity of countering aggression, especially Communist aggression, and that North Vietnam was an aggressor nation acting as part of an international Communist conspiracy predisposed U.S. officials to intervene militarily in Vietnam. The need they felt to maintain the credibility of America's willingness to fight aggression kept America in the war. It was not just falling dominos near Vietnam that mattered, but rather nations around the world, creating what one author termed the "psychological domino theory."[91]

In the effort to contain communism, the United States engaged in a broad framework of international alliances and guarantees in the post–World War II era. For this system to work, other nations had to believe that America would come to their aid. Similarly, potential adversaries, primarily the Soviet Union and China, had to believe that the United States would counter any aggressive moves they made. Thus, in the minds of decision makers there were two aspects of credibility at stake. First were commitments to U.S. allies to protect them from attack. Second, there was the credibility of threats to potential enemies that the United States would retaliate to counter aggression by the leading Communist nations, either directly or more indirectly through their support of "wars of national liberation."

Thus, a prominent theme in decision making on the war was the belief that United States had to take a forceful stand in South Vietnam to preserve its worldwide credibility. Officials repeatedly invoked this premise in memos regarding the war.[92] For example, in a memo to President Johnson on March 16, 1964, Secretary of Defense Robert McNamara concluded that because the United States was so heavily engaged in South Vietnam,

> that fact accentuates the impact of a Communist South Vietnam not only in Asia, but in the rest of the world, where the South Vietnam conflict is regarded as a test case of U.S. capacity to help a nation meet a Communist "war of liberation."[93]

The June 9, 1964, CIA study discussed earlier concluded that the loss of South Vietnam and Laos would seriously damage U.S. credibility in the

East.⁹⁴ In a report on courses of action in Southeast Asia, the high-level NSC Working Group on Vietnam wrote in November 1964,

> Essentially, the loss of South Vietnam to Communist control, in any form, would be a major blow to our basic policies. US prestige is heavily committed to the maintenance of a non-Communist South Vietnam.⁹⁵

In February 1965, as the president was considering a sustained bombing campaign against North Vietnam, his assistant for national security, McGeorge Bundy, advised him, "Even if it fails, the policy will be worth it. At a minimum it will damp down the charge that we did not do all that we could have done, and this charge will be important in many countries, including our own."⁹⁶ Other top officials shared his view. Even in defeat, they reasoned, the effort to protect South Vietnam would preserve U.S. credibility.⁹⁷

Similarly, in a paper prepared in March 1965 by John McNaughton, assistant secretary of defense for international security affairs, the author asserted that "70 percent" of the aim of U.S. support for South Vietnam was to maintain its credibility as a "guarantor." It was essential, he argued, that the United States

> avoid harmful appearances which will affect judgments by, and provide pretexts, to other nations regarding how the U.S. will behave in future cases of particular interest to those nations—regarding U.S. policy, power, resolve, and competence to deal with their problems.⁹⁸

In July, Secretary of State Dean Rusk advised the president, "The integrity of the U.S. commitment is the principal pillar of peace throughout the world. If that commitment becomes unreliable, the communist world would draw conclusions that would lead to our ruin and almost certainly to a catastrophic war."⁹⁹

These officials were preaching to the choir. President Johnson was convinced that stopping communism in Vietnam was critical for American credibility. If we failed to protect South Vietnam from communism, our allies would conclude our word was worth nothing and thus they could not count on the United States to maintain their security. "If we are driven from the field in Viet-Nam, then no nation can ever again have the same confidence in American promise, or in American protection," the president proclaimed in July 1965.¹⁰⁰ He also worried that Moscow and Peking would exploit the disarray in the United States and its alliances following a "loss" of Vietnam to expand their control in the power vacuum.[101]

By January 1966, McNaughton was arguing that it no longer mattered *why* the U.S. intervened in Vietnam. Once it was there, we had to succeed to maintain our credibility.

> The present U.S. objective in Vietnam is to avoid humiliation. The reasons why we *went into* Vietnam to the present depth are varied; but they are now largely academic. Why we have *not withdrawn* from Vietnam is by all odds, one reason: (1) to preserve our reputation as a guarantor, and thus to preserve our effectiveness in the rest of the world.[102]

Few policymakers questioned the relationship between U.S. intervention in Vietnam and its broader credibility, although they should have. On September 12, 1967, Director of Central Intelligence Richard Helms gave President Johnson a memo and analysis written by a board member of the Office of National Estimates for the president's eyes only. The study focused on the consequences of a U.S. failure to prevail in Vietnam. It concluded that the net effect would not permanently damage U.S. capacity as a world power. It ended by advising the president that "the risks are probably more limited and controllable than most previous argument has indicated." In other words, the United States could have withdrawn from Vietnam without any permanent damage to its security or that of its allies. Johnson never shared with anyone this analysis questioning this fundamental premise underlying the war.[103]

The CIA study was correct. More recent work has reached a similar conclusion. Daryl Press found that when leaders face the prospect of high-stakes military conflicts, they do not assess their adversaries' credibility by reviewing their opponents' past and evaluating their history of keeping or breaking commitments. Power and interests in the current crisis—not past actions—determine the credibility of a threat.[104] Withdrawal from Vietnam would not have harmed the United States' credibility. It would have enhanced it. By late 1964, allies and nonaligned governments were questioning not America's will but its judgment.[105]

In fact, the United States did not lose its credibility after withdrawing from the Vietnam War. Its alliances remained strong, and neither the Soviet Union nor China expanded its control. Indeed, China was occupied with Mao Zedong's Cultural Revolution until his death in 1976.[106] Thus, McNamara remembered that officials saw China as a threat, when in retrospect it was not.[107] Most significantly, in 1985, Mikhail Gorbachev came to power in the Soviet Union and sought a more cooperative relationship with the United States. The Soviet Union imploded at the end of 1991, as United States and its allies won the Cold War.

According to Ernest May, U.S. officials

> visualized their principal adversaries as nations whose behavior could not be predicted by individual past actions, but which would instead be a function of interests and capabilities. Ironically, these policymakers could not see other nations thinking the same about the United States if it withdrew from South Vietnam. They could not conceive that both enemies and friends would not revise their expectations of future American behavior and that they would assume that withdrawing from South Vietnam was not indicative of how the United States might act in other situations where its interests were clearer or the odds of success were better.[108]

"Losing" Vietnam

Inextricably linked to the containment of communism and the related premises of resisting aggression from an international Communist conspiracy to avoid other nations falling to communism and to maintain credibility to resist future aggression was the imperative not to "lose" another country to communism. In this case, the primary audience would be domestic rather than international.

Policymakers' memories of the destructive debate that occurred in the United States after the "loss" of China in 1949 added extra weight to the concern for containing communism.[109] Each post–World War II president resolved that he would not be the president who permitted the "loss" of Vietnam to communism, and their close advisors reinforced their orientations.[110] John F. Kennedy, discussing his efforts to shore up South Vietnam, explained, "Strongly in our mind is what happened in the case of China at the end of World War II, where China was lost . . . We don't want that."[111] Lyndon Johnson was haunted by the political price Harry Truman paid for "losing" China and worried that similar attacks would kill his presidency.[112] It is not surprising that right after he became president, he declared, "I am not going to lose Vietnam. I am not going to be the President who saw Southeast Asia go the way China went."[113]

Thus, President Johnson was concerned about a divisive national battle over "losing" South Vietnam, and he feared that such a conflict would with minimal pressure for escalation. According to historian Fredrik Logevall, "Had Lyndon Johnson opted for disengagement . . . he would have encountered little opposition from the leading figures in his own party."[126] He could have mobilized the many critics of the war to support pulling out of Vietnam. As William Bundy argued, the president could have carried public opinion no matter what he chose to do. Yet Johnson did not want a debate over the war. Instead, he deceived the public about the circumstances of the Gulf of Tonkin incident in August 1964[127] and withheld information about his plans for escalation during the 1964 election. He had made his decision. In fact, he had opposed pulling out of Vietnam even when he was the vice president, with little prospect of reaching the Oval Office anytime soon.[128]

A politician as experienced and canny as Lyndon Johnson surely knew he had a choice. The president was not forced by domestic politics to escalate the war; he chose to do so.

Other aspects of domestic policy played a role in policymaking on the war. Lyndon Johnson's highest priority was his Great Society legislation. He worried that a war in Vietnam could threaten his program of domestic reform because conservatives would use the war as an excuse not to support it, arguing that the war had to come first.[129] To avoid the trade-off between guns and butter, the president went to great lengths to make the costs of the war acceptable to Americans. In doing so, he deceived the public about the U.S. commitment to Vietnam and let his desire to protect the Great Society strongly influence his military strategy. Johnson did not submit policies to public or congressional debate, did not seek congressional authorization for the war, did not publicly acknowledge the shift in war policy in 1965, did not mobilize the country for war, and did not seek a tax increase to pay for it.[130] Yet he certainly did not go to war to enhance the prospects of funding his domestic policy initiatives.

In addition, the president knew he would have to worry about opposition to the war from the left, which had already begun by early 1965. He told his advisors in June 1965, "It's going to be difficult for us to very long prosecute effectively a war that far away from home with the divisions that we have here and particularly the potential divisions."[131] Johnson was correct. By May 1966, he had dipped to 46 percent approval in the Gallup Poll.[132] Needless to say, such concerns were not an incentive to prosecute a war in Vietnam.

H. R. McMaster contends that the war was not forced onto the United States by Cold War ideology. Instead, America slipped into combat primarily as the result of President Johnson's character, motivations, and relationships with his principal advisors.[133] Yet his analysis does not support such a conclusion. He is right to criticize the president's duplicity and decision-making process, which, along with the role of the Joint Chiefs of Staff, is the focus of his invaluable book. Others have also found Johnson's manner of decision making wanting.[134] Yet what McMaster actually shows is that Johnson's personal characteristics, goals, White House organization, and aides affected *how* the war was fought, not *whether* it was fought.

Fear of Provoking China or the Soviet Union

Premises determined not only that the United States would go to war but also how it would wage it. The Korea analogy alerted policymakers to the danger of Chinese intervention. With the disastrous invasion of China in the Korean War in October 1950 in mind (which I discuss in detail in chapter 4), U.S. officials were persistently concerned about provoking China as they escalated the war.[135] According to a study for the Department of Defense, "Fear of provoking Communist China to intervene on behalf of Hanoi permeated U.S. policy deliberations regarding military operations in and over Vietnam during the Eisenhower, Kennedy, and Johnson administrations."[136]

President Johnson was especially sensitive to the possibility of provoking the Chinese.[137] The result was a decision to intervene in Vietnam, but with the least force necessary. In a speech at Johns Hopkins University on April 7, 1964, the president proclaimed the objective of an independent South Vietnam, but promised, "We will do everything necessary to achieve that objective. And we will do only what is absolutely necessary."[138]

China did not want to intervene in the war,[139] but it did provide supplies and deployed a large number of support troops to North Vietnam.[140] It would have fought the U.S. to a protect a buffer zone in northern Vietnam from American occupation. The North Vietnamese were convinced that China would intervene if the U.S. bombed near the Chinese border or invaded North Vietnam.[141] Moreover, China sent a number of signals of its intentions. For example, an editorial in the *People's Daily* on February 15, 1965, warned that if the U.S. crossed the 17th parallel with ground troops, the war would expand from Vietnam to Korea.[142] Similarly, on June 1, 1965, The *People's Daily* asked, "Why should socialist China not give all-out support to socialist, fraternal Vietnam?"[143]

This belligerent rhetoric confirmed to U.S. policymakers their image of China as an aggressive and expansionist power that threatened Southeast

Asia, especially after it exploded its first atomic weapon in 1964.[144] It is easy to understand why officials were eager not to provoke China.

Policymakers were also concerned about the possible intervention of the Soviet Union.[145] The USSR preferred to keep a low profile in Vietnam and avoid a major war, but it had to show its support for the North to maintain its revolutionary credentials in its contest with China. It provided substantial aid but also sought to restrain North Vietnam rather than incite it. This behavior was ironic given that the United States blamed the Soviet Union for the war.[146]

Escalation

According to H. R. McMaster, in the fall of 1964, policymakers were operating on two critical assumptions regarding the conduct of the war. First, they concluded that the principal difficulty in South Vietnam stemmed from North Vietnam's support for the Viet Cong. Second, and crucially, they believed that the gradual application of military and diplomatic pressures on North Vietnam would persuade its leaders to terminate that support.[147] Following the thinking of Thomas Schelling, officials focused on sending threats and signals to North Vietnam about the high costs it would suffer if it did not stop its campaign to unify with South Vietnam.[148]

Avoiding the large-scale intervention of China or the Soviet Union required carefully managing the use of force in Vietnam, and top policymakers were confident they could control the escalation and not threaten either great power.[149] They also assumed that military pressures were reversible. Thus, officials looked to the North for a solution they could not find in the South, which was racked by instability. By the end of 1964, they decided on sustained bombing of North Vietnam, with an emphasis on its industrial infrastructure. On March 2, 1965, the United States began this campaign, named Operation Rolling Thunder.[150]

The president and his top advisors never considered the validity of their assumptions underlying their view of the effectiveness of graduated pressure. They did not study the relationship between ends or means, or clearly define their goals. Instead, they fixated on means rather than ends. They never seriously considered alternatives to graduated pressure or what deepening involvement might ultimately cost. The leading military officials also bore part of the blame. The Joint Chiefs of Staff left the most difficult questions unanswered and the assumptions that underlay the president's policy unchallenged.[151]

A form of wishful thinking occurs when policymakers deemphasize information inconsistent with ongoing policy and conclude that undesirable conditions will ameliorate in response to current policy. All that was needed to force the enemy to succumb, they argued, was to keep up the pressure. Thus, they resisted rigorous evaluation of their military strategy.[152] War games that concluded that air power would not destroy North Vietnam's ability to support the insurgency in the South and that graduated pressure would lead to disaster had no impact on officials' decisions.[153]

U.S. decision makers could not accept that the bombing only reinforced Hanoi's determination to conquer South Vietnam, and they failed to understand that the North Vietnamese commitment to revolution made them willing to accept losses that seemed unconscionable to Americans.[154] According to Richard Neustadt and Ernest May, "Johnson's advisors just could not conceive that the North Vietnamese would not come to terms once they saw the opposition they were likely to face and the punishment they might suffer."[155] The president expected North Vietnam would resist the bombing for a while and then be in a hurry to get it over with.[156]

He and his advisors were wrong.[157] A Defense Intelligence Agency analysis sent to Secretary of Defense Robert McNamara on November 17, 1965, reported that "The air strikes do not appear to have altered Hanoi's determination to continue supporting the war in South Vietnam." It concluded that "The idea that destroying, or threatening to destroy, North Vietnam's industry would pressure Hanoi into calling it quits, seems, in retrospect, a colossal misjudgment."[158] Although neither the Joint Chiefs of Staff nor the intelligence community projected strong possibilities of success from bombing, officials did not adjust their policy.[159] As we have seen, policymakers underestimated the determination of North Vietnam to resist and to endure hardship.[160] They also did not foresee the costs of the war to the United States.

The Impact of Premises

Early in his presidency, on May 27, 1964, Lyndon Johnson had a conversation with McGeorge Bundy. The president lamented to his national security assistant,

> I'll tell you the more that I stayed awake last night thinking of the thing, the more I think of it, I don't know what in the hell—it looks to me like we're

getting into another Korea. It just worries the hell out of me. I don't see what we can ever hope to get out of there with, once we're committed. I believe that the Chinese communists are coming into it. I didn't think we can fight them ten thousand miles from home. . . . I don't think it's worth fighting for and I don't think we can get out. It's just the biggest damned mess I ever saw.[161]

The president worried about loss of the region to communism if the United States did not intervene militarily and the potential escalation of East-West conflict if we did. He did not want Americans in combat, but he did not want to pull out.[162] His ultimate response was to go to war. He was a prisoner of his premises.

Logevall concludes, "In foreign policy matters, especially, Johnson lacked a detached critical perspective, which left him vulnerable to clichés and stereotypes about world affairs."[163] When he became president, he undertook no fundamental reassessment of the rationale for U.S. policy in Vietnam or alternatives to it. He eschewed the kind of reexamination of policy assumptions that would have been needed to initiate disengagement and tried to avoid listening to underlying rationales. The president did not like deep and wide-ranging discussions of options. Johnson also disliked dissenters, and did not welcome—and in fact, tried to elude—the opinions and advice of allied leaders.[164]

Policymakers' premises molded their decisions about U.S. participation in the Vietnam War. The doctrinal consensus on them made it difficult to challenge U.S. policy and foreclosed policy options such as a neutral unified Vietnam or a U.S. withdrawal from the conflict. As Fredrik Logevall concluded in his wide-ranging work on the choice to go to war,

> A theme of this book is that American policymakers from mid-1963 onward were not merely skeptical of the possibility of finding an early political solution to the war but acutely fearful of such a prospect and strongly determined to prevent one. Both the fear and the determination had increased by the close of 1964. Nothing—not pessimistic intelligence reporting, not allied opposition, and not pervasive South Vietnamese war-weariness and burgeoning anti-Americanism—could dissuade these men from continuing their pursuit of a military solution.[165]

Although internal U.S. government data and analysis often showed America's actions were having little impact, officials, driven by their premises, persisted in the war because of their determination to do something. Since they could not bring themselves to consider seriously the option of pulling out of the war, they could not reassess their policy.[166] As a result, "no comprehensive and systematic examination of Vietnam's importance to the United States was ever undertaken within the executive branch. Debates revolved around how to do things better and whether they could be done, not whether they were worth doing."[167]

After the war, Undersecretary of State George Ball concluded, "If our Vietnam involvement taught us anything, it is that we should beware of untested assumptions." On October 25, 1964, Ball sent a sixty-seven-page memo to Secretary of State Dean Rusk, Secretary of Defense Robert McNamara, and Special Assistant to the President on Foreign Affairs McGeorge Bundy. The memo challenged the assumptions underlying U.S. policy on Vietnam, especially the Korean analogy.[168] It had no impact of these policymakers. McNamara reports not really exploring Ball's analysis.[169] Five months later, Ball sent it to the president, who read it closely. He also was unmoved.[170] Other memos from Ball also had little effect.[171]

None of the most senior officials challenged the fundamental assumptions of the war policy.[172] McNamara, writing about the Kennedy years, remembered, "We failed to analyze our assumptions critically, then or later. The foundations of our decision making were gravely flawed." Thus, he and Rusk failed to ask basic questions, including whether the domino theory was correct and whether Communist nations in Southeast Asia would constitute a grave threat to the security of the West. McNamara recollected, "It seems beyond understanding, incredible, that we did not force ourselves to confront such issues head-on." The continued preoccupation with questions of what military course to follow rather than the broader questions of whether there should be a military course continued through the Johnson presidency.[173]

The administration also failed to debate the assumptions of its military strategy.[174] According to McNamara, "I clearly erred by not forcing . . . a knock-down, drag-out debate over loose assumptions, unasked questions, and thin analyses underlying our military strategy in Vietnam. . . . I doubt if I will ever fully understand why I did not do so."[175] The Joint Chiefs of Staff also failed to press the case for reexamination of premises.[176]

There have been many critics of our military strategy,[177] who sometimes complain that our goal was not to conquer North Vietnam; instead, it was to buy time and prevent the "loss" of South Vietnam. However, the objective of the successful Gulf War in 1991 was to remove Iraq from Kuwait, not to occupy Iraq. When we did conquer Iraq in 2003, matters did not go well, as I discuss in chapter 5. Nevertheless, it does not matter if we

ASSUMING PROBLEMS: THE WAR IN VIETNAM

could have won by risking war with China or the Soviet Union and adopting a less constrained, more robust strategy. There still would have been loss of life on all sides in a cause we should not have fought. The tragedy is not that we did not win but that we fought at all.

Eminent historian George Herring insightfully summed up the Vietnam experience.

> The United States intervened in Vietnam to block the apparent march of a Soviet-directed Communism across Asia, enlarged its commitment to halt a presumably expansionist Communist China, and eventually made Vietnam a test of its determination to uphold world order.... It elevated into a major international conflict what might have remained a localized struggle. By raising the stakes into a test of its own credibility, it perilously narrowed its options. A policy so flawed in its premises cannot help but fail, and in this case the results were disastrous.[178]

CHAPTER THREE

Ignoring and Underestimating Problems

"My God, this can't be true."—Secretary of War Henry Stimson, December 7, 1941[1]

Premises may lead decision makers to take action to solve problems that do not exist, as in the case of Vietnam. Premises may also prompt leaders to ignore or underestimate the probability of threats to a nation's well-being or to policies designed to advance the country's welfare. If officials do not think there is a problem, they are unlikely to consider options for dealing with it. Officials may also employ selective information to make inferences that a particular situation could not possibly occur. If policymakers accept this inference of impossibility, there is no need for them to consider information pointing to the opposite conclusion. Moreover, presuming away problems is likely to accord policymakers undue confidence in their current policies and thus cause them to evaluate options consistent with those policies more positively than is appropriate.

Reinforcing the power of premises is the fact that clear-cut disconfirmation of premises may not be possible.[2] There is usually a range of information from which to choose, and this data is likely to point in opposite directions. Thus, information about many important questions in politics, such as the current and future actions of hostile nations, is typically ambiguous. In such cases, leaders' views are determined more by their premises than by specific pieces of intelligence.[3] Moreover, leaders are likely to accord more credence to information that reinforces their preexisting views.

Richard Betts posed the key question of why surprise attacks are so often successful despite nations often holding evidence of an adversary's plan. To answer the question, he focused on errors in the processing of information caused by motivated bias and outlined four ways such errors may influence a prediction. Decision makers (1) look more positively on data that is reassuring and supports status quo beliefs while exhibiting more skepticism of information that challenges them; (2) often more thoroughly question the source of information when they review challenging data; (3) may accept intelligence warnings but insist on confirming evidence through fact-finding missions (which may be impossible to conduct); and (4) may rationalize and engage in wishful thinking to explain away negative data. In sum, motivated bias protects officials' premises from rigorous challenge, offering them confidence and false optimism about their views, to the detriment of those subject to surprise attacks.[4]

In World War II, some leaders of the Axis countries lived in a fantasy world—they believed their own propaganda, which argued that, for reasons of race and ideology, they were unbeatable; the Allied powers were no match.[5] For example, when the Luftwaffe commander of fighter planes informed German Reich marshal Hermann Goering that an Allied fighter had been shot down over Aachen, proving that the Allies had developed a long-range fighter that could protect their bombers over Germany, Goering responded by denying the event occurred: "I officially assert that an American fighter plane did not reach Aachen.... I herewith give you an official order that they weren't there." On another occasion, he told a German official that his report of damage in an air raid was incorrect. "Impossible," Goering claimed. "That many bombs cannot be dropped in a single night."[6]

In 1962, U.S. officials dismissed eyewitness reports of giant tubes being unloaded in Cuba because such activity was incompatible with the CIA's premise that the Soviets would not put missiles in Cuba. Similarly, officials rejected photographic evidence of the principal nuclear warhead storage center at Bejucal because it did not have security fences and guard posts similar to storage sites in the Soviet Union, which analysts expected to see.[7] The CIA concluded that they "missed the Soviet decision to put the missiles into Cuba because we could not believe that Khrushchev could make [such] a mistake."[8]

As Robert Jervis explains, officials debated the nature of Soviet intentions throughout the Cold War, and few people were swayed by intelligence or competing analysis.

> On the broadest issues of the nature and intentions of other countries and the existence and characteristics of broad historical trends, people's beliefs are determined more by their general worldviews, predispositions, and ideologies than they are by the sort of specific evidence that can be pieced together by

intelligence. The reason why CIA director John McCone expected the Soviet Union to put missiles into Cuba and his analysts did not was not that they examined different evidence or that he was more careful than they were, but that he strongly believed that the details of the nuclear balance influenced world politics and that Khrushchev would therefore be strongly motivated to improve his position.[9]

Surprise attacks by one country on another—unfortunately, not a rare occurrence—perhaps most dramatically illustrate the biased evaluation of information.[10] In April 1940, for example, the British and Norwegians were so sure that Germany would not expose its forces to British naval superiority that they ignored reports from captured German soldiers who told them truthfully that they were on their way to invade Norway.[11]

The remainder of this chapter illustrates the key role of premises in blinding capable, earnest, patriotic leaders to threats to their nations or problems with existing policies. Chapter 4 provides an in-depth examination of a classic example of the catastrophic impact of assumptions held by the policymakers who many analysts credit with establishing the framework that ultimately won the Cold War.

The Embargo

Thomas Jefferson and James Madison were two brilliant, experienced, and rigorous thinkers dedicated to avoiding war and maintaining the young nation's prosperity. Nevertheless, they launched what is surely one of the most disastrous policies in American history.

During the first decade of the nineteenth century, Britain and France engaged in a struggle for control of Europe. Central to their efforts were blockades. Britain's navy closed most European harbors to American ships unless they first traded through British ports. France responded by declaring a blockade of Britain and seizing American ships that obeyed British regulations. The British also impressed suspected British deserters and often Americans from U.S. ships and forced them into the British navy.[12]

President Thomas Jefferson did not want war and believed the United States could employ economic coercion to dissuade the European powers from interfering with American ships and sailors. On April 18, 1806, Congress passed the Non-Importation Act, which forbade the importation of certain British goods in an attempt to coerce Great Britain to suspend its impressments of American sailors and to respect American sovereignty and neutrality on the high seas. Congress suspended the implementation of the law until November 15 to allow for a British response to the threat of losing its American market.

Britain did not alter its behavior, however, and in the summer of 1807, its commercial restrictions and violations of Americans' basic rights produced a demand for war. An incident at sea further enflamed public opinion. On June 22, the HMS *Leopard* of the Royal Navy fired upon the USS *Chesapeake* for refusing to comply with a search for deserters. The short skirmish was one-sided, and the crew of the *Leopard* carried off four crewmen from the *Chesapeake*.

In December, the Non-Importation Act went into effect. More importantly, Jefferson asked Congress to pass the Embargo Act, which prohibited all American ships from departing for a foreign port. Barring American ships and goods from all overseas trade was a drastic act, but it passed Congress on December 22 with little debate and little White House justification. Over the next few months, Congress passed additional acts closing loopholes in the original law and barring all exports of any goods, whether by land or sea.

It is not clear that either Jefferson or his secretary of state, James Madison, had thought through the implications of the policy. Albert Gallatin, the brilliant secretary of the treasury, understood the economy better than either Jefferson or Madison and warned them the embargo would fail and have many negative unintended consequences, but Jefferson ignored him. Although the president originally saw the embargo as little more than a defensive device to prevent the capture of American ships, cargo, and seamen, he soon adopted Madison's view that the policy was an opportunity to transform international relations, a grand experiment in peaceful coercion to compel belligerents to remove their trade restrictions. The president seems to have had an exaggerated idea of America's international power and thought of the embargo as a means of starving the British.

As a result of the embargo, American ships rotted at the wharves, and farmers and planters could not sell their crops. American traders suffered huge commercial losses and engaged in widespread smuggling to compensate. Gallatin told the president he had to have greater powers to effectively enforce the embargo. Thus, Congress passed a draconian enforcement act that closed all loopholes and granted the president extraordinary powers to capture and punish violators, and broad discretionary authority to enforce, deny, or grant exceptions to the embargo. The law authorized port authorities to seize cargoes without a warrant and to prosecute any shipper or merchant who was thought to have merely contemplated violating the embargo. As Gordon Wood put it, "The United States government was virtually at war with its own people."[13]

Opposition to the embargo shattered the unity of the Jeffersonian party, and Jefferson signed the repeal of the embargo shortly before leaving office in March 1809. In its place, Congress enacted the Nonintercourse Act on March 1, which opened American trade with all countries except Britain and France, and their possessions. The act gave the new president, James Madison, the power to resume trade with either Britain or France should one of these countries remove its regulations against American commerce. The Nonintercourse Act proved no more effective than the embargo, and it was impossible to prevent American vessels from trading with the European belligerents once they had left American ports.

Despite the failure of the embargo, the United States made another effort at economic coercion in 1810, in the measure known as Macon's Bill Number 2, which replaced the Nonintercourse Act. The new law opened trade with both Britain and France, and the United States attempted to bargain with the two belligerents. If either power would remove its restrictions on American commerce, the United States would reapply nonintercourse against the country that had not removed them. Napoleon quickly took advantage of this opportunity, pledging to repeal his commercial restrictions, and Madison reinstituted nonintercourse against Britain in the fall of 1810 (although Napoleon did not fulfill his pledge).

When Britain finally promised to repeal its trade restrictions, it was too late to avoid war. By the time the news reached America, the United States had already declared the War of 1812 against Britain. Once again, Congress forbade all American ships from leaving port, prohibited all exports, outlawed the coasting trade, and gave government officials broad powers of enforcement. Yet, as before, the policy was not successful, and the government needed trade for revenue and diplomatic reasons. Thus, by the end of March 1814, Madison called for the repeal of the embargo and nonimportation policies.

Despite its sustained failure, Madison and Jefferson's shared premises were so strong that they continued to believe in the embargo, certain it would have worked if the United States had persevered. According to historian Gordon Wood, the embargo was perhaps, except for Prohibition, "the greatest example in American history of ideology brought to bear on a matter of public policy."[14]

French Military Planning for World War I

In the early twentieth century, the French developed Plan 17 in response to an expected war with Germany. They based their preparations for war on the fixed belief that the Germans would never use reserves in the front line. It followed, they reasoned, the Germans could not deploy enough manpower to extend their assault around French defenses and invade France through western Belgium and the French coastal provinces. They also did not believe Germany would violate Belgian territory. Thus, French leaders "resolutely ignored" evidence seeping out of Germany in 1913 that challenged their beliefs. Acting under their premises, the French concentrated their forces on attacking the Germans with an advance to the Rhine, leaving the rest of France unguarded. They planned to attack the German center and left and cut off its right (the forces operating from the northwest of Germany, the northeast of France). Certain of the validity of their strategy, the French expected and planned for quick victory.[15]

It was not as if no one could imagine what was to come. Three years before the war began, General Victor-Constant Michel, commander in chief of the French army, correctly predicted the main elements of the Schlieffen Plan, Germany's offensive strategy. When in 1911 he presented a plan to defend against an invasion through Belgium, war minister Adolphe Messimy relieved him of his command and dismissed him from the Supreme War Council.[16]

When the war began, Germany deployed reserves to the front line and advanced around the French defenses, and France's attack across the Rhine met much stiffer resistance than its generals expected. Nevertheless, the French would not adjust their plan to attack the German center, and they ignored evidence contrary to the plan. When Plan 17 failed, chief of staff General Joseph Joffre blamed his commanders, not the plan.[17] The resulting four-year war of attrition brought the most horrendous loss of life on the battlefield the world had ever known.

Fortunately for the Triple Entente, the Germans had faulty premises of their own. Their plan of attack included everything except flexibility. They could not change their basic plan of attacking France first instead of Russia (although it seems clear in retrospect that it could have been done). They mistakenly concluded that the Russians would not mobilize for war and that Belgium would not resist a German invasion. Like the French and the Russians, they expected an early victory and thus planned for a short war. They did not expect Britain to play an important role in the war, and the kaiser even believed Britain would not enter the war, despite clear evidence and advice to the contrary.[18] Policies based on each of these premises undermined the German war effort.

Operation Barbarossa

On June 22, 1941, Adolf Hitler launched Operation Barbarossa, the German code name for the invasion of the Soviet Union. This attack violated the Molotov-Ribbentrop Pact, a nonaggression treaty between the countries negotiated two years earlier, and began the largest military operation in history. The Soviet army lost two hundred divisions and suffered over 4 million casualties in 1941, the greatest losses in such a few months in the history of warfare. By the time the German advance slowed, the Soviet Union had lost roughly half its industrial and agricultural capacity.[19]

Soviet officials were highly alert to the dangers of invasion. They possessed precise and detailed intelligence information on the Nazi threat from multiple sources serving an intelligence network stretching from Berlin to Tokyo. They knew that in May and June 1941 the German army moved vast quantities of men and equipment to the Soviet border.

Nevertheless, Joseph Stalin, the general secretary of the Communist Party and the unquestioned leader of the Soviet Union, rejected this intelligence. Soviet officials who feared the dictator's wrath also sometimes pandered to Stalin's views when they presented him with intelligence reports. Moreover, the purges of the 1930s continued up to the German invasion, costing the USSR talented senior commanders and depleting the officer corps. Indeed, on the eve of war, the general secretary had around three hundred senior officers arrested.

Stalin also rejected clear warnings from Britain about the attack. He was suspicious of British plans after the Hess affair (in which Germany's deputy fuhrer Rudolph Hess parachuted into Britain in an idiosyncratic effort to negotiate peace), and his Communist ideology led him to doubt that capitalist Britain and France would work with the USSR. He thought Britain was simply trying to lure him into battle. The lessons he drew from the Crimean War and of British intervention in the Russian civil war persuaded him that the Soviet Union had more to fear from a British naval raid than from a German invasion. Stalin assumed that the capitalist powers, led by Britain, were more interested in the destruction of the Soviet Union than in the destruction of Nazi Germany. Any intelligence that pointed toward a German invasion of Russia, he believed, must therefore be disinformation emanating from British sources, who hoped to dupe the two dictators into fighting each other.

Moreover, as a dogmatic Marxist-Leninist, Stalin was convinced that Hitler's regime was the tool of German monopoly capitalism. He reasoned that if he made German businesses happy, there would be no reason for Hitler to invade. Thus, he stepped up deliveries of rubber and was supplying the Germans with phosphates, asbestos, chrome ore, manganese, nickel, and oil. Reports of an imminent invasion only convinced him that the Germans were playing hardball in their drive to extract economic concessions.

Stalin did not harbor any illusions about Hitler's ultimate ambitions to destroy the Soviet Union, but he had reasons for concluding that Germany would not attack in 1941. The Germans engaged in systematic deception, including letters from Hitler to Stalin arguing that the German troops on the Soviet Union's border were simply avoiding British bombing and that Germany was planning to invade Britain soon—not the Soviet Union.

Stalin also thought it did not make sense for Hitler to attack the USSR before attacking Britain. One of his favorite arguments was that Germany, having lost one two-front war in 1918, would never risk fighting another. Thus, so long as Britain was not defeated, Hitler would never invade Russia. (Moreover, Stalin hoped Germany would invade Britain, because he had concluded that such an attack would create a revolutionary situation he could exploit.) Some analysts contend that Stalin thought Hitler was too clever to think he could conquer the USSR, especially so late in the year as June 22, given the limited time that would remain before autumn rains turned the Russian roads into impassable quagmires.

The Soviet leader also wanted to avoid provoking Hitler, hoping to hold off a German attack until 1942, when the Soviet Union would be better prepared to defend against it. Stalin believed Tsar Nicholas II's precautionary mobilization at the outbreak of World War I had provoked a German countermobilization and thus escalation of the crisis into war, and he was determined not to make same mistake.

Although Stalin continued and even accelerated long-term preparations for war, including a massive buildup of frontline forces, he did not order a full-scale mobilization well in advance of the German attack. Soviet front lines were placed on a full state of alert, but he ordered them to avoid provocative actions. Thus, he refused to permit Soviet air defense forces to halt the massive German air reconnaissance on the eve of the invasion.

The Soviet General Staff had faulty premises as well. They grossly underestimated the scale of the initial German attack, expecting Germany to launch tactical attacks, which would be followed by two to four weeks of mobilization and concentration of forces on both sides. Again, the model was World War I. The Soviet generals knew of German blitzkrieg victories, of course, but nevertheless felt they could hold back the Wehrmacht while they mobilized. There was little place for strategic defense in the military doctrines of the Red Army, however. Instead, the Soviets were preoccupied with offensive war against Germany. Even so, the General Staff was not planning for a preemptive strike against the Germans.

Thus, Stalin operated on a set of premises that led him to conclude that Germany would not launch a strategic attack in the summer of 1941. All of his premises were incorrect, but they led him to reject accurate warnings of Hitler's plans. When an ex-Communist soldier deserted the German forces on June 21, 1941, and swam across a river to tell the Russians on the other side that his unit had been given orders to invade the following morning, Stalin had him shot for spreading "disinformation."

The inevitable uncertainty associated with predicting another nation's plans provided Stalin the opportunity to explain away the warnings. According to a careful student of Operation Barbarossa,

> it was Stalin's insistence on accepting German deception as truth, his rejection of valid intelligence from his own services, and his failure to recognize that the warnings from Western powers, themselves threatened by Hitler's aggressiveness, were both accurate and well intentioned, that led to the debacle in the summer of 1941.[20]

Even when the German attack began, Stalin took days to acknowledge the war's reality. When Georgi Zhukov, chief of the Red Army General Staff, telephoned Stalin on June 22, 1941, to tell him the Germans were attacking, Stalin refused to believe a full-scale invasion was underway. He initially thought the attack might be either the work of German generals endeavoring to force Hitler into full-scale war with the USSR or Hitler's way of pressuring him into new concessions. When it was clear that the June 22 attack was the beginning of a full-scale invasion of the Soviet Union and that Stalin had been wrong in his assessments, he focused on purging officials who knew he should have known better.

The Attack on Pearl Harbor

It is natural to assume that foreign leaders are rational as Americans understand rationality, so Americans frequently misread the intentions of other countries. It did not occur to us in 1941 that Japanese leaders thought the United States would be willing to fight and lose a limited war.[21] Tokyo hoped a quick and devastating blow at Pearl Harbor would lead Washington to pursue a limited war and allow the Japanese to establish a Pacific perimeter. This miscalculation, Richard Betts argues, was the result of "the illusions of the Japanese about American decadence and effeteness and their failure to appreciate the nation's self-confidence and absolutist view of war rooted in the liberal tradition."[22] Japanese leaders were prisoners of their premises.

Similarly, most U.S. officials believed that the Japanese could not attack Pearl Harbor. Moreover, it would not be logical for them to do so, as Japan would lose a war with the United States. These officials found evidence to support their views.[23] Roberta Wohlstetter, the author of a pathbreaking work on the Pearl Harbor assault, found, "Again and again there is this reaction, that certainly the outbreak of war with Japan was to be expected at any moment after November 27, but not to be expected at Pearl Harbor."[24]

American officials could not conceive of the type of attack the Japanese launched. They expected that if there were an air attack, it would be a softening up for a land invasion and be simultaneous with acts of sabotage.[25] Thus, the prospect of an airborne attack on Hawaii remained unthinkable to those in charge. On November 27, Admiral Husband Kimmel, commander in chief, United States Fleet, and commander in chief, U.S. Pacific Fleet, asked his war plans officer if there was any chance the Japanese would be so bold. "Absolutely none," the officer replied.[26]

A set of subsidiary premises supported the broad premise of the unlikelihood of an attack. All were faulty. U.S. officials thought the Japanese navy could not sail thousands of miles and refuel repeatedly on the high seas, and that it would not accept the risk to do so. Leaders viewed the Pearl Harbor fleet as a deterrent to an attack rather than as a target, and they felt the U.S. military could detect enemy aircraft carriers in plenty of time to prepare for an assault. Officials underestimated the skill of Japanese pilots and Japanese political and military leaders. Finally, decision makers concluded that torpedoes would not work in the relatively shallow water where the U.S. ships were docked, and thus nets were not necessary to stop them.[27]

Because they were not expecting an attack, American officials did not notice the signs pointing toward it. Instead, Wohlstetter found, they exhibited the "very human tendency to pay attention to the signals that support current expectations about enemy behavior."[28] Thus, they interpreted information pointing to an attack as consistent with their premises that it would not occur. "Human beings have a stubborn attachment to old beliefs and an equally stubborn resistance to new material that will upset them."[29] As a result, "in conditions of great uncertainty," people, even "honest, dedicated, and intelligent" ones, "tend to predict that events that they want to happen actually will happen."[30]

In the days leading up to the attack, clues of a huge Japanese initiative were circulating in Washington and made their way to Admiral Kimmel. Ten days before Japanese planes appeared over Oahu, the Navy Department sent a "war warning" to the naval forces at Pearl Harbor, asking Kimmel to execute an appropriate defensive deployment. Kimmel had been more focused on planning for an eventual move against the Japanese elsewhere in the Pacific. He largely ignored the broadly worded instructions and used his resources for training and supplying bases close to Japan rather than instituting an adequate alert system for Hawaii. After all, the assumption among government and military officials was that the Japanese would focus first on weak targets such as British and Dutch territories somewhere in the southwest Pacific or Thailand, Russia, or Korea rather than attacking thousands of miles to the east in Hawaii.[31]

It is not surprising, then, that Kimmel did not check to ensure that the army's antiaircraft and radar units were on full alert.[32] The navy knew that it had lost track of all six of Japan's aircraft carriers but its leaders did not probe the issue further.[33] No one sent long-range reconnaissance planes to the north of Hawaii, where they might have spotted the Japanese fleet.[34] Expecting sabotage to precede any Japanese attack, the commanding general ordered U.S. aircraft clustered together, making them easy targets for Japanese pilots and unable to take to the skies to combat the attackers.[35] More broadly, there was no realistic appraisal of a surprise attack or its consequences.[36]

The problem was not an absence of evidence regarding a Japanese attack. It was voluminous. The difficulty was in interpreting it. There is no doubt that it was difficult to sift through all the signals, many of them ambiguous, and identify the ones that really mattered.[37] Yet, premises posed an insurmountable obstacle to doing so. We see what we are prepared to see. U.S. officials were not sensitive to the signs of danger. To discriminate among the conflicting and ambiguous signals required a sensitivity to the signs of danger that the Americans lacked. As Wohlstetter put it, "A warning is not likely to be heard if its occurrence is regarded as so improbable that no one is listening."[38]

The premises supporting the view that the Japanese would not attack Pearl Harbor were so powerful that they blinded U.S. officials at all levels, even as the attack began. At 7:02 a.m. on December 7—less than an hour before the attack—"something completely out of the ordinary" appeared on a radar screen in Oahu. When the radar operators reported it to the lieutenant in charge, he explained away the radar event as likely caused by incoming American planes. Ultimately, the intelligence was ignored. The radar operators also tracked one of the Japanese reconnoitering planes, which was operating ahead of the bombers. Officials also ignored this information.[39]

In the weeks preceding the air raid, Kimmel had issued a general warning that an encounter with a single Japanese submarine should be regarded as sign of extreme danger, because the submarine could imply the presence of a Japanese aircraft carrier nearby. On the morning of the attack, the navy sank at least one Japanese submarine near the entrance to Pearl Harbor. However, the watch officer could not convince anyone higher up in the chain of command of the importance of this event, so no one sounded an alert.[40]

Five minutes before the Japanese attack, an operations officer at Pearl Harbor observed an aircraft dive-bombing Ford Island, at the center of Pearl Harbor. He thought, incorrectly, that it must be an American plane.[41] Most tellingly, when Secretary of War Henry Stimson was told of the Japanese attack on Pearl Harbor, he exclaimed, "My God, this can't be true. This [message] must mean Philippines," where he had expected the attack.[42]

On December 7, 1941, U.S. ships and planes were easy targets for the Japanese. There were neither fully functional radar nor any reconnaissance planes to detect the raid, which came early on a Sunday morning. Nor was there any metal netting in the harbor to protect the American fleet from torpedoes. The result of the massive failure to anticipate the Japanese attack was the day that would live in infamy. The Japanese sank or damaged nineteen U.S. Navy ships, including all eight battleships in the harbor, three cruisers, and three destroyers. There were nearly 3,600 casualties. Many military buildings were destroyed, as were 188 aircraft. At the time, it was the worst military disaster in American history.[43]

Americans were not the only ones lulled into complacency by premises of invulnerability. Singapore was of strategic importance to the British Empire, second only to the Suez Canal. It was the major British military base in Southeast Asia, essential for protecting Australia and New Zealand and controlling the Malacca Straits. Virtually simultaneous with the attack on Pearl Harbor, the Japanese launched an amphibious assault on Malaya and Thailand. The British thought Japanese forces were inferior and the Malayan jungles impassable,[44] but they were wrong. On February 15, 1942, Singapore fell to the invaders in what British prime minister

Winston Churchill called the "worst disaster and largest capitulation in British military history."[45] According to Wohlstetter, "The stunning tactical success of the Japanese on the British at Singapore was made possible by the deeply held British faith in the impregnability of that fortress."[46]

The Fall of the Philippines, 1941

The attack on Oahu was not the full story of Japanese action against the United States that day. Other war planes and their crews were poised on Formosa, waiting to attack the Philippines as soon as their commanders learned of the results of the Pearl Harbor strike. The objective of the strikes at Pearl Harbor and the Philippines was to shield Japan's drive southward to seize the oil and natural resources of Southeast Asia and the Dutch East Indies. If the Japanese could knock out U.S. Air Force assets in the Philippines, they could operate at will against the rest of the defenders—which is exactly what happened.[47]

On November 3, 1941, the United States' war plan, titled Rainbow 5, was revised to prescribe air raids launched from the Philippines against Japanese forces and installations in the event of war. On November 21, army chief of staff General George Marshall warned Douglas MacArthur, commander of the U.S. Army forces in the Far East, of a possible attack on the Philippines.

As the last wave of Japanese bombers attacked Pearl Harbor, MacArthur received a call in his Manila penthouse informing him of the airstrike. Brigadier General Leonard T. Gerow, chief of the army War Plans Division, soon called from Washington with a longer account. He told MacArthur that he "wouldn't be surprised if you get an attack there in the near future." Within an hour and a half of the attack, Marshall sent MacArthur a cablegram directing him to "carry out tasks assigned in Rainbow 5 as they pertain to Japan." The War Plans Division called again shortly afterward to check on the situation in the Philippines and to give a further warning. In addition, radar and ground observers detected the movement of Japanese aircraft, and there were reports of several preliminary Japanese attacks.

MacArthur's commander of the Far East Air Force, Major General Lewis Brereton, tried to see him immediately, seeking permission to strike the Japanese bases on Formosa. MacArthur's aides denied him access. Brereton tried other times, but it took more than five hours after receiving orders from Washington for MacArthur to call Brereton and give him the authority to make the decision on offensive air action.

By then, it was too late. Almost immediately, the Japanese attacked Philippine bases, where U.S. planes were clustered together, and over the next few days all but destroyed the U.S. Far East Air Force. The attacks effectively eliminated American air power in the western Pacific, forced the complete withdrawal of the United States Asiatic Fleet from Philippine waters, and paved the way for the Japanese invasion that followed.

How was it possible that an air force on full alert, notified of the attack on Pearl Harbor and forewarned of a force of enemy aircraft approaching, could have been caught with its planes on the ground when the attack began? As one historian put it, "there is no question that senior Army leaders in the Philippines were completely responsible for the disaster. Indecision at the highest levels resulted in hours of delay that cost the defenders of the Philippines dearly."[48]

Instead of acting decisively to prepare for a likely Japanese attack on the Philippines, MacArthur took no significant action for more than nine hours to bring his command to a proper state of readiness to resist an attack and preserve his air force. Although he ordered American planes to be sent out of harm's way, there was no sense of urgency in doing so. Accepting the prevailing belief that an attack would occur in March or April 1942, MacArthur assumed that the Japanese could not attack the Philippines for several months. He also shared the view that the Japanese Zeros could not reach the Philippines from Formosa, so they would have to be transported by aircraft carriers.[49]

A second premise also likely influenced MacArthur's failure to respond appropriately. His friend Manuel Quezon was the president of the Philippines. Quezon naively believed that his country was neither militarily nor economically important to Japan. Based on that premise, he hoped to steer the Philippines to a course of neutrality in the event of war between the United States and Japan. When Quezon first received news of the Japanese attack on Pearl Harbor, he dismissed the report as nonsense, fantasizing that Japan would not attack the Philippines. When he finally grasped reality, Quezon contacted MacArthur to urge him to avoid action that might provoke a Japanese attack on the Philippines. Despite the attack on Pearl Harbor, MacArthur's headquarters pointed out that there was as of yet no formal declaration of war against Japan. Thus, the argument was that despite the direct order from Marshall, MacArthur could not approve a counterattack on Formosan bases.[50]

Bay of Pigs

On the night of April 17, 1961, Brigade 2506, composed of about 1,300 men trained and provisioned by the CIA, invaded Cuba in an effort to overthrow the regime of Fidel Castro. Defending the island were Cuba's army of thirty-two thousand soldiers and a two-hundred-thousand-member militia. Greatly outnumbered, the invaders needed reinforcements. The CIA's inspector general wrote in his report on the episode,

> It is clear that the invasion operation was based on the hope that the brigade [the U.S.-supported invaders] would be able to maintain itself in Cuba long enough to prevail by attracting insurgents and defectors from the Castro armed services, but without having in advance any assurance of assistance from identified, known, controlled, trained, and organized guerillas.[51]

In other words, the United States based its plans for the invasion on the premise that it would be a catalyst for an uprising by an organized resistance that may or may not have existed.[52] The Joint Chiefs of Staff and other high officials advised the president that the invasion could not succeed without a popular uprising in Cuba.[53] White House officials considered an uprising essential for success, and they thought the CIA did as well.[54] Yet it was not clear how many defectors or insurgents there might be or to what use they might be put.[55]

No one expected an unarmed and unorganized spontaneous uprising as soon as the exiles hit the beaches.[56] Nevertheless, the White House, the secretary of defense, and the Joint Chiefs of Staff assumed the successful occupation of an enlarged beachhead area would soon incite an organized uprising by armed members of the Cuban resistance.[57] Top CIA officials reinforced this impression. Richard Bissell, the CIA deputy director for plans and chief of the invasion, believed the Cuban militia would not fight the invasion force and that there would be an uprising across the island, and he told President John F. Kennedy that there would be one.[58]

On March 11, 1961, Bissell argued that the invasion would cause defections from Castro's armed forces and induce widespread rebellion. In early April, the CIA claimed that more than 2,500 people belonged to resistance organizations and more than twenty thousand additional persons were resistance sympathizers. It predicted that once the brigade established a beachhead, it could expect the active support of at least a quarter of the Cuban population. On April 3, it claimed the percentage of the Cuban population opposed to Castro was much higher than the foregoing estimate, but that many would probably remain neutral until there was a strong indication of which side was winning.[59]

In a meeting on April 7, Bissell told the president that a National Intelligence Estimate (NIE) concluded the Cuban people would rise up and support the invasion and the Cuban army would not fight for Castro.[60] Five days later, the agency reported that it estimated "there are nearly 7,000 insurgents responsive to some degree of control through agents with whom communications are currently active." After the invasion, the CIA planned to supply them with arms.[61] Indeed, the U.S. Navy was waiting offshore with tanks, jeeps, and thirty thousand rifles to distribute to insurgents.[62] José Miró Cardona, head of the Cuban Revolutionary Council, thought ten thousand Cubans would come to the brigade's support.[63]

Central to the success of the enterprise, then, was the premise that Fidel Castro's regime lacked the support of the Cuban people.[64] As a result, the invasion planners assumed, Cubans would revolt and help to overthrow Castro once the invasion began. Richard Neustadt and Ernest May found this assumption to be a "classic case of presumptions unexamined." Cubans had been historically very slow to revolt. Fidel Castro did, in fact, have popular support because the life of the average Cuban had improved during his tenure, and most Cubans did not feel oppressed by communism.[65]

Evidence was readily available to decision makers that an uprising was unlikely.[66] Tellingly, on March 10, the chair of CIA Board of National Estimates wrote that Castro was in firm control of Cuba.[67] The CIA oversold and overestimated the possibility of strong indigenous support for the invaders,[68] and top policymakers failed to question this conclusion rigorously, quietly accepting the agency's reassurances. They were prisoners of their premises.

The Cuban leader arrested tens of thousands of potential insurgents and defectors even before the invasion began, knowing full well that no invasion could succeed without internal support.[69] His police arrested two hundred thousand people in Havana alone, and throughout the island, detained anyone suspected of underground connections.[70] In addition, there were few Cubans near the landing site to rise up and begin the insurrection.[71]

After the episode, Kennedy reproached himself. "How could I have been so stupid?" he asked. The president reflected that he should have canceled the entire operation once the basic premises shattered.[72] He could not forget his preinvasion conversation with former secretary of state Dean Acheson, who asked how many men were invading and how many men Castro could field against them. Kennedy replied that there were perhaps 1,500 invaders and 25,000 opponents. Acheson marveled at Kennedy's naivete: "It doesn't take Price Waterhouse to figure out that fifteen hundred aren't as good as twenty-five thousand," he told the president.[73]

The invasion was a disaster, including for the new president making his first major foreign policy decision. Virtually all of the invaders were captured or killed, and hundreds of potential allies in Cuba were executed. Friendly Latin American countries were outraged by the invasion. The Cuban victory solidified Castro's role as a national hero and pushed Cuba toward greater military cooperation with the Soviet Union, culminating in the Cuban Missile Crisis in 1962. There were many problems with the planning and decision making about the Bay of Pigs, including the ridiculous assumption that the United States could hide its role and the conclusion that it was possible to knock out the Cuban air force before the invasion.[74] It is highly unlikely, however, that the White House would have approved the invasion if the administration had not accepted the premise of its instigating a broad uprising in Cuba.

Other Surprises and Misestimates

In 1968, North Vietnam launched a massive attack on South Vietnam, creating a turning point in the U.S. public's support for the war. The American chief of intelligence in Vietnam looked back at the event and acknowledged, "Even had I known exactly what was to take place, it was so preposterous that I probably would have been unable to sell it to anybody. Why would the enemy give away his major advantage, which was his ability to be elusive and avoid heavy casualties?"[75]

The United States and Israel were surprised by Egypt's attack on Israel in 1973, because both countries assumed Egypt would not attack until it had rebuilt its air force and could mount air strikes against the Israeli air force.[76] More broadly, an attack seemed implausible because Egypt could not succeed in winning a war on the ground, so officials discounted Egyptian and Syrian deployments. Policymakers did not understand that Egyptian president Anwar Sadat saw fighting as a means of overcoming the humiliation of losses in the 1967 war and restoring his nation's self-respect as a means of opening the road to negotiations with Israel.[77] According to

Henry Kissinger, "our notion of rationality did not take seriously the notion of starting an unwinnable war to restore self-respect."[78] In addition, incentives for the ruling Israeli party engaged in an election campaign to show its deterrence strategy was successful[79] and a need for officials to achieve cognitive closure may have reinforced Israeli officials in holding firmly to the belief that an attack on Israel was unlikely. Thus, they were closed to alternative perspectives, avoided or suppressed information at odds with their own assessment, and accepted compatible speculative assessments as hard evidence.[80]

The United States did not anticipate the Soviet Union's invasion of Afghanistan in 1979, because we knew it would be a mistake—for the USSR. As the CIA's assessment of the issue concluded, the failure to predict the invasion "was *not* because of an absence of intelligence information on Soviet preparations for the move. It was that the operation being prepared was contrary to what intelligence analysts had *expected* Moscow would be willing to do."[81] The United States also did not understand that the Soviet Union saw an unstable border with Afghanistan as a threat to its security interests. It also concluded that a failure to intervene would imperil its many long-standing investments in Afghanistan and lead to a loss of prestige. In addition, the USSR thought the Afghans were about to seek American support.[82]

In the same year, U.S. leaders were surprised by the overthrow of the shah of Iran, an event that led to the detaining of American hostages for 444 days. Officials assumed the shah's position was secure because he controlled a large and effective internal security force, they expected threats to pro-Western governments to come from the left, they felt the strongest elements in Iranian society supported modernization efforts, and they assumed that religious motivations and movements were peripheral to politics.[83] All these assumptions were incorrect.

The George H. W. Bush White House was surprised when Iraq invaded Kuwait in 1990. Although the United States had detailed information on Iraqi forces poised on the Kuwaiti border, top officials still were not convinced an invasion was imminent.[84] As Secretary of State Jim Baker put it, no one believed that Saddam Hussein would attack because an attack made no sense from the perspective of those who calculated his interests.[85] After the Gulf War, the U.S. assumed incorrectly that Iraqis would overthrow Saddam.[86]

Many analysts could not believe Mikhail Gorbachev was serious about reforms because they knew such restructurings would undermine the stability of the USSR and thus his position in it.[87] India's testing of nuclear weapons in 1998, which undermined the United States' efforts to halt nuclear proliferation, took the Clinton administration by surprise. Officials assumed that it would not be rational for India to carry out such tests, so few paid attention to the signals that it indeed planned to do so.[88]

Conclusion

Premises exert a powerful influence on how even capable, responsible officials evaluate the existence of problems. In the murky world of international relations, where the intentions and reactions of other nations are difficult to evaluate, the assumptions policymakers carry in their heads often blind them to threats to the nation and other developments of strategic importance. Assuming away problems deters leaders from taking steps to avoid them. Instead, decision makers may conclude that events such as surprise attacks cannot occur, easing their cognitive life but placing the country in peril.

In chapter 4, I examine policymaking that led not just to a tactical setback for the United States, such as the attack on Pearl Harbor, but rather resulted in a strategic catastrophe.

CHAPTER FOUR

Ignoring and Underestimating Problems

The Chinese Intervention in Korea in 1950

"One of the most terrific disasters that has occurred to American foreign policy." — Secretary of State Dean Acheson, on the Chinese intervention in Korea[1]

Nine years after the attack on Pearl Harbor, the United States again suffered from surprise attacks, this time in Korea. Actually, the country was surprised twice in Korea—first, by the initial invasion of the South by the North Koreans, and then six months later by the entry of China into the war. American strategic premises inhibited policymakers from anticipating both the North Korean and the Chinese attacks, with catastrophic consequences.

In this chapter, I examine these two strategic surprises through the lens of policymakers' premises. These decision makers were giants, too. President Harry Truman and his senior officials built a new international order in the wake of World War II. Most broadly, the United States adopted the doctrine of containment, the basic framework of U.S. foreign policy for the four decades of the Cold War, culminating in the collapse of the Soviet Union. As part of this effort, the president and his advisors channeled economic and military assistance to countries vulnerable to communism under the Truman Doctrine and executed the Berlin airlift. They also constructed the modern foreign and defense policy apparatus, including the National Security Council, the CIA, and the Department of Defense. These same men adopted policies that transformed Germany and Japan into democracies and built a network of alliances in Europe and Asia that contributed to maintaining the peace. They also provided Europe the aid necessary to recover from the war under the Marshall Plan, and they established a multitude of international organizations, including the United Nations, the International Monetary Fund, the World Bank, and the General Agreement on Tariffs and Trade (the forerunner to the World Trade Organization), to help keep the peace and help humanity to prosper. The world also avoided a great power war and witnessed the spread of democracy around the globe.

Thus, this set of officials presents a best test case. If even they were prisoners of their premises, it is easier to understand how lesser mortals might fall prey to the same malady.

North Korea Attacks

In his memoirs, President Harry Truman remembered that throughout the spring of 1950 the CIA reported that North Korea might launch a full-scale invasion of South Korea.[2] These reports lacked specificity as to such an attack, and officials viewed the information of North Korean activities as just a continuation of their border raids.[3] They expected that the North would continue to rely on "guerilla and psychological warfare, political pressure and intimidation" rather than an all-out assault.[4] When the South Koreans sent a warning of a broader offensive, U.S. officials interpreted it in light of their efforts to obtain heavier military equipment. Similarly, Washington's policymakers dismissed the American ambassador to Korea's warning as a case of special pleading for his host country.[5] Thus, top officials were surprised when the North Korean army swept across the 38th parallel on June 25, 1950, and came close to uniting the Korean peninsula under the Communist regime of Kim Il-Sung.

Three premises underlay their surprise and their response to it:

- North Korea was under Russian control, and Russia did not want a war.
- It was essential to resist aggression.
- It was necessary to contain the spread of communism.

North Korea as a Soviet Agent

A principal reason the United States was surprised was its view of communism. No less than in the 1960s, policymakers in 1950 saw communism as an international conspiracy.[6] U.S. officials could not grasp that North

Korea might act on its own volition.[7] They operated on the premise that North Korea was under Russian control[8] and that war in Korea would be only an adjunct to general war with the Soviet Union. Because decision makers thought the Russians were not ready to take such a step, they concluded that no invasion would occur.[9] According to General Matthew Ridgway, the army deputy chief of staff for operations and later commander of United Nations forces in Korea, "the concept of 'limited warfare' never entered our councils."[10] Moreover, the premise that excluded the possibility of a geographically restricted war seems to have inhibited decision makers from asking just why Stalin would see supporting a limited war in Korea as a high risk or a pathway to global war.[11]

It was true that the Soviets equipped, trained, and advised the North Korean army[12] (which the United States underestimated, providing an additional reason to discount warnings of an invasion).[13] Nevertheless, it was the North Koreans who took the initiative for the war. Kim was an "intense Korea nationalist," not merely a Soviet pawn. From at least 1949, he sought Joseph Stalin's support for an invasion of South Korea. The Soviet leader put him off throughout 1949. By 1950, Stalin gave in and assented to an invasion, but he distanced himself from direct involvement. Korea was not his primary concern, and he was not willing to risk direct military confrontation with the United States to save the North Korean regime.[14] Although North Korea was largely under the Kremlin's thumb, in war "Stalin was more the accommodator than the instigator."[15]

It is also the case that the North Koreans were not subservient to the Chinese. They did not want China to dominate their country, and China had little influence on the beginning of the war, although it did approve of the concept. Kim did not even tell the Chinese the details or the timing of the June attack.[16] It was not until the U.S. counteroffensive at Inchon that the North Koreas requested substantial assistance from China.[17]

Contrary to American premises, then, the North Koreans were not an agent of a broader Communist conspiracy, nor did their invasion of the South portend global war.[18] Yet "the idea that Stalin had acquiesced to and not driven the invasion was alien" to U.S. policymakers.[19] Nearly a year after the North Korean invasion, the president told the American public, "The Communists in the Kremlin are engaged in a monstrous conspiracy to stamp out freedom all over the world." Moreover, "the attack on Korea was part of a greater plan for conquering all of Asia."[20]

Thus, despite years of provocations from the North, American officials ignored substantial evidence of a North Korean military buildup and mobilization near the border with South Korea. In fact, they were more concerned that South Korea would start a wider war by attempting to conquer North Korea, so the United States limited the size of their forces and the equipment available to them to discourage such an action and warned the South Korean president that he could not count on American support if he took aggressive action against North Korea.[21]

Resisting Aggression

Once surprised, how would the U.S. respond? Harry Truman believed that for almost all problems there were precedents that provided clear guides to principles for action. "When we are faced with a situation," the president explained, "we must know how to apply the lessons of history in a practical way."[22] As Glenn Paige put it, "With history as an unambiguous moral teacher, decision making became an exercise in applying the lessons. An occasion for decision became a stimulus to search for past analogy."[23]

But which analogy was appropriate? For President Truman and his advisors, the 1930s was the most vivid period in history. Historian Ernest May observed that "Truman saw the 1930's as teaching a plain and unmistakable lesson."[24] After learning of the North Korean attack, the president raced back to Washington from his home in Independence, Missouri. In his memoirs, he remembered thinking about previous instances "when the strong had attacked the weak."

> I recalled some earlier instances: Manchuria, Ethiopia, Austria. I remembered how each time that the democracies failed to act it had encouraged the aggressors to keep going ahead. Communism was acting in Korea just as Hitler, Mussolini, and the Japanese had acted ten, fifteen, and twenty years earlier. I felt certain that if South Korea was allowed to fall Communist leaders would be emboldened to override nations closer to our own shores. If the Communists were permitted to force their way into the Republic of Korea without opposition from the free world, no small nation would have the courage to resist threats and aggression by stronger Communist neighbors. If this was allowed to go unchallenged it would mean a third world war, just as similar incidents had brought on the second world war.[25]

By the time his plane touched down in Washington, Truman had made his basic decision. When the president surveyed his advisors, he found "complete, almost unspoken acceptance on the part of everyone that whatever had to be done to meet this aggression had to be done."[26] In their discussions, they drew historical parallels to Hitler's many aggressions, Mussolini's rape of Ethiopia, and Japan's seizure of Manchuria. At other times, they employed analogies from Greece in 1947 and the Berlin crisis in 1948.[27] As Assistant Secretary of State for Far Eastern Affairs Dean Rusk put it, "the Korean decision was in the process of being made for an entire generation since Manchuria."[28] Thus, the president and his advisors shared the premise that you could not appease aggressors. As he told the American people, "If history has taught us anything, it is that aggression anywhere in the world is a threat to the peace everywhere in the world."[29] Speaking of Communists, the president declared, "There is no telling what they will do if we don't put up a fight now."[30]

How would the U.S. resist aggression? The premise of challenging aggressors was so powerful that it dominated decision makers' thinking, even before discussions began. Prior to Truman boarding his plane in Independence, one of his aides told a reporter the president "[was] going to hit those fellows hard," and when the president landed, the first thing he said was that he was going to "hit them hard." The officials with whom the president would soon meet were also convinced that the United States would have to take action.[31]

The president told his advisors that it would take force to stop the North Koreans. The most fateful decision would be committing ground troops to the fight. Anticipating an eventual decision, in the first meeting with his advisors, Truman asked the military to prepare the necessary orders in case the UN asked for American forces.[32] Four days later, he committed troops to provide order, transportation, communications, and protection for military facilities in Korea. The next day, General Douglas MacArthur recommended using ground troops for offensive actions, and Truman immediately, and without consultation, agreed to the use of one regimental combat team. Later that day—five days after their first meeting—he found unanimous support among his advisors for giving MacArthur full authority to use the troops under his command at his discretion.[33]

Containing Communism

Two momentous events occurred in 1949: the Soviet Union exploded its first atomic bomb on August 29, and on October 1, Chinese Communist leader Mao Zedong declared the creation of the People's Republic of

China. Washington elites, having already proclaimed the Truman Doctrine and implemented the Berlin airlift, had to develop a policy to deal with these shocking developments. On April 7, 1950, President Truman received a sixty-six-page top secret National Security Council policy paper drafted by the Department of State and Department of Defense. It is commonly known as NSC-68 and was one of the most important American policy statements of the Cold War. According to the report, the United States should vigorously pursue a policy of "containing" Soviet expansion anywhere around the globe. The president signed the document into policy in September 1950.

Before the North Korean invasion, U.S. officials did not view South Korea as of strategic importance in the case of a broader war.[34] The premise of containing communism, along with a need to check aggressors and the belief in the central role of the Soviet Union in the invasion put Korea in a new light. Rather than perceiving the fighting as a localized conflict over control of the Korean peninsula, top officials saw the assault on South Korea as another battle against communism in the Cold War.[35] According to Secretary of State Dean Acheson, "It seemed close to certain that the attack had been mounted, supplied, and instigated by the Soviet Union and that it would not be stopped by anything short of force."[36] Moreover, top officials thought the North Korean attack might be an effort to divert U.S. troops from Europe, where the Russians might attack, or it might be a step toward a full-scale war.[37]

U.S. decision makers concluded that a Communist Korea posed a threat to Japanese security, not responding would send a signal to the Soviet Union that it could act elsewhere with impunity, and inaction would jeopardize the prestige and reputation of the United States as a reliable ally in fighting communism and negate five years of effort to build collective security.[38] Korea became politically significant in light of the Cold War, something that officials did not foresee.[39] Thus, the American decision to intervene was momentous, resulting in the globalization of containment, the core national security strategy for the next four decades.

Ernest May argues that the president did not have to choose to go to war. The U.S. had no special obligation to South Korea, and America would have followed him had he chosen not to go to war. Moreover, the desire to contain communism and deter aggression could have led him to conclude that Korea was a Soviet trap to involve United States in an Asian ground war where it would be at a disadvantage. Not fighting could also have reassured European allies that America would not waste scarce resources in an area of secondary concern. That is not how Truman saw matters, however. Low in the polls and suffering from criticism of the loss of China to communism, he and his advisors devoted little analysis to the differences between the 1930s and Korea in 1950, or to a more sophisticated view of containment.[40] Instead, they went to war.

The Chinese Intervene

The invasion of South Korea was only the first strategic surprise endured by the United States and its allies. Worse was yet to come. Exactly four months after the North Korean invasion, the Chinese People's Liberation Army intervened in massive numbers after American-led UN forces had pushed the North Koreans far back across the 38th parallel. U.S. military and civilian leaders were again caught by surprise, and America paid another costly price in casualties as the Chinese drove UN troops out of North Korea and almost out of South Korea as well. As Richard Betts summarized, "The war was transformed from a police action against an obscure and weak government to a conflict with the most populous nation in the world and the second ranking communist power."[41]

How could such a surprise happen? Given the success of the fight against the North Koreans, the UN's war aim changed from simply freeing South Korea of the invaders to occupying and unifying Korea as a democratic nation. In essence, decision makers concluded that the destruction of a Communist regime in North Korea would not provoke a large-scale war with China. Once again, the premises of decision makers distorted their evaluations of a major threat to their success, with tragic consequences.

Premises

As top officials made decisions regarding the fighting in Korea, they shared a consensus that:

- The Soviet Union controlled China's foreign policy.
- Chinese leaders would not view it as worthwhile to intervene militarily in Korea.
- China was too weak to conduct a large-scale military effort.

SOVIET CONTROL. The premise of the Soviet Union's control of its Communist neighbors extended to China and would influence U.S. decision makers again in the fall of 1950, distorting their analyses of whether the Chinese would enter the war. U.S. leaders reasoned that the Soviet Union did not want a general war and therefore would restrain its Chinese clients, whom they thought were under Russian control.[42] When the Chinese intervened in the war, top officials believed the Russians were behind it.[43] (Interestingly, the British disagreed.[44]) Once officials concluded that the Soviet Union would not intervene in the war, it became easier to ignore warnings about a Chinese intervention.[45]

Prominent journalist John Hersey summed up the premise of Soviet control in a story written about the White House after the Chinese attacked U.S. forces in massive numbers.

> The entire policy since June, which had seemed to be turning out for the best, was now to be more heavily tested than ever; hopes of imminent peace were gone; the willingness of the Chinese Communists, and therefore, obviously, of the Russian Communists, to risk a general war for the stake in Korea was suddenly palpable.[46]

Even after it was clear that they had made serious errors in judging what China would do, policymakers continued to assume that China was participating in a Russian-inspired conspiracy.[47]

Yet the premise was incorrect. The Chinese decided to intervene, even in the absence of Soviet support, and began redeploying troops, stockpiling material, developing strategy, and mobilizing the country soon after original North Korean invasion. Only then did Stalin agree to support a Chinese intervention in the war.[48] According to P. K. Rose, "the Chinese not only made a unilateral decision to intervene for nationalistic purposes, but also intimidated the Soviets into supporting them."[49] When Stalin reneged on his promise to provide air cover, China went ahead anyway.[50]

CHINESE MOTIVATIONS. A second premise relevant to the catastrophe that was to occur in Korea focused on Chinese motivations. Alexander George and Richard Smoke found that "estimates of Chinese intentions . . . were based on a faulty premise—namely, the belief that the Chinese leaders were calculating their interests in much the same way as we did."[51] U.S. officials did not understand that Chinese leader Mao Zedong's motivation in acting had more to do with China's traditional concerns about its borders, and fears based on previous American support of Chinese Nationalist forces, than it did with any Communist worldwide strategy. They did not consider how China might respond to American troops in Korea, and they were insensitive to the fact that Mao saw the U.S. presence in North Korea as a security threat to the existence and stability of his new Communist regime. Moreover, when the war broke out, the United States added protection for Formosa (Taiwan), undermining the tacit acceptance of allowing it to fall to mainland.[52]

Mao also saw the unification of Korea under a non-Communist regime as a threat to revolutionary prospects in the world and also to the Chinese domestic situation, which was unsettled following the long civil war. A victory of the United States in Korea would increase the prestige of the Communist party in both China and North Korea.[53]

For the first time, Western nations were employing force to eliminate a Communist regime. How could we not expect China to respond strongly to the destruction of an ally on its borders? In addition, previous experience forewarned that China would not willingly tolerate the presence of hostile armies in its backyard. The United States had not hesitated to resist aggression eight thousand miles from its shores; why should China not be expected to react to MacArthur's hostile campaign in similar fashion?[54]

U.S. officials were confident that Peking would regard its interests in Korea as quite limited, and they sent numerous reassurances to China that they had no military or political designs on the country. In addition, the United States declined offers of Chinese Nationalist troops from Formosa, and in the first months of the war did not bomb support bases in Manchuria or cross the 38th parallel or the borders of China or the Soviet Union. Thus, decision makers thought their intent not to threaten China was clear and were convinced they were not threatening legitimate Chinese interests by occupying and unifying North Korea. It followed, to them, that the Chinese would see their actions in the same light or could be persuaded to do so. Even in the face of warnings from China and evidence of the buildup and deployment of Chinese troops (see below) policymakers continued to believe their reassurances would work.[55]

Moreover, top American leaders did not consider how the Chinese might view the more hostile declarations issued by MacArthur and those who agreed with him that contradicted their limited aims or the administration's efforts to curb such statements.[56] The Chinese found it hard to believe that U.S. officials such as MacArthur could be advocating a policy that did not represent the views of those at the highest level.[57] Similarly, officials believed that neither the Soviet Union nor China would intervene if only South Korean soldiers were in control of the extreme north of the country.[58] However, the United States could not successfully constrain MacArthur's use of American troops in those areas.[59]

There was no challenge to leaders' understanding of China's frame of reference, no examination of the assumptions on which it rested. Although diplomat George Kennan and a few others below the top level of officials did disagree, there was no systematic reevaluation.[60] Moreover, Kennan was concerned about Russian, not Chinese, intervention.[61] George and Smoke found that instead of reexamining assumptions, "Washington's reluctance to accept information that challenged the premises and wisdom of its policy strongly encouraged its tendencies to misread the frame of reference with which Peking perceived events in Korea, to misinterpret available intelligence, and to underestimate Peking's motivation and willingness to take risks."[62]

CHINESE WEAKNESS. A third faulty premise was that China was too weak to conduct a large-scale military effort. Thus, decision makers did not believe the Chinese would intervene because it would require a large number of trained troops, it might weaken the Chinese government both internally and internationally, and there was no real advantage to China for such an action.[63] American officials routinely underestimated China's military capabilities, concluding that it could not organize, train, equip, or transport a large ground army.[64] They also thought the best time for a Chinese intervention had passed, and that China's entry into the war would make it more dependent on the Soviet Union, a situation that it wished to avoid.[65]

In sum, as Chen Jian put it, "American policymakers simply could not imagine that Beijing would gain anything by involving itself in a major confrontation with the United States."[66] They were wrong.

Warnings

Despite their premises, it is not as if U.S. decision makers had no inkling of a Chinese attack. Harvey DeWeerd noted that the warnings of a Chinese intervention "showered down upon us in connection with Korea in 1950 seem strident and compelling."[67] These alerts of possible Chinese intervention included the following:[68]

- July 6: the army chief of staff told President Truman there were about two hundred thousand Chinese troops in Manchuria.

- By late August and for the next three months, numerous studies from the Joint Intelligence Reports of the Far East Command, the primary source of intelligence for Washington decision makers, warned of the possibility of Chinese intervention.
- September 5: Secretary of State Dean Acheson was told that Chinese premier and foreign minister Zhou Enlai (Chou En-lai) warned that if UN forces approached the Chinese border, China would intervene in Korea.
- September 25: China communicated through India that it would intervene if the UN forces crossed the 38th parallel. The British ambassador to the United States passed the same message to the State Department.
- September 30: Zhou Enlai branded the United States as China's worst enemy and declared that China would not allow a neighbor to be invaded.
- End of September: according to the U.S. ambassador in Moscow, Soviet and Chinese contacts told both the British and Dutch ambassadors that if foreign troops crossed the 38th parallel, China would intervene.
- October 2: Zhou Enlai again warned that China would respond to an invasion of North Korea.
- October 3: the UN Command reported evidence that twenty Chinese divisions had been in Korea since September 10.
- October 3: Zhou Enlai repeated China's threat to the Indian ambassador in Peking. There were similar reports from Stockholm, Moscow, and New Delhi.
- October 8–14: UN Command reported that the massing of Chinese troops in Manchuria "appear[ed] conclusive."
- October 10: Radio Peking repeated the warning of October 3.
- October 25: the first large-scale Chinese attack was carried out on South Korean troops.
- October 26–27: the United States reported its first engagements with Chinese troops.
- October 28: newly captured Chinese prisoners of war said they were from large units.
- October 31: Russian-made MiGs flying from Manchuria appeared in combat.
- November 1–2: major Chinese attacks befell U.S. forces.
- November 4: the United States identified the presence of seven Chinese army divisions in the Korean theater.
- November 4: General MacArthur termed Chinese intervention "a distinct possibility of the gravest international importance."
- November 5: MacArthur reported hostile contact with Chinese troops.
- November 6: MacArthur alerted Washington, "Men and material in large force are pouring across all bridges over the Yalu, from Manchuria. This movement not only jeopardizes but threatens the ultimate destruction of the forces under my command."

- November 6: the CIA reported two hundred thousand Chinese troops massing across the North Korean border in Manchuria.
- November 7: MacArthur reported hostile air operations from Manchuria against his forces. He warned that if the Chinese build-up continued, he might have to retreat.
- November 7: the U.S. identified the presence of twelve Chinese army divisions in the Korean theater.
- November 24: the CIA predicted Chinese action that would nullify the U.S. efforts and preserve the North Korean state in some form.

In addition, throughout the summer and autumn of 1951, the Chinese openly engaged in the build-up and movement of troops on a massive scale. They expected the United States to see these actions—and it did.

Dismissing Warnings

Even after China repeatedly warned that it would enter the war with a full-scale effort, and after seeing Chinese mass troop movements, American officials viewed Chinese warnings as bluffs or diplomatic pressure and dismissed the possibility of a major intervention.[69] On October 12, four days after Mao had issued his order for China to enter the war, the CIA concluded that Chinese intervention "was not probable."[70] The strategic surprise of Chinese intervention was not the result of intelligence failure but, as DeWeerd put it, the "unwillingness to draw unpleasant conclusions . . . we refused to believe what our intelligence told us was in fact happening because it was at variance with the prevailing climate of opinion in Washington and Tokyo" (MacArthur's headquarters).[71] Decision makers were blinded by their premises.

For example, on October 3, when Zhou Enlai sent, through the Indian ambassador, a warning to the U.S. not to cross the 38th parallel, Secretary of State Dean Acheson inexplicably concluded it was "not to be disregarded but, on the other hand, not an authoritative statement of policy." Perhaps it was just a public relations attempt to save the North Korean regime.[72] Similarly, President Truman thought Zhou's message could be little "more than a relay of Communist propaganda."[73]

At their meeting on Wake Island on October 15, 1950—just as the Chinese were entering North Korea—General MacArthur told President Truman there was little chance of a large-scale Chinese intervention. Moreover, MacArthur claimed, should China enter the war, it would do so with only limited numbers of troops, and his air power would destroy the Chinese forces. The "greatest slaughter" would occur. Indeed, the general proclaimed, victory was won, all resistance would end by Thanksgiving, and he could withdraw one of his armies by Christmas.[74]

We have seen that the UN commander at times issued his own warnings, but he also discounted them. On both November 5 and November 7, the mercurial MacArthur altered his pessimistic assessments of the days before and concluded that the Chinese military actions did not constitute a full-scale intervention. It appears that the general raised the issue of Chinese intervention to convince Washington to let him bomb the bridges across the Yalu and continue his offensive.

An additional complicating factor was that MacArthur's intelligence officials played down the threat of Chinese intervention so as not to upset him and alarm the South Koreans. They also distorted the evidence of Chinese activity. Similarly, American field commanders did not exercise appropriate caution in probing Chinese strength because they were unwilling to defy MacArthur. The general himself suppressed and then minimized the significance of the evidence of Chinese intervention.[75]

On November 7, MacArthur announced he was planning on moving forward. Two days later, he wrote Secretary of Defense George Marshall that the Chinese were first-class soldiers representing an aggressively imperialistic country which allied with the Soviet Union for its own purposes.[76] He was correct in his analyses, but he did not draw the appropriate conclusion. Instead, the general expressed confidence he could deny the enemy reinforcements and destroy him. This statement was especially ironic because, in the words of Secretary of State Acheson, "In fact, his troops were being secretly surrounded by overpowering numbers of Chinese."[77]

Over the period of August and September, American officials gradually began discussing the possibility of Chinese intervention. During mid-September, American officials across the national security bureaucracy openly acknowledged that MacArthur's successful invasion at Inchon and his movement up the Korean peninsula had significantly increased the likelihood of China entering the war on a large scale. These concerns increased in October in light of the growing evidence of People's Liberation Army activity in Korea. A November 8 National Intelligence Estimate recognized that Chinese ground troops were engaging UN forces in North Korea and that China had accepted an increased risk of war, which was probably going to occur.[78] Unsurprisingly, there were disagreements between MacArthur, who wanted to reunite Korea, and those who felt that to move further north would lead to a larger and more aggressive Chinese intervention.[79]

Nevertheless, the United States and the UN pursued a policy that ensured China would enter the fray. The great American landing at Inchon occurred on September 15. That same day, Truman directed MacArthur to force the North Korean army back across the 38th parallel or destroy it altogether. If the Soviet Union or China had not entered the war, or if there was no indication or threat of their entry, he could extend his operations beyond the 38th parallel and occupy North Korea.[80]

MacArthur's forces had to move across the border because the border itself offered a poor defensive line. To break off the UN offensive when its forces reached the border was to invite a new attack from the North Koreans. Yet, it was not necessary to occupy North Korea to find a suitable defensive position. Eager to reach the Yalu River before it froze, which would make it easier for the Chinese to cross and occupy all of North Korea, MacArthur proclaimed that to draw a line at the narrow neck of the peninsula would be appeasement that found its "historic precedence in the action taken at Munich." Domestic critics of the Truman administration would also have seen not crossing the border as appeasement.[81]

On September 27, Washington again told MacArthur his objective was to destroy the North Korean armed forces, and gave him permission to cross the 38th parallel as long as major Soviet or Chinese forces did not enter the war, made no announcement of their intent to enter, and made no threat to counter UN forces militarily. In the event of major Chinese forces fighting *south* of the 38th parallel, he could continue as long as he had a reasonable chance of successful resistance.[82]

There were warnings, of course, but the United States only hardened its policy of unifying Korea. On October 7, 1950, the First Cavalry Division crossed the 38th parallel, and the UN passed a resolution calling for a "unified, independent and democratic Korea." For the first time, the West had decided to move beyond containment to the elimination of a Communist regime. Unbothered by the threat of Chinese intervention, the administration drifted into this expanded war aim without an explicit, well-formulated decision to do so. Given MacArthur's success at Inchon, unification seemed the only way to end the war, and it was an attractive and low-risk bonus of the UN counterattack.[83] Richard Neustadt described the decision to occupy North Korea as a "passing fancy, taken and abandoned as the war news changed."[84]

This change in the aim of the war provided China a strong motivation to prevent the UN from achieving it. On October 8, Mao issued the official order to enter the war. Nevertheless, on October 9, the president gave MacArthur extraordinary discretion, directing him that in the event of a major Chinese entry into the war, he should continue his efforts to unify Korea and resist Chinese troops anywhere in Korea as long as he had a reasonable chance of success.[85] Truman did not indicate that he consulted with anyone in this decision.

MacArthur's messages about Chinese troops pouring across the Yalu aroused immense anxiety in Washington.[86] By November 8, in light of the evidence of Chinese military activity, the president's advisors recognized the UN probably could not unify Korea by military means and it would be necessary to negotiate with the Chinese to salvage as much as possible. However, they rationalized that they would prefer to negotiate from a position of strength. They also recognized the risk to MacArthur's forces, and the president gave the general permission to bomb bridges across the Yalu River to stem the flow of Chinese troops into Korea.[87]

Nevertheless, after months of dismissing warnings of Chinese intervention,[88] Truman's top advisors did not suggest he send new instructions to the general, ordering him to halt his advance to the Yalu River and pull back to less vulnerable positions.[89] Instead, they recommended, and obtained presidential approval, to keep the mission assigned to MacArthur under review.[90] Dean Acheson later recalled,

> Here, I believe, the Government missed its last chance to halt the march to disaster in Korea. All the President's advisers in this matter, civilian and military, knew that something was badly wrong, though what it was, how to find out, and what to do about it they muffed.[91]

Once the participation of Chinese troops was finally accepted, the question became how to interpret their presence. Consistent with the prevailing premises, the new narrative was that China's goal was to stall the UN advance and provide a buffer zone on its border rather than mount an offensive to defeat it.[92] Unsurprisingly, on November 17, MacArthur reported that he would begin his push to the Chinese border "to end the war" on November 24th. According to Truman, he even told one of his commanders to inform his troops they would be home by Christmas.[93] The Chinese intervened with a massive force on the 25th, but MacArthur was so convinced the Chinese would not intervene that it took him days to accept the fact that they had indeed done so.[94] In the end, the Chinese forced the general to conduct the "longest military retreat in American military history."[95]

Obstacles to Reexamining Premises

Several factors complicated reexamining the war aim and the premises on which it was based. First, there was a broadly shared reluctance to override a theater commander in the field. According to President Truman, "You pick your man, you've got to back him up."[96] Moreover, Acheson felt that under this obvious truth lay an uneasy respect for the MacArthur mystique. Army chief of staff and World War II hero General Omar Bradley later admitted that MacArthur's stature was so great that the Joint Chiefs of Staff felt literally incapacitated to deal with him.[97] Moreover, the threat of Chinese intervention only encouraged rapid movement north so MacArthur could establish good defense lines.[98] U.S. troops crossed the 38th parallel on October 8, and the clearest evidence of Chinese action came after that, when the commander was in battle mode.[99]

Perhaps the sorcerer of Inchon could pull off a five-thousand-to-one shot. Between October 26 and November 17, Acheson lamented,

> all the dangers from dispersal of our own forces and intervention by the Chinese were manifest. We were all deeply apprehensive. We were frank with one another, but not quite frank enough. I was unwilling to urge on the President a military course that his military advisers would not propose. They would not propose it because it ran counter to American military tradition of the proper powers of the theater commander since 1864.

If military officials had recommended withdrawal to a more southern line, disaster would probably have been averted. But such an action would have meant a fight with the commanding general and possibly the relief of him. So the president's advisors hesitated, and the chance was lost.[100]

Defaulting to MacArthur's Yalu River plan and minimizing the warnings of Chinese intervention allowed policymakers to pursue an aggressive stance against the Chinese Communists, a strategy that was more politically advantageous domestically than a more modest goal of driving the North Koreans from the South. Responding to the evidence of Chinese intervention would have required admitting that the administration's war aims of unifying Korea under a non-Communist government were wrong, which would incur severe political costs as long as Chinese intervention did not seem inevitable.[101]

Officials also knew that the public had become disenchanted with Truman's foreign policy. The Communist takeover in China, the unexpected Soviet detonation of an atomic bomb, and the outbreak of the Korean War aggravated a feeling of insecurity, and the Republicans were exploiting this angst for partisan advantage in the November elections. Thus, a victory over communism was appealing.[102]

Adding to the momentum of U.S. policy was the fact that the Chinese forces disengaged from fighting and disappeared in the period of November 9–24. This disappearance reduced anxiety in Washington and encouraged the view that the Chinese had only defensive purposes, nourishing MacArthur's illusions and encouraging him to gamble with occupying the North.[103] The secretary of state thought, "The most elementary caution would seem to warn that they [the Chinese troops] might, indeed probably would, reappear as suddenly and harmfully as they had before." MacArthur, however, was taking no precautions.[104]

In addition, the Soviet Union responded with moderation to the war. It gave modest aid to the North Koreans and was circumscribed and conciliatory toward the United States. This behavior inspired risk-taking, as it strengthened the view of American officials that Russia would not intervene.[105] China also seemed to exhibit restraint. It did not attempt to take Formosa or intervene in North Korea in the summer, when, in the view of U.S. officials, it would have been most propitious to do so, especially because the North Koreans were still an effective fighting force.[106]

With victory in their grasp, the intervention of major powers unlikely, and American military prowess clear, taking risks seemed acceptable. Reinforcing the predilections of policymakers were the broader advantages of unifying Korea. Japan would be heartened, Sino-Soviet divisions might emerge in an avalanche of recriminations at the loss of a Communist nation, and Soviet satellites in Eastern Europe might feel an incentive to distance from Moscow.[107] Truman believed the reunification of Korea would inflict a momentous defeat on the strategy of Soviet expansion.[108]

Governing routines, domestic politics, international strategy, misperceptions, and enemy deception were obstacles to challenging the premises on which the UN fought the Korean War. Once established, the premises on which leaders base their war aims are not easily changed. It takes time and commitment, openness to change, and the cooperation of commanders. Moreover, officials are less likely to revise strategic assumptions if disconfirming evidence accrues in piecemeal fashion rather than in a sudden jolt.[109] The Chinese were not so obliging. Thus, a number of factors abetted the miscalculation of Chinese actions.

The point remains that the policymakers' premises held and determined their choices. In the words of George and Smoke, "Behind the administration's wishful thinking lay its reluctance to accept and weigh properly information that challenged the premises and wisdom of occupying North Korea as a prelude to unification of the country."[110]

Groupthink

President Truman and his top advisors demonstrated mutual support for risk-taking (occupying North Korea) and tenaciously held to erroneous assumptions, even in the face of mounting evidence to challenge them. I have argued that the core explanation for these decision-making failures was the faulty premises held by these officials.

Irving Janis offers a different explanation. In his influential *Groupthink*,[111] he finds a major defect in cohesive decision-making groups. Although they are not sycophants and freely speak their minds, members of such groups nevertheless suffer from subtle constraints that prevent them from fully exercising their critical powers and openly expressing doubts when most others have reached consensus. Cohesive groups tend to evolve informal norms to preserve friendly intragroup relations. The greater the cohesion in the group, the more power it has to produce "mindless conformity" that leads group members to exhibit a lack of vigilance regarding problems with their decisions and excessive risk-taking in them. Indeed, the concurrence-seeking tendency can be maintained only at the expense of ignoring realistic challenges.[112]

According to Janis, then, groupthink is "a mode of thinking that people engage in when they are deeply involved in a cohesive in-group, when the members' strivings for unanimity override their motivation to realistically appraise alternative sources of action." Thus, "the more amiability and esprit de corps among the members of a policy-making in-group, the greater is the danger that independent critical thinking will be replaced by groupthink, which is likely to result in irrational and dehumanizing actions directed against out-groups."[113]

Janis knows that common failures in decision making, such as not properly evaluating options and the information supporting them and considering too narrow a range of options, "can arise from other common causes of human stupidity as well." Nevertheless, he "assumes" such failures result from groupthink, because when there is a cohesive group and defective decision making, there is a "better-than-chance likelihood that one of the causes" of the defective decision is a strong concurrence-seeking tendency, which is the motivation that gives rise to all the symptoms of groupthink."[114]

He offers five case studies to illustrate "fiascoes" resulting from groupthink. One case is Vietnam, on which his discussion is tentative. The second of these cases focuses on the Korean War, in which virtually all analysts agree that decision makers took great risks and indulged in wishful thinking. Janis leaves no doubt as to the explanation.

> The main reason for the members' concurrences on the ill-considered escalation decision was that Truman's advisory group was adhering to a set of norms that were promoted by the leader and that all willingly accepted. These shared norms enabled the members to maintain a sense of group solidarity at the expense of suffering from the major symptoms of groupthink. The most prominent were excessive risk-taking based on a shared illusion of invulnerability, stereotypes of the enemy, collective reliance on ideological rationalizations that supported the belligerent escalation to which the group became committed, and mindguiding to exclude the dissident views of experts who questioned the group's unwarranted assumptions.[115]

Were there "illusions of invulnerability"? I can find nothing in the record to support such an assertion. We know that many of Truman's advisors were fully aware that the United States would be sorely strained if the Chinese intervened. Even MacArthur—despite his bravado at Wake Island in mid-October—understood that a Chinese intervention would change the war and prevent him from reunifying Korea. Military officials played a key role in the deliberations on Korea, and they routinely pointed out the challenges of confronting a large-scale Chinese intervention.

What about stereotypes of the enemy and ideological rationalizations about it? We have seen that Truman and his advisors operated under three faulty premises:

1. The Soviet Union controlled China and would restrain its junior partner.
2. Chinese leaders would not see the United States occupying North Korea as threat.
3. China was too weak to conduct a large-scale military effort and thus would not intervene.

These premises are what Janis refers to as stereotypes.[116]

He admits that Truman's advisors' views of China's independence, military strength, and intentions were based on ideological presumptions that they shared with all leading members of the administration and many other Americans as well.[117] Yet, because these premises were so widely shared, they did not require groupthink to protect them from challenges. The heated debate that Janis advocates to correct these stereotypes[118] may have been an excellent idea, but who was going to participate?

Just as importantly, by November, top officials were cognizant of Chinese military activity and its implications for their plans for the unification of Korea and as a threat to MacArthur's forces. They just could not figure out how great the problem was. There were disagreements between MacArthur, who wanted to reunite Korea, and those who felt that to move further north would lead to a larger and more aggressive Chinese intervention. Thus, Truman and his advisors took the precaution of keeping the mission assigned to the commander under review. Their premises inhibited effectively reading information, but groupthink did not prevent them from considering changing conditions and thinking about how to respond to them.

It is no doubt true, as Janis claims, that the failure to correct their misconceptions can be linked with the advisors' propensity to support each other in taking excessive risks. Of course they can. The real question is whether we need to resort to groupthink to explain such behavior. As we have seen, there is plenty of evidence that once having held widely shared premises, policymakers generally resist changing them in light of new and challenging information. We would have predicted the same behavior if we had never heard of groupthink.

Were there "mindguards" who protected the group from adverse information by excluding the dissident views of experts who questioned the group's unwarranted assumptions? The *only* example Janis offers is the concerns of George Kennan and Director of Policy Planning Paul Nitze about the UN troops crossing the 38th parallel and occupying North Korea. Janis claims that Secretary of State Dean Acheson kept them from access to top officials.[119] We simply do not know whether the views of Kennan and Nitze were known beyond their department, but it seems unlikely that the concerns of such visible officials went no further than Acheson. We do know, however, that Kennan was concerned about Russian, not Chinese, intervention,[120] and that he did not make an argument about such a danger. Moreover, Kennan had left the government by August, before the warnings of Chinese intervention—indeed, before MacArthur had landed at Inchon. In July, Nitze's "Policy Planning Staff urged caution but did not forswear opportunities should they arise."[121]

Janis also discusses in detail the conditions under which groupthink is likely to arise. Were such conditions present in the Korean War case? The *sine qua non* for groupthink to occur is a cohesive decision-making group. There is broad agreement that Truman and his advisors formed such a harmonious group.[122]

The first antecedent condition for the emergence of groupthink is structural faults in the decision-making process, such as insulation of the group, a lack of a tradition of impartial leadership and a priority on open, unbiased inquiry into the available alternatives, the lack of norms requiring methodical procedures, and homogeneity of members' background and ideology.[123]

There is no evidence that Truman tried openly or more subtlety to influence the advice he was given. Moreover, he and his advisors routinely received information, evaluations, and recommendations from the Departments of State and Defense, the CIA, the Joint Chiefs of Staff, MacArthur's headquarters in Tokyo, and other relevant organizations. Truman and his advisors were not isolated.

In addition, there is no evidence of pressures to conform to a view on the likelihood of Chinese intervention. Truman encouraged open and candid discussion, even if he evaluated information in terms of his premises. Even Janis reports that the president "was highly responsive to his advisors' recommendations" and that the judgments expressed by his advisors were sincere.[124] One example related to Korea is changing his mind on accepting help from the Nationalist Chinese on Formosa, which his advisors opposed.[125] Army Chief of Staff General J. Lawton Collins, who, along with the other service heads, met regularly with the president during the war, termed Truman a "remarkable man" who listened carefully, heard all sides on an issue, got to the root of a problem, and then acted in a decisive manner.[126] It was premises, not process, that was at the heart of the decision-making problem.

In general, however, there is little evidence of sloppy (as opposed to incorrect) staff work. Nevertheless, there are some worrisome indications of process failures. For example, the record does not indicate discussion of Truman's October 9 decision to give MacArthur discretion in the event of a major Chinese entry into the war. Such a momentous decision surely deserved the most careful attention. There may simply be a gap in the record, or Truman may have thought previous discussion was sufficient. Nevertheless, as we have seen, the administration seems to have drifted into the decision to occupy North Korea.

It is true that discussion occurred among men of similar background and ideology. In particular, Janis notes that these men shared the same basic values and beliefs, particularly the need to contain the spread of communism.[127] It is important to note that this core view was widely held in Western society. It was hardly likely that there would be people in positions of influence who would have thought that the spread of communism was a positive development.

The second antecedent condition encouraging groupthink is the incentive to maintain group cohesiveness to provide a source of security for members, reducing anxiety and heightening self-esteem.[128] Indeed, Janis assigns "preeminence" to the impact of high stress and low self-esteem (constituting an internal source of stress) in explaining why groupthink occurs.[129] He further suggests that conformist tendencies may be strongest in persons who are most fearful of disapproval and rejection. Nevertheless, anyone can get caught up at times in group madness that produces symptoms of groupthink.[130]

According to Janis, a "provocative situational context" (high stress) occurs when there are serious external threats and low hope of a better solution than the leader's. Low self-esteem may be induced temporarily by recent failures that make members' inadequacies salient, excessive difficulties with current decision-making tasks that lower each member's sense of self-efficacy, and moral dilemmas such as an apparent lack of feasible alternatives except those that violate ethical standards.[131] The symptoms of groupthink, then, "might be best understood as a mutual effort among the members of a group to maintain emotional equanimity in the face of external and internal sources of stress arising when they share responsibility for making vital decisions that pose threats of failure, social disapproval, and self-disapproval."[132]

Were Truman and his advisors likely to have felt unusual stress? Was their self-esteem at risk? There is little evidence to suggest it. It would be difficult to find a set of leaders more secure than Harry Truman, Dean Acheson, George Marshall, Omar Bradley, and their colleagues. Moreover, they were not operating in a peculiarly stressful environment. According to Glenn Paige, the response to the initial decision to commit U.S. troops to defend against the North Korean invasion was "overwhelmingly favorable" with the U.S.[133] Thus, this was not an agonizing or painful decision.[134] Similarly, there was widespread international support for the UN resolution to counter the attack. When these officials erred in not heeding warnings of Chinese intervention, they were operating in an environment of near euphoria at MacArthur's success after his landing at Inchon. Thus, there was "little agonizing" over the decision to cross the 38th parallel, which was favored by most Americans, including Joseph McCarthy.[135]

Janis also argues that "the chances of groupthink developing during crisis period of high stress will be markedly reduced if the leader conducts the policy deliberations in a relatively impartial way, so as to set the norm for the discussion of a wide range of alternatives."[136] As we have seen, Truman met this norm.

In sum, groupthink provides a plausible explanation for the failure to challenge premises. In the case of the Chinese intervention in the Korean War, however, it adds little to an explanation focused on the power of premises themselves. President Truman and his advisors displayed a high degree of consensus on key decisions. They generally considered only a single course of action and had minimal conflict over it. They may have decided on a course even more rapidly, but they lacked information in the early days of the conflict. Nevertheless, there was never any question about challenging aggression and containing Communist advances. Military officials pointed out the difficulties of military action but never opposed it.[137] Premises, right or wrong, prevailed.

Conclusion

The officials in charge of American national security policy in the Truman administration are renowned for their perspicacity. Yet even such Olympian figures were prisoners of their premises. They greatly underestimated the probability of Chinese intervention in Korea, dismissing warnings of impending conflict while holding fast to faulty beliefs and allowing Douglas MacArthur to attempt to unify the peninsula. The result was a catastrophe for America. Secretary of State Dean Acheson later summarized the consequences of the Chinese intervention, calling it

> one of the most terrific disasters that has occurred to American foreign policy, and certainly.... the greatest disaster which occurred to the Truman administration. It did more to destroy and undermine American foreign policy than anything that I know about.[138]

CHAPTER FIVE

Assuming *and* Ignoring Problems: The Invasion of Iraq

"We all should have pushed harder on the intelligence and revisited our assumptions."
—President George W. Bush[1]

The most significant American national security policy in the twenty-first century has been the invasion of Iraq for the purpose of overthrowing Saddam Hussein's dictatorship. As such, it deserves careful and extended attention. The United States accomplished its immediate goal of regime change in short order, but it was soon apparent that the primary justification the Bush administration articulated for the war, removing Iraq's weapons of mass destruction (WMD), was faulty. There were no WMD. Was the war the result of incompetent and mendacious officials manipulating the nation into a war it did not need to fight? Or can we explain the genesis of the invasion by examining the sincere premises of the major figures in the George W. Bush administration? The aftermath of the war proved to be a protracted nightmare of instability, death, and wasted resources. Was the failure to anticipate this outcome the result of inept, overoptimistic policymakers, or was it once again the result of the premises on which they rested their policy?

In this chapter I analyze the government's decision making about invading Iraq and the postwar occupation and reconstruction of the country. In the first instance, decision makers assumed a problem that did not exist, and in the second, they ignored the likelihood of serious troubles arising from their decision to remove Saddam Hussein.

Invading Iraq

The Bush administration was understandably highly risk averse in the wake of the 9/11 terrorist attacks.[2] Top officials, including the president, concluded that they had failed to protect the country and could not tolerate a terrorist state with WMD. George W. Bush feared that if America failed to act against terrorists and those states that harbored them, such inaction would encourage further attacks. In an address on October 7, 2001, he informed his audience, "Failure to act would embolden other tyrants, allow terrorists access to new weapons, new resources, and make blackmail a permanent feature of world events."[3] Vice President Dick Cheney and national security assistant Condoleezza Rice believed that U.S. credibility was at stake after the country failed to respond to Saddam Hussein's massacre of Shiites in 1991 and his toying with UN weapons inspectors following the Gulf War, the Khobar Towers explosion and African embassy attacks in 1996, and the bombing of the USS *Cole* in 2000.[4] Cheney summed up the administration's orientation when he declared that the United States needed to act if there were only a 1 percent chance of terrorists getting their hands on nuclear weapons.[5]

Aversion to loss is not a substitute for analysis, however. Unfortunately, most high-level decision makers did not rigorously examine the following critical questions: (1) Did Iraq possess WMD? (2) Would Iraq use WMD to harm the United States? and (3) Would Iraq share WMD with terrorists? Instead, officials *assumed* the answers, which provided the basis for going to war. At the core of policymakers' thinking were three premises:

- Iraq possessed weapons of mass destruction.
- Iraq posed a threat to the United States.
- Saddam Hussein would be more cooperative with inspections if he lacked weapons of mass destruction.

Weapons and Threats

It is highly unlikely that the United States would have invaded Iraq in 2003 in the absence of the fear of WMD.[6] Top officials, including the president, knew the public would not support war unless it felt the country was in danger of a devastating attack. It was this necessity that sparked President Bush's disappointment when CIA officials could not make a convincing case for the public regarding Iraq's WMD programs and Saddam Hussein's connections with terrorists.[7]

Most high-level administration officials were certain that Saddam Hussein possessed weapons of mass destruction and posed a threat to the United States, either directly or indirectly through his sharing of WMD with terrorist organizations. Invading Iraq to remove Saddam followed logically from these premises.

Vice President Cheney addressed the VFW National Convention on August 26, 2002. He assured the gathering, "There is no doubt that Saddam now has weapons of mass destruction," and there was "no doubt" that he was amassing them to use against the United States. Cheney added, "Many of us are convinced that Saddam will acquire nuclear weapons fairly soon."[8] He repeated the same claims three days later in a speech in San Antonio.[9] When he learned that Osama bin Laden was working on developing an advanced chemical and biological weapons program and also seeking nuclear capability, he concluded that Saddam Hussein was the most likely to furnish these WMD to the architect of the 9/11 attacks.[10]

At a press conference on September 26, 2002, Secretary of Defense Donald Rumsfeld proclaimed, "We know they have weapons of mass destruction. We know they have active programs. There isn't any debate about it."[11] On February 5, 2003, Secretary of State Colin Powell addressed the United Nations and told the delegates that Saddam Hussein possessed WMD, was seeking more, had close connections with terrorists, and posed a threat to the American people.[12]

Most importantly, President Bush addressed the nation on October 7, 2002, making his most comprehensive argument for war. In definitive terms, he told Americans that Iraq "possesses and produces chemical and biological weapons. It is seeking nuclear weapons. It has given shelter and support to terrorism."[13] Announcing the invasion of Iraq on March 19, 2003, he told the American people that the United States would not "live at the mercy of an outlaw regime that threatens the peace with weapons of mass murder."[14]

Top officials were not alone in being prisoners of their premises. Most key leaders among U.S. allies believed Saddam Hussein would accept inspectors and abide by UN resolutions only under the threat of military force.[15]

The intelligence community reported with what policymakers viewed as near total confidence that Iraq possessed weapons of mass destruction, a view shared by other intelligence agencies around the world.[16] Intelligence agencies had been wrong in the past about Iraq's WMD, and after

9/11, it was an unpardonable sin to underestimate threats to the nation. In addition, Iraq had possessed and used WMD in the past and lied repeatedly to UN inspectors in an effort to conceal its weapons program. Iraq also had not fully accounted for the weapons it claimed it had destroyed.[17] It was also true that since 2000, Saddam Hussein had become the benefactor of Palestinian radicals and terrorists in Israel. As a result of this pattern of behavior, the intelligence community shared a consensus that Iraq retained some WMD, had the ability to produce more, and had ambitions to do so. Years of similar judgments may have also made it more difficult to question basic assumptions.

Other information pointed to similar conclusions about the presence of WMD. The outgoing secretary of defense, William Cohen, warned that Saddam Hussein had rebuilt Iraq's weapons infrastructure. On September 7, 2001, the State Department's Bureau of Intelligence and Research produced a document identifying progress in weapons development Iraq had made in the previous few years, including keeping weapons inspectors at bay.[18] Richard Haass, the State Department's director of policy planning, reported that he never heard anyone claim that Iraq had no WMD.[19]

Lack of Systematic Debate and Analysis

Because it was certain that Saddam possessed WMD and was a threat to the United States, the Bush administration never organized a systematic internal debate on the fundamental questions of whether Iraq actually possessed weapons of mass destruction, whether the Iraqi threat was imminent, whether it was necessary to overthrow Saddam, and, if so, the likely consequences of such an action. Instead—hauntingly reminiscent of decision making about Vietnam—it focused on the question of how to invade successfully.[20] As Condoleezza Rice put it, "We had planned and planned and even tested our plans in war games. But we had not—I had not—done a good enough job of thinking the unthinkable."[21]

George Tenet, the director of the CIA, remembers a lack of asking the core questions that would have challenged the administration's premises of the need to attack.

> There was never a serious debate that I know of within the administration about the imminence of the Iraqi threat.... Nor was there ever a significant discussion regarding enhanced containment or the costs and benefits of such an approach versus full-out planning for overt and covert regime change.[22]

Instead, the agenda focused on how to attack. "What never happened, as far as I can tell, was a serious consideration of the implications of a US invasion."[23]

Paul Pillar, the national intelligence officer for the Near East and South Asia from 2000 to 2005, was responsible for coordinating assessments on Iraq from all fifteen agencies in the intelligence community. In his view, "The most extraordinary aspect of [the] George W. Bush administration's launching of a war in Iraq in March 2003 was the absence of any apparent procedure for determining whether the war was a good idea." There was no discussion as to whether it was in the nation's interests to go to war. Instead, discussion focused on how to sell the policy and how to implement the decision.[24] Journalist George Packer described the decision process well: "It was an accretion, a tipping point. A decision was not made—a decision happened, and you can't say when or how." Thus, "by the early spring of 2002, a full year before the invasion, the administration was inexorably set on a course of war."[25]

There was a broad lack of opportunity for relevant components of the government, such as intelligence agencies, the State Department, and the military, and experts outside of the government to offer input on the core premise of the need to go to war. The issue was never raised.[26] When Richard Haass began to express the State Department's reservations about a war with Iraq, the president's national security advisor, Condoleezza Rice, interrupted him: "You can save your breath, Richard. The president has already made up his mind on Iraq."[27] In an interview on April 4, 2002—nearly a year before the invasion—Bush told his interlocutor, "I made up my mind that Saddam needs to go."[28]

Confident in its premises regarding WMD, the administration did not order an intelligence estimate on WMD. Indeed, it never requested any intelligence estimate on Iraq before the invasion. (Democrats on the Senate Intelligence Committee requested the National Intelligence Estimate [NIE] that the CIA produced in October 2002.) In fact, there was no administration call for any classified assessment on anything to do with Iraq from any official until a year into the war.[29] As intelligence analyst Paul Pillar summed up the situation, the administration "went to war without requesting ... any strategic-level intelligence assessments on any aspect of Iraq."[30]

The CIA produced the October 2002 NIE in just nineteen days, as opposed to the many months it typically devotes to such a document. Given the accelerated time frame, it could only summarize existing views, not reexamine the evidence and analysis. The NIE was really a political document masked as an intelligence assessment. Intelligence officials knew that Saddam Hussein was a liar and that the president had decided to go to war, so this fatalistic assumption set in motion a "high-stakes descent into circular reasoning."[31]

There is some question whether the president or his national security advisor studied closely the NIE, which was only ninety-two pages, or followed up on the dissents and caveats in the assessment.[32] If they did read it, they apparently did not notice the weakness of the evidence. Although the NIE contained stark assertions about WMD, it was laden with doubt. The phrase "we don't know" appeared thirty times. The definitive "we know" appeared only three times. Forty percent of the assessments were made with low confidence, including when Saddam Hussein would use WMD, whether he would attack the U.S. homeland, and whether he would share WMD with al-Qaeda.[33]

Intelligence pointing to Iraqi WMD would have benefited from careful scrutiny. The evidence underlying conclusions about Iraqi WMD was badly outdated, almost completely circumstantial, unreliable, and often fabricated. The CIA had few human resources in Iraq,[34] and it overestimated the number of independent sources on WMD. As a result, its conclusions reflected more certainty than was warranted, failed to stress the limited direct evidence, and did not clearly explicate the grounds for reaching conclusions. It also failed to consider the significance of negative reports and the absence of evidence of WMD. Moreover, analysts did not make it clear that the inferences about WMD were based on plausibility rather than on reports from valid and unambiguous sources. In addition, those at the top of the agency became more confident because they had a source of information that analysts did not—although it proved to be unreliable. Analysts also did not consider alternative explanations for Saddam Hussein's behavior.[35] Charles Duelfer, who headed the Iraq Survey Group, which was tasked with establishing the truth about WMD after the war, lamented, "In retrospect, we envisioned this whole nuclear program based on two wobbly data points."[36]

In a review of the U.S. intelligence community's performance on determining Iraq's possession of WMD, senior CIA officials concluded that U.S. intelligence collection strategies contributed to the failure to correctly assess Iraq's weapons arsenal. Intelligence officials did not focus on questioning the validity of the premise that Iraq's WMD programs were continuing. Indeed, as former deputy director of the CIA Richard Kerr concluded, "of all the methodological elements that contributed ... to the Intelligence Community's performance, the most important seems to be an uncritical acceptance of established positions and assumptions."[37]

When analysts look for information on a subject with a preconception of what is needed, they are almost certain to find data that reinforces their assumptions. Thus, the intelligence community directed its collection capabilities to filling in what it thought were gaps in information about WMD programs, monitoring progress, looking for new developments in weapons and delivery systems, and identifying efforts to acquire materiel and technology abroad. Even the growing need to acknowledge gaps in knowledge and caveat judgments to explain the absence of direct intelligence did not provoke an internal review within the intelligence community. Although intelligence analysts acknowledged certain gaps in their information, their qualified results did not call into question the accuracy of their basic assumptions regarding the existence of WMD, hastening the conversion of heavily qualified judgments into accepted fact.[38]

Yet, the weakness of the data on Iraq's WMD never encouraged the consumers of intelligence to reappraise their premise.[39] Expecting to find evidence of WMD, officials did not discern the significance of the failure to find it. As Secretary of Defense Donald Rumsfeld famously declared in 2002, "the absence of evidence is not evidence of absence."[40] Rumsfeld himself later reflected that top officials did not hear enough about what the intelligence community did not know one way or the other about the existence of Iraqi WMD.[41]

The premise of Iraqi WMD became nonfalsifiable. Once decision makers discarded probabilities for mere possibilities, as Cheney had, there was no need for information or analysis. For example, Bush administration hawks opposed UN weapons inspections and did not seem interested in inspection results. They did little to provide intelligence to help the inspectors. When the inspections uncovered no WMD, White House officials engaged in circular reasoning, arguing that the absence of evidence of WMD was actually evidence that Saddam Hussein was hiding them—not that he did not have any. In reality, the Iraqi leader was not obstructing weapons inspectors. The irony was that Saddam's compliance was going up while our confidence in his doing so was going down.[42]

Officials saw what they expected to see. Policymakers tend not to question judgments that fit their preconceptions or preferences.[43] Worse, it appears as though some administration officials were cherry-picking intelligence to justify a decision they had already reached based on their premises.[44] The vice president, for example, "repeatedly referred to uncertain and ambiguous intelligence reporting as if it were fact."[45]

In the months before the Iraq war, leading administration officials, including George W. Bush, Colin Powell, Donald Rumsfeld, and Condoleezza Rice, depicted significant ties between Saddam and al-Qaeda.[46] In his 2003 State of the Union message shortly before the invasion, the president darkly suggested that Saddam "aids and protects terrorists, including members of al-Qaeda. Secretly and without fingerprints, he could provide one of his hidden weapons to terrorists or help them develop their own."[47] However, the intelligence community never offered any analysis that supported the notion of an alliance between the Iraqi president and al-Qaeda,[48] and George Tenet told the president the CIA was skeptical about the principal piece of supposed evidence of the link.[49] Key intelligence agencies concluded that the probability of transferring weapons of mass destruction to terrorists was very low.[50] Similarly, the NIE concluded that Iraq was probably several years away from developing nuclear weapons and unlikely to use any weapons of mass destruction against the United States unless Saddam's regime was placed in mortal danger.[51]

George W. Bush rarely expressed skepticism at the evidence of WMD,[52] but, to his credit, he found a December 21, 2002, CIA briefing regarding Iraq's possession of WMD unconvincing (other White House and Pentagon officials had a similar reaction)—and not useful for selling the war to the public. He also wanted a tie between Saddam Hussein and terrorists. The CIA officials providing the briefing knew they had no smoking gun, but CIA director George Tenet famously replied that making a better case was a "slam dunk." Instead of pushing the CIA to reexamine its data or obtain better information—as opposed to making a more convincing case for the public—Bush relied on Tenet's reassurance, as well as the judgments of intelligence agencies around the globe.[53]

Bush also asked Condoleezza Rice to review the evidence again. This assignment was of little help to the president, however, and she later remembered, "I had never seen a stronger case."[54] When CIA officials briefed her on December 28, 2002, they thought she seemed to be hearing the specific conclusions of the case for the first time. She noticed that there were lower levels of confidence in the findings than she saw in the President's Daily Briefings, but she did not report this disparity to the president or press the CIA as to which version was more accurate.[55]

Interpreting Saddam Hussein

Viewing Iraq through their shared premises, U.S. officials construed Saddam Hussein's efforts to remove any residue from his old WMD-development programs as efforts to hide the weapons rather than destroy them. As a result, U.S. intelligence agencies misinterpreted Saddam's directions that his military do away with weapons of mass destruction or their elements. In 2002, when U.S. intelligence intercepted an internal message between two Iraqi commanders talking about removing the words "nerve agents" from "wireless instructions," the analysts did not understand that this communication reflected the regime's attempt to ensure it was in compliance with UN resolutions. Similarly, when U.S. intelligence learned of instructions to the Iraqi military to search "for any chemical agents" in order to "make sure the area is free of chemical containers," officials viewed this information through the prism of a decade of deceit. When Secretary of State Colin Powell addressed the UN Security Council in February 2003, he offered evidence from photographs and intercepted communications that the Iraqis were rushing to sanitize suspected weapons sites. In one of the supreme ironies of the entire episode, U.S. officials viewed the steps the Iraqi government was taking to reduce the prospect of war as evidence against it, increasing the odds of a military confrontation.[56]

President Bush and others did not account for Saddam's view that he could not be too open about his compliance with disarmament for fear of showing weakness in a dangerous part of the world.[57] The Iraqi leader even feared that clarity regarding the removal of WMDs might encourage an Israeli attack.[58] In addition, officials remembered that the United States had underestimated Iraq's progress in developing nuclear weapons in the late 1980s and early 1990s, and inferred that Iraq had WMD because it had such a complex organization dedicated to concealing them.[59] In other words, they saw what they expected to see.

Moreover, it seemed implausible that Saddam would risk destruction of his regime if he had actually met international demands regarding weapons of mass destruction.[60] Bush argues in his memoirs that the only logical conclusion was that Saddam was hiding something.

> In retrospect, of course, we all should have pushed harder on the intelligence and revisited our assumptions. But at the time, the evidence and the logic pointed in the other direction. If Saddam doesn't actually have WMD, I asked myself, why on earth would he subject himself to a war he will almost certainly lose?[61]

The president, like all officials, had a personal understanding of politics and of human nature. Because facts do not speak for themselves, his political judgment interpreted them in a way that made sense to *him*.

It is often a mistake to assume that foreign officials are rational as Americans understand rationality—as we saw with the Chinese in 1950 and the North Vietnamese throughout the war in Vietnam—but it is difficult to properly interpret information when the truth is implausible and when others' beliefs and behavior are strange and self-defeating. More broadly, one can sympathize with officials, who would have found it difficult to believe the following:

- Iraq could not account for missing anthrax because Iraqi bureaucrats feared Saddam's anger if he learned that they dumped it near one of his palaces.
- Saddam had convinced himself that the United States would not invade because it already had a military presence in the region.
- Saddam resisted private meetings between weapons inspectors and Iraqi scientists because he saw such meetings as threats to his regime.
- Saddam did not want to declare anything regarding the use of chemical weapons against Iran for fear this evidence might be used in lawsuits against Iraq.
- Saddam feared inspections would allow the United States to pinpoint his location and assassinate him.
- Many of the suspicious ways Iraq purchased equipment were the result of fear, incompetence, and corruption.
- The U.S. suspected aluminum tubes the Iraqis had purchased were being used for producing nuclear fuel because they had such precise specifications. Yet they were actually for building rockets. Iraqi engineers needed to compensate for problems that could not be addressed more directly because doing so would involve quarreling with one of Saddam's cronies, who was in charge of the rocket program.[62]

No one offered alternative explanations for Saddam's behavior or challenged whether it was appropriate to infer his current actions from his past conduct. Moreover, as we have seen, others would probably not have viewed such explanations as credible.[63]

Attributing meaning to the scattered and unreliable evidence of the connections between Iraq and al-Qaeda depended on what policymakers found reasonable from the Iraqi point of view, and this type of analysis varied among officials.[64] The president, vice president, Pentagon civilian officials, and others who strongly held the premise of Iraq possessing WMD, saw a connection.[65] Intelligence analysts specializing in terrorism were more likely to see links than were regional experts.[66]

Politicization of Intelligence

The intelligence community denied any collaboration between Saddam and al-Qaeda or any role of Iraq in the 9/11 attacks, and it was very skeptical about the possibility that Saddam would turn over WMD to terrorists—

which were accurate assessments.[67] It also resisted presenting an optimistic evaluation of the aftermath of an invasion (although it was not asked for such an assessment) and noted that invading might increase support for terrorists.[68]

Nevertheless, the Bush administration's certainty about the Iraqi threat encouraged the intelligence community to provide data to support the president's policy.[69] It was not that officials directly intimidated the intelligence community to provide data to support its plans, although there was certainly pressure to do so.[70] The Senate Select Committee on Intelligence and the Silberman-Robb commission asked analysts whether administration officials twisted their arms. They reported no evidence that analysts shaped or altered their judgments in response to political pressures, although they conceded they worked in an atmosphere of "intense" policymaker interest.[71] Of course, it is unlikely that analysts would acknowledge that their judgments were politicized. In any case, politicization is usually a more subtle process.

Moreover, reports that conform to policy preferences have an easier time making it through the gauntlet of coordination and approval than ones that do not. Managers wanted to avoid the unpleasantness of laying unwelcome analysis on a policymaker's desk, so they often sugarcoated what otherwise would have been an unpalatable message in the hope that policymakers would pay attention to a report. However, they diminished the clarity of the analysis in the process.[72]

Many observers note that it was clear well before March 2003 that the Bush administration would frown on or ignore analysis that called into question going to war and welcomed analysis that supported such a decision. (President Bush did not know that high-level officials including Colin Powell, George Tenet, Condoleezza Rice, and several generals had concluded that war was a *fait accompli*.[73]) The desire to bend with this wind is natural and strong—and often unconscious. Moreover, there are many opportunities for intelligence analysts to bias their judgments when they have fragmentary and uncertain evidence and express their views with caveats and fine distinctions. Thus, the perception that the administration would not welcome challenges to their premises regarding an Iraqi threat created an atmosphere that was not conducive to critical analysis, encouraged excessive certainty, and eroded subtleties and nuances.[74]

And that is what happened. CIA analysts were told by their bosses that the White House did not want qualifiers. The president's daily intelligence briefings became increasingly alarmist, vivid, and lacking in nuance.

In October 2002, CIA director George Tenet gave the administration the benefit of the doubt and testified to Congress that there was a connection between Saddam Hussein and al-Qaeda. He had told the president the same thing, and he told Bush that Iraq had WMD, was seeking UAV mapping software to plan attacks against the United States, and was actively seeking a nuclear capability. Moreover, in October 2002, Tenet issued a statement saying there was no difference between the CIA's view of Iraq's growing threat and that of the White House, and he did not let naysayers near Colin Powell as he wrote the speech he delivered to the UN on February 5, 2003.[75] Sir Richard Dearlove, Britain's head of foreign intelligence, wrote in July 2002 that military action was seen as inevitable—and intelligence and facts were being fixed around the policy.[76]

In addition, political leaders insisted that the intelligence community continually reassess its conclusions, such as that there were no significant links between Saddam and al-Qaeda, not only because they wanted a different answer but because their premises of how the world worked led them to expect such a connection, and they thought that assessments to the contrary were based less on detailed evidence than on misguided political sensibility.[77]

Moreover, officials' repeated urgings of analysts to look at certain matters biased the intelligence gathering process. The Bush administration "repeatedly called on the intelligence community to uncover more material that would contribute to the case for war," especially information on the supposed connection between Saddam and al-Qaeda, which analysts had discounted. The intelligence community responded to these requests by concentrating its resources on them, producing a body of reporting and analysis that, thanks to its quantity and emphasis, left the impression that what it studied was a bigger part of the problem than it really was.[78]

Undersecretary of Defense Douglas Feith was dedicated to finding every possible link between Saddam and al-Qaeda, even if this meant relying on raw, unvetted data. The effort began with the premise of a connection and then sought support to confirm it by producing results that the intelligence community, including the Defense Intelligence Agency, would not provide. His group placed suspicion on par with knowledge, and its briefings—sometimes piped directly to the White House—accused the intelligence community of faulty analysis for failing to see the supposed alliance.[79] The vice president's office also produced a case relying on raw intelligence and was often critical of professional intelligence analysts.[80]

Paul Pillar argues that, for the most part, the intelligence community's own substantive judgments do not seem to have been compromised by these criticisms (with the possible exception of its judgments of Saddam providing jihadists with chemical or biological training). However, some administration supporters accused the intelligence community of attempting to sabotage the president's policies. This atmosphere reinforced the disinclination within the intelligence community to question the prevalent view about WMD. Any such challenge would have served merely to reaffirm the presumptions of the accusers.[81]

Post-Invasion Iraq

The primary immediate goal of the invasion of Iraq—and the one articulated by the Bush administration—was to remove WMD from the hands of a brutal dictator. There was a broader goal driving the policy, however. President George W. Bush and other top officials shared the premise that it was necessary to topple Saddam Hussein and transform the Middle East. According to Richard Haass, the State Department's director of policy planning, Bush simply wanted to destroy Iraq, and nothing else mattered—or was window dressing to build support for war.[82]

From the very beginning of its tenure, the administration had a long-term goal of implanting a pro-U.S. democratic regime in Iraq that would lead to the political transformation of neighboring authoritarian regimes, solving a number of the United States' problems in the Middle East all at once. According to Michael Gordon and Bernard Trainor,

> For the Bush Administration, Iraq was an inviting target for preemption not because it was an immediate threat but because it was thought to be a prospective menace that was incapable of successfully defending itself against a U.S. invasion. For an administration that was determined to change the strategic equation in the Middle East and make Saddam an object lesson to other proliferators, Iraq was not a danger to avoid but a strategic opportunity.[83]

Thus, the desire for regime change in Iraq was based on the broad premise of the impact it would have on both potential terrorists and other nations in the region. Such a strategy of regional transformation flowed logically from the premise that the spread of democracy is a panacea and its absence a threat.[84]

Early Interest in Toppling Saddam

Although overthrowing Saddam was not an initial foreign policy priority for Bush, Powell, Rumsfeld, and Rice,[85] it was for some ranking members of the new administration. Shortly after Bush's inauguration, the Office of the Vice President asked the Defense Intelligence Agency for a memo on Iraqi support for terrorism, and Saddam Hussein's involvement in the 1993 plot to assassinate President George H. W. Bush and the attack on the World Trade Center that same year.[86] Donald Rumsfeld and his deputy Paul Wolfowitz had been among the signatories of an open letter to Bill Clinton on January 26, 1998, advocating the removal of Saddam's regime from power because of his potential for acquiring WMD.[87]

Even for Bush, removing Saddam Hussein was not far from his mind. On January 30, 2001, in his first meeting with his National Security Council, Bush raised the need to design a policy toward Iraq aimed at removing Saddam rather than containing him. The president ordered Secretary of Defense Donald Rumsfeld to provide him an outline of military options.[88] In April, at the first deputy secretary meeting on terrorism, Richard Clarke, the national coordinator for security, infrastructure protection, and counter-terrorism, found that officials, especially Wolfowitz, were far more interested in the threat from states like Iraq than from al-Qaeda.[89]

The 9/11 attacks reinforced the inclinations of policymakers to topple Saddam Hussein. From the time of the attacks, Wolfowitz and Douglas Feith thought Iraq was involved. Rumsfeld was ready to start bombing the country. Shortly after 9/11, Dick Cheney asked the CIA if Saddam Hussein was involved and was displeased when he was told he was not.[90] At a meeting at Camp David on September 15, Wolfowitz kept returning to Iraq as the most important target for the initial U.S. response, until Bush took the option off the table.[91]

Covering his bases but also reflecting his suspicions, on September 12, 2001, the day after the terrorist attacks, Bush asked Clarke about Iraq's role in the assaults—the only country about which the president inquired. (Clarke told the president there was no cooperation between al-Qaeda and Iraq).[92] On September 16, the president told his national security advisor he wanted a plan for invading Iraq in case it was implicated in the 9/11 attacks or attempted to take advantage of them. The next day he told his war council, "I believe Iraq was involved,"[93] and directed the Pentagon to begin planning military options for dealing with Iraq if that were necessary.[94] The president asked Rumsfeld to review the existing battle plans for Iraq in November 2001,[95] and that same month, the secretary of defense instructed the Pentagon's Central Command to begin planning for a war.[96] In his State of the Union message on January 29, 2002, Bush declared Iraq among those constituting the "axis of evil"—countries that sponsored terrorism and sought WMD.[97] The next month, the president approved covert deployment of CIA teams to northern Iraq, and his deputy national security advisor, Stephen Hadley, began interagency lunches to discuss going to war, creating momentum for an option that was never debated.[98] By mid-2002, it appears that Bush had effectively decided to invade.[99] On September 7, 2002, he told the National Security Council that there would be war unless Saddam Hussein turned over his WMD.[100]

Establishing a New Regime

For a superpower to overthrow a government is one thing. Establishing a new regime is a much more difficult task. Doing so requires a complex and sustained effort. The Bush administration operated on several basic premises regarding the aftermath of the invasion of Iraq, each of which appeared to simplify the mission and lower the cost of the enterprise. These premises included that:

- Iraqis would greet Americans as liberators.
- Iraq's infrastructure would be in serviceable condition.
- The Iraqi army would remain in whole units capable of being used for reconstruction.
- The Iraqi police were trustworthy and professional, capable of securing the country.
- The U.S. invasion force would be sufficiently large to secure the country.
- The country would remain largely orderly.
- Iraq's oil revenues would continue to finance much of the government.
- There would be a smooth and rapid transition for Iraq to become a democratic nation.
- Sectarian grievances would give way to a desire to preserve a free Iraq.

In addition, some officials thought the Iraqis would welcome expatriates, many of whom had not been in the country for decades, as new leaders of their country, and they anticipated expatriates forming the Free Iraqi Forces to help fight the war. Others, including the president, felt Iraq was teeming with leaders who would gladly lead the country to democracy.[101]

LACK OF ANALYSIS. Each of these premises was faulty,[102] but the administration made no systematic evaluation of them before the war. It had no intelligence to support the premises, and it did very little research into Iraqi culture and psychology.[103] Instead, decision makers assumed them to be true[104] and rejected predictions of widespread resistance and disorder. When on February 27, 2003, army chief of staff General Eric Shinseki told Congress several hundred thousand U.S. ground troops were needed to secure Iraq after the invasion succeeded, Deputy Secretary of Defense Paul Wolfowitz told Congress, "It's hard to conceive that it would take more forces to provide stability in post-Saddam Iraq than it would take to conduct the war itself.... Hard to imagine."[105] Wolfowitz's statement sent a message throughout the Pentagon that it was better not to challenge the assumptions underlying the invasion.[106] The administration then named Shinseki's successor, making the general a lame duck. According to an air force officer involved in planning the invasion, "After seeing Wolfowitz chew down a four-star, I don't think anyone was going to raise their head up and make a stink about it."[107]

Richard Haass commissioned studies from the National Intelligence Council about what the United States should expect to encounter in a liberated Iraq. Two were completed before the invasion, predicting a difficult road ahead. They had no impact on U.S. policy. He reflected later,

> The human tendency to pay attention to those predictions that buttress preferences and discount those that do not was on full display. And largely missing was any rigorous mechanism to scrutinize and challenge preferences held by those in policy-making positions of responsibility.[108]

On its own, the intelligence community considered the principal challenges the post–invasion authority in Iraq would face. It concluded that Iraq was not a fertile ground for democracy and would have a long, difficult, and turbulent transition to becoming a democratic state. Intelligence officials also projected the need for a great expenditure of resources to restore Iraq's economy and forecast a significant chance of violent conflict. Moreover, a foreign occupying force would be the target of resentment and attacks unless it established security and put Iraq on road to prosperity immediately after Saddam's fall. In addition, the war and the U.S. occupation would boost political Islam and increase sympathy for terrorists' objectives—and Iraq would be a magnet for extremists from elsewhere in the Middle East.[109] An assessment completed in August 2004 warned that the insurgency in Iraq could evolve into a guerrilla war or civil war. After it leaked to the media in September during the presidential campaign, Bush, who had told voters that the mission in Iraq was going well, described the assessment to reporters as "just guessing."[110]

The Council on Foreign Relations, the Center for Strategic and International Studies, RAND, the Army War College, the U.S. Institute of Peace, and the National Defense University's Institute for National Strategic Studies also produced reports on post-invasion Iraq. They were striking in their unanimity of opinion that the security and reconstruction of Iraq would require large numbers of troops for an extended period and international cooperation would be essential, but none of the reports penetrated the Oval Office or Pentagon.[111]

It is ironic that decision makers were alert to technical intelligence regarding WMD, where the analysis was wrong, but apparently paid little attention to intelligence on cultural and political issues vital to understanding the challenges of post-invasion Iraq, where the analysis was correct.[112]

LACK OF PLANNING. The faulty premises regarding the aftermath of the invasion of Iraq led not only to intractable problems for those charged with establishing and maintaining civil society but also discouraged planning for doing so. Despite intelligence to the contrary, top administration officials believed that the political and economic reconstruction of Iraq would be easy and that they needed neither short-term plans to maintain order nor long-term preparations to put down an insurgency and create a stable polity.[113] According to George Packer, "Plan A was that the Iraqi government could be quickly decapitated, security would be turned over to remnants of the Iraqi police and army, international troops would soon arrive, and most American forces would leave within a few months. There was no plan B."[114]

President Bush assigned the Department of Defense the responsibility for postwar Iraq, but Donald Rumsfeld gave the matter little thought and did not cooperate with other elements of government, such as the Department of State. Neither he, Vice President Cheney, nor General Tommy Franks had an interest in post-invasion matters. It was not until December 2002 that Stephen Hadley asked the Department of Defense about plans for running postwar Iraq, and in February 2003, Condoleezza Rice told the president there was no plan for the post-invasion period. Nevertheless, the president did not press the Pentagon to produce one. The little planning that did occur was insufficient, late, underresourced, and disorganized. Moreover, internal administration debates over who would exercise power in in Iraq paralyzed even the modest planning effort.[115] In essence, no one in charge was asking the most basic question: what will we do if it all goes wrong?[116]

Bush did not receive comprehensive briefings on a postwar plan until March 10 and 12, 2003, barely a week before the war. He ignored reports concluding that it would be hard work to rebuild Iraq and spent his time on the easier victory of toppling Saddam rather than the more demanding job of rehabilitating and securing Iraq. Thus, the United States lacked an adequate number of troops, even though there were hundreds of suspected WMD sites and long, porous borders to secure. There was a direct link between the way the Pentagon planned the war and the bitter insurgency it soon confronted. Rumsfeld's plan to transform the military by emphasizing speed over mass proved to be at odds with the goal of transforming Iraq.[117]

The Bush administration never had a plan or program for running postwar Iraq.[118] Jay Garner, the Director of the Office for Reconstruction and Humanitarian Assistance for Iraq immediately following the invasion, explained to the House International Relations Committee, "This is an ad hoc operation, glued together over about four or five weeks' time"; "[We] didn't really have enough time to plan."[119] As one scholar put it, "The Bush administration had goals for Iraq, but no coherent strategy for accomplishing them. Its policy was based on a combination of naivete, misjudgment, and wishful thinking."[120]

In his memoirs, Secretary of Defense Donald Rumsfeld makes clear the importance of examining the fundamental premises of policies and of evaluating options in light of these assumptions. In hindsight, he found that several key premises regarding the aftermath of the war in Iraq were false. The possibility of an insurgency was not in policymakers' or the military's assumptions in the spring of 2003. Contrary to officials' beliefs, which formed the basis of policy, the Iraqi infrastructure was not in serviceable condition, the army did not remain in whole units capable of being used for reconstruction, the police were not trustworthy or professional and thus incapable of securing the country, and there was no oil money for reconstruction. Although Rumsfeld read a list of potentially false premises—a "Parade of Horribles"—to senior officials in the autumn of 2002, there was never a systematic review of his list (or a similar effort in the State Department), and the president never saw it.[121] Moreover, Bush never asked for such an analysis. Rumsfeld himself was maddeningly unclear about his views regarding the war.[122]

Similarly, Condoleezza Rice recalled that she had not been insistent enough when the president accepted the Department of Defense's assumptions about what it could achieve in Iraq with the number of troops it was deploying.[123] Officials in the State Department tried to slow down the juggernaut to war. Colin Powell warned the president of the dangers of invading Iraq in a two-hour meeting on August 5, 2002, but he did not say, "Don't invade." He also did not argue against Rumsfeld and other principals who supported the invasion. Indeed, although he opposed going to war, he said he was with Bush when the president asked for his support on January 13, 2003.[124]

The acceptance of an easy occupation and reconstruction of Iraq and thus the lack of planning and careful evaluation of policy had additional dire consequences. For example, top officials never systematically discussed the critical matters of disbanding the Iraqi army or de-Baathification of the Iraqi public service[125] or the controversial questions regarding detainees and electronic surveillance.[126] Thus, Bush did not foresee the psychological impact of de-Baathification and the disbanding army on the Sunnis, and he was surprised to learn how deep de-Baathification cut. In retrospect, the president concluded that he should have insisted on more debate on these decisions.[127] Donald Rumsfeld had the same view—after the fact.[128]

Reevaluating Premises in Face of Failure

The nineteenth century British statesman Lord Salisbury reflected that "the commonest error in politics is sticking to the carcasses of dead policies."[129] Leaders are heavily invested in their policies, and reappraisal may be politically and psychologically painful. In the case of Iraq, a public reevaluation would have provided ammunition to the war's legion of critics. It would also have forced leaders to face the fact that there would be no quick or painless solution to the insurrection.[130] In early 2007, Senator John McCain explained, "It's just so hard for me to contemplate failure that I can't make the next step."[131] Secretary of State Colin Powell reflected that that the administration was dangerously protective of decisions regarding rebuilding Iraq. He felt that no one in the White House could break through and insist on a realistic reassessment of the situation in Iraq. The hardest of all tasks, he believed, was to go back to fundamentals and question your own judgment.[132]

The president had an additional incentive to persevere in his policy. He told Bob Woodward, "I know it is hard for you to believe, but I have not doubted what we're doing [in Iraq]." Months later, he added, "[A] president has got to be the calcium in the backbone. If I weaken, the whole team weakens.... If my confidence level in our ability declines, it will send ripples throughout the whole organization. I mean, it's essential that we be confident and determined and united."[133] The president's emphasis on expressing certainty and optimism rather than engaging in substantive policy debate discouraged officials from reconsidering policy, even when it was clear that it was failing.[134] Shades of gray analysis is incompatible with certainty.

It is easy to understand that it would have been painful for the president to admit mistakes on the war. More importantly, the president did not want to appear weak and open himself and his party to additional criticism.[135] When conviction drives process, however, it severely limits the rigorous consideration of options, because it locks a leader into a particular course of action, inhibiting adjustments to unexpected turns of events.[136] In Bush's case, it allowed the president to rely on his instincts,[137] a flimsy basis for decision making.

Nevertheless, reappraisal was necessary, and it is troubling—but not surprising—that the same decision makers who went to war on the basis of faulty premises were also slow to challenge them when faced with widespread violence.[138] Adhering rigidly to a flawed plan, the administration did not adapt to developments on the ground and remained wedded to its prewar analysis even after the Iraqis showed an early penchant for guerilla warfare.[139]

The administration had not planned for lawlessness after toppling Saddam Hussein, and the president was surprised when it occurred. "What the hell is happening?" Bush asked at a National Security Council meeting. "Why isn't anyone stopping these looters?" After leaving office, Bush concluded that cutting troop levels too quickly was the most important failure of execution in the war.[140] Calculations of troop needs depended on the assumptions of the Iraq army remaining in place and Arab nations contributing troops. When both proved to be false, the administration made no adjustment. As Stephen Hadley, the president's national security assistant, put it, "We never connected it up ... I don't know why. It seems in retrospect, very clear."[141] Bush also felt that failing to respond more quickly or aggressively when the security situation deteriorated was very damaging to the U.S. effort, which had failed to protect Iraqis and allowed the insurgency to gain momentum and al-Qaeda operatives to flock to Iraq in search of a new safe haven.[142]

According to the president, for three years the premise underlying policy in Iraq was that political progress was the measure of success. Because U.S. officials presumed (1) civil order would be maintained after the fighting ended, (2) they could train Iraqis quickly to take over security responsibilities, and (3) they could rely on coalition forces for help in the meantime, they concluded they had sufficient troops and could reduce troop strength after the war. All these premises were incorrect. Nevertheless, when Paul Bremer, the head of the Coalition Provisional Authority, requested more troops, the president denied his request on the advice of the secretary of defense and military leaders. Only in 2006 did it become clear to Bush that more security was needed before political progress could continue.[143]

It was not until August 17, 2006, that the president authorized his now–national security assistant, Steven Hadley, to formalize a review that the National Security Council Iraq team was doing. He initiated "deep dives" with national security specialists in which he actively probed and questioned analysts and dug into the details of policy.[144] "I wanted to challenge every assumption behind our strategy and generate new options," the president recalls. According to Bush, he gathered facts and options from inside and outside the administration, challenged assumptions, and weighed all the options carefully. Ultimately, he decided on a surge in troops and chose to change the commanders in Iraq and the leadership of the Department of Defense.[145] The thorough decision-making process the president described, including the challenging of premises, seemed to pay off, as violence in Iraq diminished substantially after the adjustment in policy.

Intuition

Other factors may exacerbate the problems of premises. The George W. Bush White House portrayed the president and his top advisors as consumers of imprecise intelligence, making the best decisions they could in a murky world of secret plots and illicit programs. There is another view, however. President Bush often described himself as an instinctual decision maker—"I'm not a textbook player. I'm a gut player,"[146] a view shared by other close observers.[147] Thinking with one's gut is really acting on premises.

A drawback to relying on instincts is acting impulsively rather than delving deeply into a range of possible options. Some, but not all,[148] close observers viewed Bush as intellectually passive, lacking inquisitiveness and resisting reflection.[149] To the extent it was true, it would have also discouraged tough questioning and thorough analysis. Rather than complicated, rigorous policy analysis of what policies should be, his intellectual curiosity focused on reaching the bottom line of a solution and knowing what he needed to do to sell and implement his policies.[150] The president's decision-making orientation seems inappropriate for issues such as a war on terrorism that are laced with subtlety and nuance. It also discouraged tough questioning and thorough analysis, not only of policy options but, more importantly, of the fundamental premises of policies.

Instinctual reactions also discourage investing time in soliciting and cultivating the views of others and asking probing questions of advisors. When the CIA briefed the president on August 6, 2001, about the threat from al-Qaeda, he did not follow up with questions, instructions, or discussions with his top advisors.[151] Well-placed officials in the administration were skeptical about the intelligence on WMD in Iraq, but an effective expression of these views apparently did not reach Bush,[152] at least partly because he did not encourage dissenting views.

The president often failed to ask experts and relevant officials probing questions, including what they thought about an issue.[153] For example, when the president met with David Kay, the chief U.S. weapons inspector, who reported on the lack of evidence of WMD, Bush seemed disengaged. "I'm not sure I've spoken to anyone at that level who seemed less inquisitive," Kay recalled.[154] Jay Garner was surprised that Bush did not ask him any questions as he briefed the National Security Council before leaving for the Middle East right before the war. When he returned to the United States, he tried to give Bush a report of his experiences in running postwar Iraq, but the president said he did not need one, and asked Garner just to tell him some stories. Garner was unable to alert the president to mistakes he thought Paul Bremer was making. Neither Bush, Cheney, or Rice *ever* solicited his thoughts or asked for his advice.[155]

Similarly, Bush did not formally request the views of many of his top national security advisors on going to war in Iraq,[156] the most important decision of his presidency (although he said he knew where they stood).[157] As a result, although both Secretary of State Colin Powell and CIA Director George Tenet opposed going to war, neither ever told Bush.[158] Thinking you already know where your advisors stand, as Bush did,[159] is not the same as having them debate an issue in front of you.

Conclusion

The invasion and occupation of Iraq did not have to occur. Yet it did, largely because patriotic and able officials uncritically accepted premises that led them to conclude that invading Iraq was necessary and they could easily manage the post-invasion period. As a result of their decisions, more than 4,500 American servicemen and women and perhaps 3,000 people working for U.S. contractors died, and over 32,000 service members and many thousands of contractor employees were wounded.[160] As many as three hundred thousand U.S. military suffered from post-traumatic stress disorder.[161] The U.S. taxpayers were left with a bill for more than $2 trillion.[162] Just as important were the more than four hundred thousand Iraqis who died as a result of the insurrection and its attendant instability.[163]

Bush administration officials brought to office strongly held premises regarding Iraq and its possession of WMD, and the 9/11 attacks increased their salience. The administration's flawed national security decision-making process[164] (which operated contrary to the president's wishes),[165] and the president's lack of inquisitiveness, failure to ask probing questions, and disinterest in rigorous policy analysis discouraged carefully assessing them. Yet, in the end, it was officials' premises that a problem existed that drove the decision to go to war. They were the *sine qua non* for the invasion and the tragedy that followed.

Ironically, once Saddam was defeated, officials ignored many of the core problems they faced. Despite the violence in the wake of the invasion of Iraq, the Bush administration did not readily challenge its basic premises regarding the aftermath of the war. Thus, in the president's words, it "took four painful, costly years" to change U.S. military policy in post-invasion Iraq.[166] The president's projection of absolute confidence, and the fierce loyalty he bestowed and demanded, limited critical thinking, as did his rejection of advice that ran counter to his instincts. Nevertheless, it was premises that once again determined the starting point for policy, encouraged a lack of planning and analysis, and discouraged rapid adaptation to realities on the ground.

CHAPTER SIX

No Silver Bullet

"What government needs is great askers." —Barbara Tuchman[1]

In his landmark work, *Perception and Misperception in International Politics*, Robert Jervis concludes, "Analysis of policies that failed indicated that many crucial errors occur not because decision-makers arrive at the wrong answers, but because they ask the wrong questions"[2] Capable, diligent, well-intentioned officials often fail to question their premises, yet those beliefs are often faulty. Catastrophe may result, bleeding nations of their youth and treasure. We have seen that the secretaries of defense during the major commitments to a war in Vietnam and the invasion of Iraq both testified that the deliberations of policymakers focused on how to fight the war, not *whether* to fight it.

Premises are not the only influence on decisions. Policymakers' personalities, styles of decision making, advisory processes, group dynamics, limited time for deliberations, resource constraints, and other features of decision making at the pinnacle of government may also play a role in the choices officials make. Nevertheless, the premises leaders carry in their heads at the beginning of the decision-making process exert extraordinary influence on the decisions they make. Often, these premises put them on the path to a decision, no matter what else follows.

The first step in decision making is identifying a problem. As we have seen in the cases of Vietnam and Iraq, premises often encourage decision makers to assume the presence of problems that actually do not exist. Premises may also blind policymakers to problems that require their attention or cause them to underestimate the likelihood of problems arising, as we saw in the surprise attacks in 1941, the Chinese intervention in

Korea, and other policy debacles. Just as importantly, not all policies are successful. The premises officials hold may encourage them to resist even clear evidence of a policy's failure, as in Jefferson's Embargo Act and the wars in Vietnam and Iraq. Disaster frequently follows.

Premises may influence domestic as well as national security policy. Basic views about the impact and fairness of various forms of taxation, the most effective way to stimulate the economy, the deservingness of those receiving social welfare benefits, the state of race relations, and the threat posed by climate change, for example, are at the heart of the decisions officials make about these matters. Policymakers often dismiss arguments that contradict their premises as unworthy of consideration.

Revaluating Premises

Given the significance of premises in policymaking, it is not surprising that there is widespread agreement about the importance of identifying and examining the major assumptions underlying the identification of policy problems and then evaluating alternatives in light of such analyses.[3] Is there anything policymakers can do to counter the danger of becoming prisoners of their premises? Can they increase the probability they will choose to face the facts and thoroughly analyze a range of options rather than simply relying on their premises?

The answer is as obvious as it is difficult to execute. Officials should identify and clearly articulate the key assumptions of a policy choice.[4] After adopting a policy, they need to continue to carefully explore the relationships between ends and means rather than assuming them. The more central a premise is to a policy, the more important it is to analyze it rigorously.[5]

In effect, decision makers should ask what it would take to disconfirm their views and what evidence should be present if their views are correct. They need to carefully scrutinize the information they used to support their assumptions. To engage in this exercise requires not only a self-critical mindset but also a search for information. We have seen that too often officials have the arrogance of ignorance. As Barbara Tuchman concluded in *The March of Folly*, "No one is so sure of his premises as the man who knows too little."[6]

People are generally not closed-minded, consciously deceiving themselves to preserve their prior beliefs. Our cognitive biases do not free us to reach a conclusion simply because we want to reach that conclusion. Instead, we have accuracy goals that motivate us to be rational and construct persuasive justifications for our judgments, seeking and carefully considering relevant evidence to reach the best conclusion.[7] Strong, salient, and credible counterevidence may persuade even those committed to their positions.[8]

Constraints on Challenging Premises

It is not easy to question premises, however. It is psychologically difficult to change one's fundamental beliefs. According to Secretary of State George Shultz, for example, once President Ronald Reagan came to an "understanding" of an event, "no fact, no argument, no plea for reconsideration would change his mind."[9] Similarly, Lyn Nofziger, a longtime advisor to Reagan, said that his boss could "convince himself that the truth is what he wants it to be."[10]

Cognitive biases are powerful because they are not volitional, occurring unconsciously and automatically.[11] Beliefs fulfill a need for cognitive simplicity and help busy officials cope with complex decisions. The tension between the drives for accuracy and the perseverance of existing beliefs underlies all human reasoning. Once attitudes are crystallized, change is unlikely. It is inevitable that the perception and interpretation of new information will be influenced by established ideas.[12] Our beliefs can bias our constructions of justifications for our decisions, making them seem more rational than they really are.[13] We typically rationalize our accuracy goals to make our decisions compatible with our premises.

Information about many important questions in politics, such as the current and future actions of hostile nations, is typically ambiguous and open to multiple interpretations. There is usually a range of information from which to choose, and this data is likely to point in opposite directions. The truth may seem implausible, and the actions of adversaries may be unexpected or appear to be self-defeating. In such situations, the assumptions policymakers carry in their heads often blind them to threats to the nation and other developments of strategic importance, and their views are determined more by their premises than by specific pieces of information.[14] Moreover, leaders are likely to accord more credence to information that reinforces their preexisting views.

Clear-cut disconfirmation of premises may not be possible.[15] It is difficult to disconfirm beliefs that an enemy will not attack, as it was to refute the view that the North Vietnamese would eventually capitulate, or that the shah of Iran was in control of his country. It also is often sensible to dismiss information as deceptions.[16] It is possible that premises may become unfalsifiable, and that evidence of disconfirmation will lead decision makers to the wrong conclusion. We saw this in both the escalation of fighting in Vietnam and the assessments of weapons inspections in Iraq, for example.

Discrediting the source of information and options is a means of reducing the complexity and resolving the contradictions with which policymakers must deal.[17] At first, President Johnson handled the critics of his Vietnam policy quite well, inviting them to his office and talking to them for hours. However, as opposition increased and polls indicated a dip in his popularity, he responded to criticism by discrediting its source. He maintained that Senator William Fulbright (the chairman of the Senate Foreign Relations Committee) was upset at not being named secretary of state; that the liberals in Congress were angry at him because he had not gone to Harvard, because the Great Society was more successful than Kennedy's New Frontier, and because he had blocked Robert Kennedy from the presidency; that columnists opposed him in order to make a bigger splash; and that young people were hostile because they were ignorant.

It is rare for negative evidence to be solicited, reported, or noticed.[18] Sometimes, leaders may simply avoid information they fear will force them to face disagreeable decisions that will complicate their lives and produce additional stress. Richard Nixon is a classic example. In his memoirs, he wrote of putting off a confrontation with his own attorney general, John Mitchell, because of Mitchell's hypersensitivity and Nixon's own desire to remain ignorant about Mitchell's involvement in Watergate in case it would prove harmful for him to know about it. Referring to Nixon's ability to engage in self-delusion and avoid unpleasant facts, White House Chief of Staff H. R. Haldeman argued that the "failure to face the irrefutable facts, even when it was absolutely clear that they were irrefutable, was one of our fatal flaws in handling Watergate at every step."[19]

Former secretary of state George Shultz has described his boss, Ronald Reagan, as engaging in wishful thinking regarding issues and events, sometimes rearranging facts and allowing himself to be deceived—for example, when he insisted that he had not traded arms for hostages in the Iran-Contra Affair.[20] Wishful thinking also played a prominent role in decision making about the ill-fated invasion of Cuba at the Bay of Pigs at the beginning of the Kennedy administration and the lack of adequate planning for the U.S. peacekeeping operation in Iraq in 2003 following the war.[21]

A form of wishful thinking occurs when information inconsistent with ongoing policy is deemphasized and policymakers conclude that undesirable conditions are only temporary and will ameliorate in response to current policy. Officials used this type of reasoning to garner support for the continued escalation of the Vietnam War. All that was needed to force the enemy to succumb, they argued, was to keep up the pressure. Thus, they resisted rigorous evaluation of their military strategy.[22] Policymakers found it comforting to believe in the strategy of escalating the war.[23]

Information alone is not sufficient for challenging premises, however. Presidents and other top officials need to encourage debate if they are to effectively identify and challenge their premises. Debates are most likely to draw out implicit premises and force policymakers to acknowledge them directly and make explicit judgments about them. Such deliberations require a variety of analysts holding a variety of views.

There are challenges to making premises explicit and evaluating them carefully, however. Officials may lack the time or energy to examine all the assumptions underlying a policy (some of which may be correct anyway). In addition, there may not be relevant officials holding divergent views, especially if an issue, such as resistance to communism, is well-established and believed to be well-understood. Moreover, as the secrecy and urgency of a decision increases, the number of participants advising the president decreases. There is also, inevitably, pressure toward homogeneity, especially among those closest to the president, both in the White House and in the bureaucracy. The president is likely to have chosen aides and cabinet members who generally agree with him, and they are likely to be highly responsive to his perspectives and preferences. It is possible to appoint a devil's advocate, but it is highly unlikely that the White House would ask someone not at the center of the administration to serve in such a position. Moreover, it is easy to dismiss devil's advocates as simply playing a role.

Sources of Premises

Another reason for the strength of premises is their sources. Many premises arise from officials' reading—or misreading—of history. The imperative to resist aggression and to maintain credibility, which was key in both

Korea and Vietnam, arose from the experience with Hitler before World War II. In Vietnam, decision makers' fear of provoking China or the Soviet Union was a lesson learned from the Korean War. Officials' unwillingness to tolerate a brutal dictator who had possessed weapons of mass destruction was certainly largely the result of leaders' risk aversion after the 9/11 attacks and Saddam Hussein's history of possession of WMD, deception about them, and support for terrorism.

Analogical reasoning is a cognitive shortcut that employs metaphors and similes to simplify a complex and ambiguous reality by relating it to a relatively simple and well-understood example or concept. Most typically, policymakers rely on historical analogies[24] — events that are familiar and salient, and thus readily accessible.[25] They are also relatively easy to communicate to both elites and the general public in the effort to build political support for policy.[26] At their best, such analogies offer insights derived from previous events.[27]

The use of analogies poses substantial risks, however. A. J. P. Taylor warned that "men use the past to prop up their own prejudices."[28] Decision makers may choose their analogies on the basis of superficial similarities to match the premises of their current policy preferences, undermining their ability to gain historical insights. At the very least, analogies may be oversimplified and inappropriate to a current situation, as decision makers who are ignorant or insensitive to the context of an analogy or its difference from present circumstances draw inappropriate inferences.[29] Decision makers may also employ seemingly persuasive but ultimately inappropriate similes, such as Vietnam as a falling domino, to buttress their historical analogies.

Robert Jervis argues that officials do not necessarily choose analogies to buttress their predispositions. In his view, the lessons officials draw from history filter their evaluation of current information.[30] Nevertheless, he agrees that inappropriate analogies may obscure aspects of a current situation that differ from one in the past and thus hinder decision making. Events that serve as analogies may not be the best guides to the future. Lessons from analogies are often superficial and overgeneralized, and decision makers typically do not examine a range of analogies before selecting one they think sheds the most light on their situation. Moreover, when an interpretation of the past is strikingly incorrect, it is more likely that the interpretation is influenced by current preferences rather than the other way around.[31]

The conclusions supported by analogical reasoning seem to have strength independent of the available evidence, probably because the analogies simplify and provide a coherent framework for ambiguous and inconsistent information. Analogies help policymakers define the nature of a situation confronting them, clarify the stakes involved in the issue, provide prescriptions, assess the alternatives, and evaluate their moral rightness. Once chosen, analogies allow officials to go beyond the knowledge available to them and process information to fit into existing schema or analogies. Thus, analogies persevere, even in the face of contradictory information.[32]

In other instances, officials appeared to be ignorant of history. Vietnam's long aversion to both Chinese and Western hegemony seemed to be a cipher to policymakers. The fact that communism was not a monolithic conspiracy also seemed to have little impact on policy. The potential for sectarian strife in Iraq played little role in the thinking about the aftermath of an invasion. A related type of ignorance is underestimating the capabilities of potential adversaries, as U.S. officials did with Japan in 1941 and China in 1950.

Another source of faulty premises is viewing the intentions and assessments of hostile states through the prism of U.S. calculations instead of those of their leaders. In Korea, officials misestimated how both Mao and Stalin saw their stakes in war. Similarly, in Vietnam, policymakers could not understand the willingness of the North to suffer the human and material costs of war. In Iraq, U.S. officials failed to evaluate Saddam Hussein's lack of cooperation with weapons inspections from *his* perspective, and they did not consider how various interests in Iraq would react to a more democratic system.

Agents of Change?

Actors outside the executive branch may play a prominent role in encouraging officials to reexamine their premises. Most critical is the loss of public support. In a democracy, leaders cannot sustain indefinitely a costly policy against the wishes of the public. Presidents wish to be reelected, and do not want to be seen as pursuing a highly visible failing and costly policy. The media is not as dependent on official sources as in the past century and is more activist in challenging leaders. Moreover, the fragmentation of the media, including social media, provides journalists ample opportunities and incentives to challenge policies.

Members of the president's party in Congress are usually supportive of the White House, but they do not want to risk their reelections or their majorities, if they have them. Thus, they may quietly push officials toward reexamining their policies. Senators and representatives of the opposition party have no such hesitancy in criticizing the president and his aides and have strong incentives to call for change once a policy goes sour, as often happens. In addition, congressional opposition both reinforces and encourages public opposition.

Experts outside the government and dissident officials within the executive branch may also advocate substantial reassessments of policy. Lyndon Johnson's panel of "wise men" influenced his thinking about Vietnam. Private individuals and some generals successfully encouraged George W. Bush to rethink his strategy in Iraq.

Nevertheless, policymakers find it especially difficult to change their minds when they have invested substantially in their policies and sacrificed for decisions. Instead, they are likely to wish to continue to expend resources to make a policy work or even expand their objectives to justify the costs the nation has incurred.[33] Vietnam and Iraq are examples of officials resisting change, even when it was clear that their policies were not working. Instead, the nation endured years of costly and fruitless conflict.

Leaders must usually suffer a major loss of political support and incur serious programmatic failure before they will reevaluate their policies and the premises on which they are based. When belief change does occur, it typically follows the cognitive consistency principle of least resistance. First officials change their tactical beliefs about the best means to achieve particular ends. They change their strategic assumptions and orientation only after the failure of tactical solutions and reconsider their basic goals or objectives only after repeated strategic failures.[34] Surprise attacks are dramatic examples of such failures. Even in such cases, however, officials often at first do not believe their own eyes.

We have come full circle. There is no simple solution to the problem of faulty premises. Making good decisions is an uphill battle. Even the most able and diligent decision makers labor under cognitive limits and the psychological and social needs that trigger motivated reasoning. Both factors will always have the potential to distort leaders' processing information and bias them against changing their minds. Thus, premises continually pose the risk of catastrophe, especially in the identification and definition of problems. Nevertheless, both policymakers and their critics should be alert to the key assumptions underlying a policy decision and do their best to insist on subjecting them to rigorous analysis. The nation's well-being depends on them doing so.

Notes

Chapter One

1. For other aspects of beliefs, see Robert Jervis, "Understanding Beliefs," *Political Psychology* 27 (October 2006): 641–663; Nils J. Nilsson, *Understanding Beliefs* (Cambridge, MA: MIT Press, 2014).

2. See, e.g., Elizabeth N. Saunders, *Leaders at War: How Presidents Shape Military Interventions* (Ithaca, NY: Cornell University Press, 2013).

3. See, e.g., Richard E. Neustadt and Ernest R. May, *Thinking in Time: The Uses of History for Decision Makers* (New York: Free Press, 1986), pp. 135–136.

4. Barbara W. Tuchman, *The March of Folly: From Troy to Vietnam* (New York: Ballantine Books, 1984), pp. 7, 23-24.

5. Tuchman, *March of Folly*, pp. 7, 23–24.

6. The classics in this substantial literature are Herbert A. Simon, "A Behavioral Model of Rational Choice," in *Models of Man: Social and Rational; Mathematical Essays on Rational Human Behavior in a Social Setting*, ed. Herbert A. Simon (New York: Wiley, 1957); James G. March and Herbert A. Simon, *Organizations* (New York: Wiley, 1958); Charles E. Lindblom and David Braybrooke, *A Strategy of Decision: Policy Evaluation as a Social Process* (New York: Free Press, 1963); Herbert A. Simon, "Bounded Rationality and Organizational Learning," *Organization Science* 2 (March 1991): 125–134. See also Daniel Kahneman, "Maps of Bounded Rationality: Psychology for Behavioral Economics," *American Economic Review* 93 (December 2003): 1449–1475.

7. See Susan T. Fiske and Shelley E. Taylor, *Social Cognition*, 2nd ed. (New York: McGraw-Hill, 1991).

8. See Herbert A. Simon, *Administrative Behavior: A Study of Decision-Making Processes in Administrative Organization* (New York: Macmillan, 1947); Herbert A. Simon, "Rational Choice and the Structure of the Environment," *Psychological Review* 63 (March 1956): 129–138.

9. See Daniel Kahneman and Amos Tversky, "On the Psychology of Prediction," *Psychological Review* 80 (July 1973): 237–251; Amos Tversky and Daniel

Kahneman, "Availability: A Heuristic for Judging Frequency and Probability," *Cognitive Psychology* 5 (September 1973): 207–232; Amos Tversky and Daniel Kahneman, "Judgment under Uncertainty: Heuristics and Biases," *Science* 185 (September 1974): 1124–1131; Robert Jervis, *Perception and Misperception in International Politics* (Princeton, NJ: Princeton University Press, 1976); Richard E. Nisbett and Lee Ross, *Human Inference: Strategies and Shortcomings of Social Judgment* (Englewood Cliffs: NJ: Prentice-Hall, 1980); Daniel Kahneman and Jonathan Renshon, "Hawkish Biases," in *American Foreign Policy and the Politics of Fear: Threat Inflation Since 9/11*, ed. Trevor Thrall and Jane Cramer (New York: Routledge, 2009), 79–96; Thomas Gilovich, Dale Griffin, and Daniel Kahneman, eds., *Heuristics and Biases: The Psychology of Intuitive Judgment* (Cambridge: Cambridge University Press, 2002); Reid Hastie and Robyn M. Dawes, *Rational Choice in an Uncertain World: The Psychology of Judgment and Decision Making* (Thousand Oaks, CA: Sage, 2001); Max Bazerman, *Judgment in Managerial Decision Making*, 6th ed. (Hoboken, NJ: Wiley, 2006); Hulda Thórisdóttir and John T. Jost, "Motivated Closed-Mindedness Mediates the Effect of Threat on Political Conservatism," *Political Psychology* 32 (June 2011): 785–811; Daniel Kahneman, *Thinking, Fast and Slow* (New York: Farrar, Straus and Giroux, 2011).

10. The classic works on cognitive dissonance and consistency are Leon Festinger, *A Theory of Cognitive Dissonance* (Palo Alto, CA: Stanford University Press, 1957); Jack Brehm and Arthur Cohen, *Explorations in Cognitive Dissonance* (New York: Wiley, 1962); and Robert P. Abelson et al., *Theories of Cognitive Consistency: A Sourcebook* (Chicago: Rand-McNally, 1968).

11. Silvia Knobloch-Westerwick, Cornelia Mothes, and Nick Polavin, "Confirmation Bias, Ingroup Bias, and Negativity Bias in Selective Exposure to Political Information," *Communication Research* 47 (February 2020): 104–124; Matthew L. Stanley et al., "Resistance to Position Change, Motivated Reasoning, and Polarization," *Political Behavior* 42 (September 2020): 891–913; Milton Lodge and Charles S. Taber, *The Rationalizing Voter* (New York: Cambridge University Press, 2013); James N. Druckman, Jordan Fein, and Thomas J. Leeper, "A Source of Bias in Public Opinion Stability," *American Political Science Review* 106 (May 2012): 430–454; Rune Slothuus and Claes H. de Vreese, "Political Parties, Motivated Reasoning, and Issue Framing Effects," *Journal of Politics* (July 2010): 630–645; Charles S. Taber, Damon Cann, and Simona Kucsova, "The Motivated Processing of Political Arguments," *Political Behavior* 31 (June 2009): 137–155; Charles S. Taber and Milton Lodge, "Motivated Skepticism in the Evaluation of Political Beliefs," *American Journal of Political Science* 50 (July 2006): 755–769; John T. Jost, "The End of the End of Ideology," *American Psychologist* 61, no. 7 (2006): 651–670; Richard R. Lau and David P. Redlawsk, *How Voters Decide: Information Processing in Election Campaigns* (New York: Cambridge University Press, 2006); Milton Lodge and Charles S. Taber, "The Automaticity of Affect for Political Leaders, Groups, and Issues: An Experimental Test of the Hot Cognition Hypothesis,"

Political Psychology 26 (June 2005): 455–482; David P. Redlawsk, "Hot Cognition or Cool Consideration: Testing the Effects of Motivated Reasoning on Political Decision Making," *Journal of Politics* 64 (November 2002): 1021–1044; Ziva Kunda, "The Case for Motivated Reasoning," *Psychological Bulletin* 108 (November 1990): 480–498; Ziva Kunda, "Motivated Inference: Self-Serving Generation and Evaluation of Causal Theories," *Journal of Personality and Social Psychology* 53, no. 4 (1987): 636–647; Milton Lodge and Ruth Hamill, "A Partisan Schema for Political Information Processing," *American Political Science Review* 80 (June 1986): 505–519; Charles Lord, Lee Ross, and Mark R. Lepper, "Biased Assimilation and Attitude Polarization: The Effects of Prior Theories on Subsequently Considered Evidence," *Journal of Personality and Social Psychology* 37 (November 1979): 2098–2109; Jervis, *Perception and Misperception*, chap. 11.

12. Irving L. Janis and Leon Mann, *Decision Making: A Psychological Analysis of Conflict, Choice, and Commitment* (New York: Free Press, 1977), pp. 57–58, 74–79, 107–133.

13. Ashley L. Schiff, *Fire and Water: Scientific Heresy in the Forest Service* (Cambridge, MA: Harvard Press, 1962), pp. 169–173.

14. Lodge and Taber, *Rationalizing Voter*. On the ability and tendency of more knowledgeable people to resist new information, also see John R. Zaller, *The Nature and Origins of Mass Opinion* (New York: Cambridge University Press, 1992), pp. 102–113; Dan M. Kahan et al., "Motivated Numeracy and Enlightened Self-Government," *Behavioural Public Policy* 1 (May 2017): 54–86; Christopher Achen and Larry Bartels, *Democracy for Realists: Why Elections Do Not Produce Responsive Government* (Princeton, NJ: Princeton University Press, 2016), chap. 10.

15. On this process, see Charles Taber, "Information Processing and Public Opinion," in *The Oxford Handbook of Political Psychology*, ed. David O. Sears, Leonie Huddy, and Robert Jervis (New York: Oxford University Press, 2003), pp. 433–476; and Milton Lodge and Charles Taber, "Implicit Affect for Political Candidates, Parties, and Issues: An Experimental Test of the Hot Cognition Hypothesis," *Political Psychology* 26 (December 2005): 455–482; Charles Taber, Milton Lodge, and Jill Glather, "The Motivated Construction of Political Judgments," in *Citizens and Politics: Perspectives from Political Psychology*, ed. James Kuklinski (New York: Cambridge University Press, 2001), pp. 198–226.

16. Francis Bacon, *New Organon, Book One (Aphorisms Concerning the Interpretation of Nature, and the Kingdom of Man)* (1621), aphorism XLVI.

17. See, e.g., Charles S. Taber and Milton Lodge, "Motivated Skepticism in Political Information Processing," *American Journal of Political Science* 50 (July 2006): 755–769.

18. Ziva Kunda, *Social Cognition: Making Sense of People* (Cambridge, MA: MIT Press, 1999), pp. 242–246.

19. For overviews of motivated reasoning, see Jack S. Levy, "Political Psychology and Foreign Policy," in *The Oxford Handbook of Political Psychology*,

ed. David O. Sears, Leonie Huddy, and Robert Jervis (New York: Oxford University Press, 2003); Milton Lodge and Charles S. Taber, "Three Steps Towards a Theory of Motivated Reasoning," in *Elements of Reason: Understanding and Expanding the Limits of Political Rationality*, ed. Arthur Lupia, Matthew D. McCubbins, and Samuel L. Popkin (New York: Cambridge University Press, 2000); Richard R. Lau, "Models of Decision-Making," in *The Oxford Handbook of Political Psychology*, ed. Sears, Huddy, and Jervis.

20. Daniel Kahneman, *Thinking*, pp. 201, 45ff.

21. Joshua D. Kertzer, "Re-Assessing Elite-Public Gaps in Political Behavior," *American Journal of Political Science* (forthcoming), and sources cited therein.

22. Richard K. Herrmann and Jong Kun Choi, "From Prediction to Learning: Opening Experts' Minds to Unfolding History," *International Security* 31 (Spring 2007): 132–161; Gregory Herek, Irving Janis, and Paul Huth, "Decision Making during International Crises: Is Quality of Process Related to the Outcome?" *Journal of Conflict Resolution* 31 (June 1987): 203–226; Joseph de Rivera, *The Psychological Dimension of Foreign Policy* (Columbus, OH: C. E. Merrill, 1968), p. 57.

23. Philip E. Tetlock, "Theory-Driven Reasoning about Plausible Pasts and Probable Futures in World Politics: Are We Prisoners of Our Preconceptions?" *American Journal of Political Science* 43 (April 1999): 335–366.

24. See, e.g., Janice Gross Stein, "Building Politics into Psychology: The Misperception of Threat," *Political Psychology* 9 (June 1988): 262; de Rivera, *Psychological Dimension*, 57. See also John W. Patty, "The Politics of Biased Information," *Journal of Politics* 71 (April 2009): 385–397.

25. Jervis, *Perception and Misperception*, pp. 195–201; Kunda, *Social Cognition*, p. 231.

26. For an overview of presidential decision making, see George C. Edwards III, Kenneth R. Mayer, and Stephen J. Wayne, *Presidential Leadership*, 11th ed. (New York: Rowman and Littlefield, 2020), chap. 9, and sources cited therein.

27. For a discussion of the challenges of studying decision making, see Patrick J. Haney, "Foreign-Policy Advising: Models and Mysteries from the Bush Administration," *Presidential Studies Quarterly* 35 (June 2005): 289–302.

28. John F. Kennedy, preface to *Decision-Making in the White House*, by Theodore C. Sorensen (New York: Columbia University Press, 2005), pp. xxix and xxxi.

29. Nathan Leites, *A Study of Bolshevism* (Glencoe, IL: Free Press, 1953).

30. Alexander L. George, "The 'Operational Code': A Neglected Approach to the Study of Political Leaders and Decision-Making," *International Studies Quarterly* 13 (June 1969): 190–222.

31. Ole R. Holsti, "The 'Operational Code' Approach to the Study of Political Leaders: John Foster Dulles' Philosophical and Instrumental Beliefs," *Canadian Journal of Political Science* 3 (March 1970): 123–157; Stephen G. Walker, "The Interface between Beliefs and Behavior: Henry Kissinger's Operational Code and the Vietnam War," *Journal of Conflict Resolution* 21 (March 1977):

129–168; Alexander L. George, "The Causal Nexus between Cognitive Beliefs and Decision-Making Behavior: The 'Operational Code' Belief System," in *Psychological Models in International Politics*, ed. Lawrence S. Falkowski (Boulder, CO: Westview, 1979); Stephen G. Walker, "Psychodynamic Processes and Framing Effects in Foreign Policy Decision-Making: Woodrow Wilson's Operational Code," *Political Psychology* 16 (December 1995): 697–717.

32. See Stephen G. Walker, "A Cautionary Tale: Operational Code Analysis as a Scientific Research Program," in *Progress in International Relations Theory*, ed. Colin Elman and Miriam Fendius Elman (Cambridge, MA: MIT Press, 2003).

33. David R. Mayhew, *Congress: The Electoral Connection*, 2nd ed. (New Haven, CT: Yale University Press, 2004).

Chapter Two

1. Robert S. McNamara, James G. Blight, and Robert K. Brigham, *Argument without End: In Search of Answers to the Vietnam Tragedy* (New York: Public Affairs, 1999), p. 221.

2. For a detailed overview of this period, see George McT. Kahin, *Intervention: How America Became Involved in Vietnam* (New York: Alfred A. Knopf, 1986).

3. McNamara, Blight, and Brigham, *Argument without End*, pp. 353–354.

4. Lyndon Baines Johnson, *The Vantage Point: Perspectives of the Presidency, 1963–1969* (New York: Holt, Rinehart, and Winston, 1973), p. 153.

5. Doris Kearns, *Lyndon Johnson and the American Dream* (New York: HarperCollins, 1976), pp. 238–331; McNamara, Blight, and Brigham, *Argument without End*, p. 368; Herbert Y. Schandler, *America in Vietnam* (Lanham, MD: Rowman & Littlefield, 2009), pp. 47–48, 153, 156, 173–174. See also Harry G. Summers Jr., *On Strategy: A Critical Analysis of the Vietnam War* (Novato, CA: Presidio Press, 1982).

6. Johnson, *Vantage Point*, p. 151.

7. Yuen Foong Khong, *Analogies at War: Korean, Munich, Dien Bien Phu and the Vietnam Decisions of 1965* (Princeton, NJ: Princeton University Press, 1992), chap. 7.

8. Khong, *Analogies at War*, pp. 11, 134, chap. 7. See also Ernest R. May, *"Lessons" of the Past: The Use and Misuse of History in American Foreign Policy* (New York: Oxford University Press, 1973), pp. 112–114.

9. Lyndon B. Johnson, "The President's News Conference of July 28, 1965," *Public Papers of the Presidents of the United States: Lyndon B. Johnson, 1965*, book 1 (Washington, DC: Government Printing Office, 1966), p. 794. See also Lyndon B. Johnson, "Address at Johns Hopkins University: 'Peace without Conquest'," April 7, 1965, *Public Papers of the Presidents of the United States: Lyndon B. Johnson, 1965*, book 1 (Washington, DC: Government Printing Office, 1966), pp. 394–395.

10. Quoted in Kearns, *Lyndon Johnson*, p. 252.

11. Quoted in Kearns, *Lyndon Johnson*, p. 329. See also Townsend Hoopes, *The Limits of Intervention* (New York: David McKay, 1969), pp. 100–101.

12. Khong, *Analogies at War*, pp. 58–62, chap. 5. See also May, *"Lessons" of the Past*, pp. 113–114.

13. Johnson, *Vantage Point*, pp. 47–48, 573.

14. Khong, *Analogies at War*, p. 104.

15. Khong, *Analogies at War*, p. 11, chap. 5.

16. See, e.g., Leslie H. Gelb and Richard K. Betts, *The Irony of Vietnam: The System Worked* (Washington, DC: Brookings Institution, 1979), p. 2, chap. 6; Khong, *Analogies at War*, pp. 192–195; John C. Donovan, *The Cold Warriors: A Policy-Making Elite* (Lexington, MA: Heath, 1974).

17. See, e.g., McNamara, Blight, and Brigham, *Argument without End*, pp. xv, 13; James C. Thomson Jr., "How Could Vietnam Happen? An Autopsy," *Atlantic Monthly*, April 1968, in *To Reason Why: The Debate about the Causes of U.S. Involvement in the Vietnam War*, ed. Jeffrey P. Kimball, (Philadelphia: Temple University Press, 1990), p. 219.

18. McNamara, Blight, and Brigham, *Argument without End*, p. 28.

19. May, *"Lessons" of the Past*, pp. 100–101. See also George C. Herring, *America's Longest War: The United States and Vietnam, 1950–1975* (New York: Wiley, 1979), pp. x, 114–115, 270; Gelb and Betts, *Irony of Vietnam*, pp. 2, 25; Khong, *Analogies at War*, chap. 4; McNamara, Blight, and Brigham, *Argument without End*, pp. 28, 30–31.

20. Herring, *America's Longest War*, p. xi.

21. Johnson, *Vantage Point*, p. 152.

22. Quoted in McNamara, Blight, and Brigham, *Argument without End*, p. 155. See also Johnson, "Address at Johns Hopkins," p. 395; Johnson, "President's News Conference of July 28, 1965," p. 974.

23. Kearns, *Lyndon Johnson*, pp. 238–331; Khong, *Analogies at War*, pp. 229–233; McNamara, Blight, and Brigham, *Argument without End*, pp. 43–44, 54, 57, 66; Schandler, *America in Vietnam*, pp. 6, 157–158.

24. The BDM Corporation, *A Study of Strategic Lessons Learned in Vietnam: Omnibus Executive Summary*, 1980, p. III–8; Fredrik Logevall, *Choosing War: The Lost Chance for Peace and the Escalation of War in Vietnam* (Berkeley: University of California Press, 1999), p. 32; Nancy Bernkopf Tucker, "Threats, Opportunities, and Frustrations in East Asia," in *Lyndon Johnson Confronts the World: American Foreign Policy, 1963–1968*, ed. Warren I. Cohen and Nancy Bernkopf Tucker (New York: Cambridge University Press, 1994), p. 103.

25. See Harold P. Ford, "Why CIA Analysts Were So Doubtful about Vietnam," *Studies in Intelligence* no. 1 (1997): 85–95.

26. See, e.g., Logevall, *Choosing War*, pp. 290–291, 385; Michael Beschloss, *The Crisis Years: Kennedy and Khrushchev 1960–1963* (New York: HarperCollins, 1991), pp. 63, 160, 330, 355, 659.

27. Neil Sheehan et al., *The Pentagon Papers* (New York: Bantam Books, 1971), pp. 8-9.

28. Schandler, *America in Vietnam*, p. 156; BDM Corporation, *Strategic Lessons*, p. III-7; Michael H. Hunt, *Lyndon Johnson's War: American's Cold War Crusade in Vietnam, 1945–1968* (New York: Hill and Wang, 1996), pp. 104–105.

29. Hunt, *Lyndon Johnson's War*, p. 41.

30. McNamara, Blight, and Brigham, *Argument without End*, pp. 73, 80, 83, 87–88.

31. BDM Corporation, *Strategic Lessons*, p. III-8.

32. McNamara, Blight, and Brigham, *Argument without End*, p. 177; Logevall, *Choosing War*, p. 10.

33. Quoted in McNamara, Blight, and Brigham, *Argument without End*, p. 81.

34. Khong, *Analogies at War*, pp. 232–233.

35. Ford, "CIA Analysts."

36. McNamara, Blight, and Brigham, *Argument without End*, p. 177.

37. Nayan Chanda, *Brother Enemy: The War after the War* (New York: Harcourt Brace Jovanovich, 1986).

38. Michael Tatu, "Moscow, Peking, and the Conflict in Vietnam," in *The Vietnam Legacy*, ed. Anthony Lake (New York: Pegasus, 1976); Logevall, *Choosing War*, p. 191.

39. Kahin, *Intervention*, pp. 278–279, and sources cited therein.

40. McNamara, Blight, and Brigham, *Argument without End*, p. 81; Logevall, *Choosing War*, p. 322.

41. Robert S. McNamara, *In Retrospect: The Tragedy and Lessons of Vietnam* (New York: Times Books, 1995), pp. 31, 48, 321–322.

42. Herring, *America's Longest War*, p. 270. See also Khong, *Analogies at War*, pp. 233, 240–245.

43. Khong, *Analogies at War*, pp. 189–190.

44. McNamara, Blight, and Brigham, *Argument without End*, p. 66.

45. Schandler, *America in Vietnam*, pp. 21–22, 25; McNamara, Blight, and Brigham, *Argument without End*.

46. William Turley, *The Second Indochina War* (Boulder, CO: Westview Press, 1986); Timothy Lomperis, *The War Everyone Lost—and Won* (Baton Rouge: Louisiana State University Press, 1984).

47. Gelb and Betts, *Irony of Vietnam*, pp. 338–339; Kahin, *Intervention*; Chanda, *Brother Enemy*; Stanley Karnow, *Vietnam: A History* (New York: Viking Press, 1983); Khong, *Analogies at War*, pp. 233–240; George McT. Kahin and John W. Lewis, *The United States in Vietnam*, rev. ed. (New York: Dial Press, 1969), esp. chap. V, pp. 304–305; McNamara, Blight, and Brigham, *Argument without End*, pp. 33, 35–37, 41–42, 58, 217, 319, 402; Schandler, *America in Vietnam*, pp. 153–154.

48. Quoted in Kearns, *Lyndon Johnson*, p. 328.

49. McNamara, Blight, and Brigham, *Argument without End*, p. 95; Schandler, *America in Vietnam*, p. 58.

50. McNamara, Blight, and Brigham, *Argument without End*, pp. 33, 42, 58.

51. Memorandum from the Under Secretary of State (Ball) to President Johnson, "Keeping the Power of Decision in the South Viet-Nam Crisis," June 18, 1965, *Foreign Relations of the United States, 1964–1968, Volume III, Vietnam, June–December 1965* (Washington, DC: Government Printing Office, 1996), pp. 16–21. See also George W. Ball, *The Past Has another Pattern: Memoirs* (New York: W. W. Norton, 1982), pp. 395–396.

52. Memorandum from George Ball to Dean Rusk, Robert McNamara, McGeorge Bundy, William Bundy, and Leonard Unger, "A Plan for Cutting Our Loses in South Viet-Nam," discussed in Khong, *Analogies at War*, pp. 153–154; Ball, *Past Has Another Pattern*, pp. 396–397.

53. Memorandum from the President's Special Assistant for National Security Affairs (Bundy) to President Johnson, "France in Vietnam, 1954, and the United States in Vietnam, 1965 — A Useful Analogy?" June 30, 1965, *Foreign Relations of the United States, 1964–1968, Volume III, Vietnam, June–December 1965* (Washington, DC: Government Printing Office, 1996), pp. 79–85.

54. See Khong, *Analogies at War*, chap. 6; Ball, *Past Has another Pattern*, p. 376; May, *"Lessons" of the Past*, pp. 104–105.

55. Khong, *Analogies at War*, pp. 184–185, 230.

56. See, e.g., Schandler, *America in Vietnam*, pp. xv–xvi, 17, 156–157, 174; H. R. McMaster, *Dereliction of Duty* (New York: HarperCollins, 1997), pp. 206–207; Paul R. Pillar, *Intelligence and U.S. Foreign Policy: Iraq, 9/11, and Misguided Reform* (New York: Columbia University Press, 2011), p. 102; Thomson, "How Could Vietnam Happen?" p. 218.

57. Transcript, Clark Clifford Oral History Interview II, July 2, 1969, by Paige Mulhollan, p. 10, LBJ Library Online.

58. Dean Acheson, *Present at the Creation: My Years in the State Department* (New York: Norton, 1969), p. 219.

59. Cited in Sheehan et al., *Pentagon Papers*, p. 9.

60. "Report to the National Security Council by the Department of State," February 27, 1950, *Foreign Relations of the United States, 1950, East Asia and the Pacific*, vol. VI (Washington, DC: Government Printing Office, 1976), pp. 744–747. This report was approved by President Truman on April 24, 1950.

61. "Memorandum by the Assistant Secretary of State for Far Eastern Affairs (Rusk) to the Deputy Under Secretary of State (Matthews)," January 31, 1951, *Foreign Relations of the United States, 1951, East Asia and the Pacific*, vol. VI, part 1 (Washington, DC: Government Printing Office, 1977), p. 20.

62. "Statement of Policy by the National Security Council on United States Objectives and Courses of Action with Respect to Southeast Asia," June 25, 1952, *Foreign Relations of the United States, 1951, East Asia and the Pacific*, vol. XII, part 1 (Washington, DC: Government Printing Office, 1984), pp. 127–134.

63. Cited in Sheehan et al., *Pentagon Papers*, p. 7. See also p. 35.

64. Arthur Radford, Memorandum for the Secretary of Defense, "Preparation of Department of Defense Views Regarding Negotiations on Indochina for the Forthcoming Geneva Conference," March 12, 1954, *Foreign Relations of the United States, 1952–1954, The Geneva Conference*, vol. XVI (Washington, D.C: Government Printing Office, 1981), pp. 473–474.

65. "Memorandum of Discussion at the 192nd Meeting of the National Security Council, Tuesday, April 6, 1954," *Foreign Relations of the United States, 1952–1954, Indochina*, vol. XIII, part 1 (Washington, DC: Government Printing Office, 1982), p. 1261.

66. Robert H. Ferrell, ed., *The Eisenhower Diaries* (New York: W. W. Norton, 1981), p. 190.

67. Dwight D. Eisenhower, "The President's News Conference of April 7, 1954," *Public Papers of the Presidents of the United States: Dwight D. Eisenhower: 1954*, no. 73 (Washington, DC: Government Printing Office, 1960), p. 383. See also his comments in a memorandum the day before his press conference.

68. See, e.g., Chester Cooper, *The Lost Crusade* (New York: Dodd, Mead & Co., 1970), pp. 64, 107.

69. See, e.g., John McCone, Memorandum for the Record, May 10, 1962. "Discussion with General Eisenhower." (S/Eyes Only). CIA/DCI files, Job No. 80B01285A, DCI McCone, Folder No. 2.

70. "Memorandum of Conversation, Eisenhower-Kennedy meeting on Laos," in *Vietnam: The Definitive Documentation of Human Decisions*, vol. 2, ed. Gareth Porter (Stanfordville, NY: E. M. Coleman Enterprises, 1979), p. 90.

71. "Transcript of Broadcast on NBC's 'Huntley-Brinkley Report,' September 9, 1963," *Public Papers of the Presidents of the United States, John F. Kennedy: Containing the Public Messages, Speeches, and Statements of the President, January 1 to November 22, 1963* (Washington, DC: Government Printing Office, 1964), p. 659.

72. "Draft Memorandum for the President," November 8, 1961, *Foreign Relations of the United States, 1961–1963*, vol. 1, *Vietnam, 1961* (Washington, DC: Government Printing Office 1988), p. 561.

73. L. L. Lemnitzer, Memorandum for the Secretary of Defense, "The Strategic Importance of the Southeast Asia Mainland," January 13, 1962, *United States–Vietnam Relations, 1954–1967, U.S. Involvement in the War, Internal Documents, The Kennedy Administration: January 1961–November 1963*, book 2 (Washington, DC: Office of the Secretary of Defense, n.d.), pp. 448–450.

74. Johnson, *Vantage Point*, p. 151. See also p. 136.

75. Johnson, *Vantage Point*, p. 120. See also Kearns, *Lyndon Johnson*, p. 330.

76. "Memorandum from the Board of National Estimates to the Director of Central Intelligence (McCone)," Washington, June 9, 1964, *Foreign Relations of the United States, 1964–1968*, vol. 1, *Vietnam, 1964* (Washington, DC: Government Printing Office, 1992), pp. 484–487.

77. "National Security Action Memorandum No. 288," March 17, 1964, *Foreign Relations of the United States, 1964–1968*, vol. 1, *Vietnam, 1964* (Washington, DC: Government Printing Office, 1992), p. 173; "U.S. Objectives in South Vietnam," National Security Action Memorandum No. 288, March 17, 1964; Sheehan et al., *Pentagon Papers*, p. 284; Harold P. Ford, *CIA and the Vietnam Policymakers: Three Episodes 1962–1968* (Washington, DC: CIA History Staff, 1998), p. 56.

78. Memorandum from the Secretary of Defense (McNamara) to the President, "South Vietnam," March 16, 1964, *Foreign Relations of the United States, 1964–1968*, vol. 1, *Vietnam, 1964* (Washington, DC: Government Printing Office, 1992), p. 154.

79. McNamara, *In Retrospect*, pp. 124–125.

80. Logevall, *Choosing War*, p. 236.

81. Khong, *Analogies at War*, p. 230.

82. Gordon M. Goldstein, *Lessons in Disaster: McGeorge Bundy and the Path to War in Vietnam* (New York: Holt, 2008), pp. 138–140. See also Pillar, *Intelligence and U.S. Foreign Policy*, pp. 102–103.

83. Paper Prepared by the National Security Council Working Group, "Courses of Action in Southeast Asia," November 21, 1964, *Foreign Relations of the United States, 1964–1968*, vol. 1, *Vietnam, 1964* (Washington, DC: Government Printing Office, 1992), p. 918. See also Logevall, *Choosing War*, pp. 246–247.

84. "Memorandum of the Meeting of the Executive Committee," November 24, 1964, *Foreign Relations of the United States, 1964–1968*, vol. 1, *Vietnam, 1964* (Washington, DC: Government Printing *Office*, 1992), p. 944. More broadly, see Kahin, *Intervention*, pp. 126, 166, 239, 314, 387.

85. "Implications of an Unfavorable Outcome in Vietnam, 11 September 1967," in *Estimative Products on Vietnam, 1948–1975* (Washington, DC: National Intelligence Council, 2005), pp. 394–426. See also Richard Helms, *A Look over My Shoulder: A Life in the Central Intelligence Agency* (New York: Random House, 2003), 314–315.

86. McNamara, Blight, and Brigham, *Argument without End*, p. 40.

87. McNamara, Blight, and Brigham, *Argument without End*, pp. 41, 94, 101.

88. McNamara, Blight, and Brigham, *Argument without End*, pp. 38, 40–41, 58, 84, 95.

89. McNamara, Blight, and Brigham, *Argument without End*, p. 22.

90. See Khong, *Analogies at War*; Peter T. Leeson and Andrea M. Dean, "The Democratic Domino Theory: An Empirical Investigation," *American Journal of Political Science* 53 (July 2009): 533–531.

91. Jonathan Schell, *The Time of Illusion* (New York: Knopf, 1976), pp. 9–10.

92. Pillar, *Intelligence and U.S. Foreign Policy*, p. 102. See also Ball, *Past Has Another Pattern*, p. 402; May, *"Lessons" of the Past*, pp. 103–104; Terry L. Deibel and John Lewis Gaddis, eds., *Containing the Soviet Union: A Critique of U.S. Policy* (Washington, DC: Pergamon-Brassy, 1987), p. 3; Herring, *America's Longest War*,

pp. 115, 270; Kahin, *Intervention*, pp. 312–314, 361; McMaster, *Dereliction of Duty*, pp. 184, 206, 300–302, 306, 332; McNamara, Blight, and Brigham, *Argument without End*, p. 99; Schandler, *America in Vietnam*, pp. 56, 158; Logevall, *Choosing War*, p. 31.

93. Memorandum from the Secretary of Defense (McNamara) to the President, "South Vietnam," p. 154.

94. Memorandum from the Board of National Estimates to the Director of Central Intelligence (McCone), p. 485.

95. Paper Prepared by the National Security Council Working Group, "Courses of Action in Southeast Asia," November 21, 1964, *Foreign Relations of the United States, 1964–1968*, vol. 1, *Vietnam, 1964* (Washington, DC: Government Printing Office, 1992), p. 917.

96. "A Policy of Sustained Reprisal," Memorandum from McGeorge Bundy to President Lyndon B. Johnson, annex A., February 7, 1965, Sheehan et al., *Pentagon Papers*, p. 426.

97. McMaster, *Dereliction of Duty*, pp. 180, 184–185, 219; Herring, *America's Longest War*, p. 129.

98. Paper Prepared by the Assistant Secretary of Defense for International Security Affairs (McNaughton), "Action for South Vietnam," March 10, 1965, *Foreign Relations of the United States, 1964–1968*, vol. 2, *Vietnam, January–June 1965* (Washington, DC: Government Printing Office, 1996), pp. 427, 431.

99. Dean Rusk, "Paper by Secretary of State Rusk," July 1, 1965, *Foreign Relations of the United States, 1964–1968*, vol. 3, *Vietnam, June–December 1965* (Washington, DC: Government Printing Office, 1996), pp. 105.

100. Johnson, "The President's News Conference of July 28, 1965," p. 974. See also Johnson, "Address at Johns Hopkins," p. 395; McNamara, *In Retrospect*, p. 191; Logevall, *Choosing War*, pp. 31, 272–273.

101. Johnson, *Vantage Point*, p. 152. See also Ball, *Past Has another Pattern*, p. 401.

102. Memo from Assistant Secretary of State John McNaughton, "Some Paragraphs on Vietnam," January 19, 1966, Sheehan et al., *Pentagon Papers*, pp. 491–492.

103. McNamara, *In Retrospect*, pp. 292–294. The report can be found in CIA Files, Job No. 80B01285A, Box 11, DCI/Helms, Folder 4: "1 Aug-31 Dec '67."

104. See, e.g., Daryl G. Press, *Calculating Credibility: How Leaders Assess Military Threats* (Ithaca, NY: Cornell University Press, 2005).

105. Logevall, *Choosing War*, pp. 289–290, 380.

106. See, e.g., Kahin and Lewis, *United States in Vietnam*, chap. 11.

107. McNamara, *In Retrospect*, pp. 215, 218–219.

108. May, *"Lessons" of the Past*, pp. 119–120.

109. Gelb and Betts, *Irony of Vietnam*, pp. 221–225; Brian VanDeMark, *Into the Quagmire* (New York: Oxford University Press, 1991), p. 216.

110. BDM Corporation, *Strategic Lessons*, p. III-4.

111. Quoted in May, *"Lessons" of the Past*, p. 99. See also Logevall, *Choosing War*, pp. 31, 38–39.

112. Johnson, *Vantage Point*, pp. 151–152; Kearns, *Lyndon Johnson*, p. 252–253. Richard Neustadt and Ernest May disagree, arguing that Johnson separated himself from Truman as a junior senator. See Neustadt and May, *Thinking in Time*, p. 164. Johnson's own views seem more persuasive.

113. Quoted in Robert A. Caro, *The Passage of Power* (New York: Knopf, 2012), p. 402.

114. See, e.g., Gelb and Betts, *Irony of Vietnam*, p. 223; Logevall, *Choosing War*, p. 78.

115. Daniel Ellsberg, *Papers on the War* (New York: Simon and Schuster, 1972), pp. 80–104.

116. May, *"Lessons" of the Past*, p. 112. See also Kahin, *Intervention*, pp. 216, 313.

117. Neustadt and May, *Thinking in Time*, p. 162.

118. See Khong, *Analogies at War*, pp. 200–204.

119. Gelb and Betts, *Irony of Vietnam*, pp. 225–226.

120. Hubert H. Humphrey, *The Education of a Public Man: My Life and Politics* (Garden City, NY: Doubleday, 1976), p. 323. See also Neustadt and May, *Thinking in Time*, p. 163.

121. John P. Burke and Fred I. Greenstein, *How Presidents Test Reality: Decisions on Vietnam, 1954 and 1965* (New York: Russell Sage Foundation, 1989) pp. 147–149; Logevall, *Choosing War*, pp. 55–59, 66–68, 73, 82–83, 91–92, chap. 5, 145–155, 167–169, 254, 282–289, 305–310, 333–334, 340–341, 349–352, 358–362, 370, 377–378.

122. Logevall, *Choosing War*, pp. 283, 333–334, 377; John E. Mueller, *War, Presidents and Public Opinion* (New York: John Wiley & Sons, 1973), pp. 35, 52–58.

123. Logevall, *Choosing War*, pp. 236–237, 381.

124. Logevall, *Choosing War*, pp. 292–295. See also p. 39.

125. William C. Westmoreland, *A Soldier Reports* (New York: Dell, 1980), p. 255.

126. Logevall, *Choosing War*, p. 139.

127. McNamara, Blight, and Brigham, *Argument without End*, pp. 23–24, 166–170, 184–186, 202–205; McMaster, *Dereliction of Duty*, pp. 121–136; Kahin, *Intervention*, pp. 219–226; Logevall, *Choosing War*, 196–201.

128. Logevall, *Choosing War*, pp. 51, 139, 194–201, 208, 242–243, 306–307, 407.

129. Kearns *Lyndon Johnson*, p. 252.

130. See, e.g., McMaster, *Dereliction of Duty*; Gelb and Betts, *Irony of Vietnam*; Herring, *America's Longest War*, pp. 133–134, 141–142; Larry Berman, *Planning a Tragedy: The Americanization of the War in Vietnam* (New York: W. W. Norton, 1982), pp. 143–150; Goldstein, *Lessons in Disaster*, p. 132.

131. McNamara, *In Retrospect*, p. 190.

132. George C. Edwards III, *Presidential Approval* (Baltimore: John Hopkins University Press, 1990).

133. McMaster, *Dereliction of Duty*, pp. 323-324.

134. See, e.g., Burke and Greenstein, *How Presidents Test Reality*.

135. Khong, *Analogies at War*, pp. 115–117, 136–137, 141–143, 147, 189–190. See also May, *"Lessons" of the Past*, pp. 105–108; Herring, *America's Longest War*, pp. 126, 140–141; Kahin, *Intervention*, pp. 207, 210, 212, 238, 246, 280, 287, 320, 332, 338–341, 351, 356, 384–385; "Statement of Policy by the National Security Council on *United States Objectives and Courses of Action With Respect to Southeast Asia"*; Schandler, *America in Vietnam*, pp. 47, 54, 66, 68, 70, 73, 75, 77, 83, 104–105, 157–158.

136. BDM Corporation, *Strategic Lessons*, p. III-3.

137. Johnson, *The Vantage Point*, pp. 115, 117, 125, 131, 134-135, 140, 149, 152. See also Ball, *Past Has another Pattern*, p. 377; Kearns, *Lyndon Johnson*, p. 282.

138. Lyndon B. Johnson, "Address at Johns Hopkins University: 'Peace without Conquest,'" April 7, 1965, no. 172, *Public Papers of the Presidents of the United States: Lyndon B. Johnson, 1965*, book 1 (Washington, DC: U.S. Government Printing Office, 1966), pp. 395. See also Gelb and Betts, *Irony of Vietnam*, p. 25, ff.

139. McNamara, Blight, and Brigham, *Argument without End*, p. 177; Logevall, *Choosing War*, pp. 207–208, 364–366.

140. Kahin, *Intervention*, pp. 337–341.

141. McNamara, Blight, and Brigham, *Argument without End*, p. 177.

142. Schandler, *America in Vietnam*, pp. 104–105.

143. Kahin, *Intervention*, p. 339.

144. VanDeMark, *Into the Quagmire*, pp. 24–25; Thomson, "How Could Vietnam Happen?" p. 218.

145. Schandler, *America in Vietnam*, pp. 47, 54, 66, 70, 73, 75, 83, 157–158; Herring, *America's Longest War*, p. 141; Henry F. Graff, *The Tuesday Cabinet: Deliberation and Decision on Peace and War under Lyndon B. Johnson* (Englewood Cliffs, NJ: Prentice-Hall, 1970), p. 39.

146. Logevall, *Choosing War*, pp. 17, 290, 323.

147. McMaster, *Dereliction of Duty*, pp. 138–139.

148. McNamara, Blight, and Brigham, *Argument without End*, p. 160; McMaster, *Dereliction of Duty*, pp. 326–327. See also Thomas C. Schelling, *The Strategy of Conflict* (Cambridge, MA: Harvard University Press, 1960).

149. McNamara, Blight, and Brigham, *Argument without End*, p. 160; Herring, *America's Longest War*, p. 126.

150. For overviews of this period see McMaster, *Dereliction of Duty*, chaps. 10–12; Herring, *America's Longest War*, pp. 125–130.

151. McMaster, *Dereliction of Duty*, especially pp. 177–178, 189, 196, 214, 219, 226, 232, 256, 261.

152. See, e.g., Goldstein, *Lessons in Disaster*, pp. 172–173, 179–180, 186, 188–190, 215, 226.

153. McMaster, *Dereliction of Duty*, chap. 8.

154. McMaster, *Dereliction of Duty*.

155. Neustadt and May, *Thinking in Time*, p. 84.

156. Kearns, *Lyndon Johnson*, p. 266.

157. Schandler, *America in Vietnam*, chap. 6 and sources therein; McNamara, Blight, and Brigham, *Argument without End*, pp. 344–346.

158. Quoted in Sheehan et al., *Pentagon Papers*, p. 469. See also *Bombing as a Policy Tool in Vietnam: Effectiveness*, A Staff Study Based on the Pentagon Papers, Committee on Foreign Relations, United States Senate, October 12, 1972 (Washington, DC: Government Printing Office, 1972); Institute for Defense Analyses, "The Effects U.S. Bombing on North Vietnam's Ability to Support Military Operations South Vietnam: Retrospect and Prospect," August 29, 1966; Ford, *CIA and Vietnam Policymakers*; Thomas Ahern Jr., *Good Questions, Wrong Answers: CIA's Estimates of Arms Traffic Through Sihanoukville, Cambodia, During the Vietnam War*, February 2004, https://ia800400.us.archive.org/20/items/GoodQuestionsWrong AnswersCIAsEstimateOfArmsTrafficThroughSihanoukvilleCambodiaDuringThe VietnamWar/Vietnam%20Histories%204%20-%20Good%20Questions%2C%20 Wrong%20Answers%20-%20CIA%27s%20Estimate%20of%20Arms%20 Traffic%20Through%20Sihanoukville%2C%20Cambodia%2C%20During%20 the%20Vietnam%20War.pdf .

159. Sheehan et al., *Pentagon Papers*, pp. 331–332.

160. Herring, *America's Longest War*, pp. 143–144.

161. Quoted in McNamara, Blight, and Brigham, *Argument without End*, p. 155.

162. McNamara, Blight, and Brigham, *Argument without End*, p. 156.

163. Logevall, *Choosing War*, pp. 78–79.

164. Logevall, *Choosing War*, pp. 77–79.

165. Logevall, *Choosing War*. The quote is on p. 295.

166. Logevall, *Choosing War*; McNamara, *In Retrospect*, pp. 114, 142, 154–155. See also Tuchman, *March of Folly*, chap. 5.

167. Gelb and Betts, *Irony of Vietnam*, pp. 190, 353–354, 365–367. See also Goldstein, *Lessons in Disaster*, pp. 172–190, 215–218, 226.

168. Ball, *Past Has Another Pattern*, pp. 380–385. The memo was printed in "Top Secret: The Prophecy the President Rejected," *Atlantic Monthly*, July 1972, pp. 35–49.

169. McNamara, *In Retrospect*, pp. 156–158.

170. Ball, *Past Has Another Pattern*, pp. 380–384, 392; Khong, *Analogies at War*, pp. 106–112.

171. Khong, *Analogies at War*, p. 118; Ball, *Past Has Another Pattern*, chap. 25.

172. Ball, *Past Has Another Pattern*, pp. 375–376, 422; Pillar, *Intelligence and U.S. Foreign Policy*, p. 102; McNamara, *In Retrospect*, pp. 95, 101–102, 148.

173. McNamara, *In Retrospect*, pp. 29, 39–41, 101, 108, 156, 158, 164, 300, 311, 323. See also, Ball, *Past Has Another Pattern*, p. 384.

174. McNamara, *In Retrospect*, pp. 39, 107–109, 122, 152–153, 162, 203, 210–211, 243, 264; McMaster, *Dereliction of Duty*; Goldstein, *Lessons in Disaster*, p. 140.

175. McNamara, Blight, and Brigham, *Argument without End*, p. 325. See also McNamara, *In Retrospect*, p. 203.

176. McMaster, *Dereliction of Duty*, p. 167.

177. See, e.g., Harry G. Summers Jr., *On Strategy: A Critical Analysis of the Vietnam War* (Novato, CA: Presidio Press, 1982); Bruce Palmer Jr., *The 25-Year War: America's Military Role in Vietnam* (Lexington: University Press of Kentucky, 1984); McMaster, *Dereliction of Duty*.

178. Herring, *America's Longest War*, p. 270.

Chapter Three

1. Quoted in Harry H. Ransom, *Central Intelligence and National Security* (Cambridge, MA: Harvard University Press, 1958), p. 54

2. Ziva Kunda, *Social Cognition: Making Sense of People* (Cambridge, MA: MIT Press, 1999), p. 235.

3. See Paul R. Pillar, *Intelligence and U.S. Foreign Policy: Iraq, 9/11, and Misguided Reform* (New York: Columbia University Press, 2011), pp. 170–171.

4. Richard K. Betts, *Surprise Attack: Lessons for Defense Planning* (Washington, DC: Brookings Institution, 1982), pp. 123–124, 126.

5. Victor Davis Hanson, *The Second World Wars: How the First Global Conflict Was Fought and Won* (New York: Basic Books, 2017).

6. Albert Speer, *Inside the Third Reich* (New York: Avon, 1970), pp. 364–365, 377–378. For other examples, see pp. 377–379.

7. Michael Dobbs, *One Minute to Midnight: Kennedy, Khrushchev, and Castro on the Brink of Nuclear War* (New York: Knopf, 2008), pp. 351–352.

8. Sherman Kent, "A Crucial Estimate Relived," *Studies in Intelligence* 8 (Spring 1964): 1-18, https://www.cia.gov/readingroom/docs/CIA-RDP80M01009A000300420003-8.pdf.

See also Klaus Knorr, "Failures in National Intelligence Estimates: The Case of the Cuban Missiles," *World Politics* 16 (April 1964): 455–467.

9. Robert Jervis, "Why Intelligence and Policymakers Clash," *Political Science Quarterly* 125 (Summer 2010), p. 199.

10. Betts, *Surprise Attack*.

11. Robert Jervis, "Understanding Beliefs," *Political Psychology* 27 (October 2006), p. 651.

12. This example relies on Gordon S. Wood, *Empire of Liberty: A History of the Early Republic, 1789–1815* (New York: Oxford University Press, 2009), pp. 648–658, 664–670; and Dumas Malone, *Jefferson the President: The Second Term* (Boston: Little, Brown, 1974), chap. 26.

13. Wood, *Empire of Liberty*, p. 656.

14. Wood, *Empire of Liberty*, p. 649.

15. Barbara W. Tuchman, *The March of Folly: From Troy to Vietnam* (New York: Ballantine Books, 1984), p. 7; Barbara W. Tuchman, *The Guns of August* (New York: Ballantine Books, 1962), chap. 3, p. 142.

16. Tuchman, *Guns of August*, pp. 42–45.

17. Tuchman, *Guns of August*, chaps. 11, 13, and 14.

18. Geoffrey Blainey, *The Causes of War*, 3rd ed. (New York: Free Press, 1988), pp. 36–37; Tuchman, *Guns of August*, pp. 27, 32, 88, 94, 130, 140–144, 198.

19. This example relies on Gabriel Gorodetsky, *Grand Delusion: Stalin and the German Invasion of Russia* (New Haven, CT: Yale University Press, 1999); Constantine Pleshakov, *Stalin's Folly: The Tragic First Ten Days of World War II on the Eastern Front* (Boston: Houghton Mifflin, 2005); Robert Service, *Stalin: A Biography* (Cambridge, MA: Harvard University Press, 2005); David E. Murphy, *What Stalin Knew: The Enigma of Barbarossa* (New Haven, CT: Yale University Press, 2005); Geoffrey Roberts, *Stalin's Wars* (New Haven, CT: Yale University Press, 2006); Richard J. Evans, *The Third Reich at War* (New York: Penguin Press, 2009); and Barton Whaley, *Codeword Barbarossa* (Cambridge, MA: MIT Press, 1973).

20. Murphy, *What Stalin Knew*, p. 249.

21. Robert Jervis, *Why Intelligence Fails* (Ithaca, NY: Cornell University Press, 2010), p. 177; Brendan Simms and Charlie Laderman, *Hitler's American Gamble: Pearl Harbor and Germany's March to Global War* (New York: Basic Books, 2021), p. 159.

22. Betts, *Surprise Attack*, pp. 130–132.

23. Betts, *Surprise Attack*, pp. 46–48.

24. Roberta Wohlstetter, *Pearl Harbor: Warning and Decision* (Stanford, CA: Stanford University Press, 1962), p. 46. See also 66, 136.

25. Gordon W. Prange, *At Dawn We Slept* (New York: Penguin Books, 1982), pp. 125–126.

26. Steve Twomey, *Countdown to Pearl Harbor: The Twelve Days to the Attack* (New York: Simon and Schuster, 2016), p. 57. See also Irving L. Janis, *Groupthink*, 2nd ed. (Boston: Houghton Mifflin, 1982), pp. 72–73, 75, 92–94; Prange, *At Dawn We Slept*, 96–99, 122, ff.

27. Twomey, *Countdown to Pearl Harbor*, p. 280; Wohlstetter, *Pearl Harbor*, pp. 26, 69, 69n, 89-90, 230-231, 250, 278, 337-338, 369-370; Janis, *Groupthink*, pp. 73, 83-87; Prange, *At Dawn We Slept*, chap. 19; Simms and Laderman, *Hitler's American Gamble*, pp. 43, 155, 215, 230, 267, 298–299, 357–358, 371.

28. Wohlstetter, *Pearl Harbor*, p. 392.

29. Wohlstetter, *Pearl Harbor*, p. 393.

30. Wohlstetter, *Pearl Harbor*, especially pp. 392–393, 397.

31. Wohlstetter, *Pearl Harbor*, pp. 23–24, 45, 55, 48–49, 71n, 77, 109, 128, 158, 161, 249–250, 252, 256, 258, 266, 270, 275–276, 293-297, 302, 325, 328, 332, 296, 302–303, 322, 328, 335, 371; Janis, *Groupthink*, pp. 73, 75, 93.

32. Janis, *Groupthink*, p. 76. See also Wohlstetter, *Pearl Harbor*, pp. 47–48, 403–404.

33. Wohlstetter, *Pearl Harbor*, pp. 41–42.

34. Wohlstetter, *Pearl Harbor*, pp. 14, 19–28; Prange, *At Dawn We Slept*, pp. 409–413.
35. Prange, *At Dawn We Slept*, pp. 412–413.
36. Wohlstetter, *Pearl Harbor*, p. 69.
37. Wohlstetter, *Pearl Harbor*.
38. Wohlstetter, *Pearl Harbor*, pp. 56, 68–70, 304.
39. Wohlstetter, *Pearl Harbor*, pp. 11–12; Prange, *At Dawn We Slept*, pp. 500–501.
40. Wohlstetter, *Pearl Harbor*, pp. 14–18.
41. Wohlstetter, *Pearl Harbor*, p. 18. See also p. 12.
42. Quoted in Ransom, *Central Intelligence*, p. 54. See also Simms and Laderman, *Hitler's American Gamble*, p. 151, 151n32.
43. The most detailed version of the entire event is Gordon W. Prange, with Donald M. Goldstein and Katherine V. Dillon, *At Dawn We Slept: The Untold Story of Pearl Harbor*, 2nd ed. (New York: Penguin Books, 1991).
44. Tim Moreman, *The Jungle, the Japanese and the British Commonwealth Armies at War, 1941–45: Fighting Methods, Doctrine and Training for Jungle Warfare* (London: Frank Cass, 2005).
45. Winston Churchill, *The Hinge of Fate* (Boston: Houghton Mifflin, 1950), p. 81.
46. Wohlstetter, *Pearl Harbor*, 398–399.
47. This example relies on William H. Bartsch, *December 8, 1941: MacArthur's Pearl Harbor* (College Station, TX: Texas A&M Press, 2003), especially pp. 257–263; Daniel R. Mortensen, "Delaying Action or Foul Deception," in *War in the Pacific: Pearl Harbor to Tokyo Bay*, ed. Bernard C. Nalty (New York: Salamander Books, 1991), chap. 3; Louis Morton, *The Fall of the Philippines* (Washington, DC: Center of Military History, 1953), chap. 5; Richard Connaughton, *MacArthur and Defeat in the Philippines* (New York: Overlook Press, 2001); John Burton, *Fortnight of Infamy: The Collapse of Allied Airpower West of Pearl Harbor* (Annapolis, MD: U.S. Naval Institute Press, 2006), chap. 6.
48. John Gordon, *Fighting for MacArthur: The Navy and Marine Corps' Desperate Defense of the Philippines* (Annapolis, MD: U.S. Naval Institute Press, 2011), p. 38.
49. Wohlstetter, *Pearl Harbor*, pp. 366–367, 396.
50. Wohlstetter, *Pearl Harbor*, p. 396.
51. Lyman B. Kirkpatrick, *Inspector General's Survey of the Cuban Operation*, October 1961, p. 54. See also Lyman B. Kirkpatrick Jr., "Paramilitary Case-Study-The Bay of Pigs," *Naval War College Review* 25 (November–December 1972): 31–42.
52. Jim Rasenberger, *The Brilliant Disaster: JFK, Castro, and America's Doomed Invasion of Cuba's Bay of Pigs* (New York: Scribner, 2011), p. 229; James G. Blight and Peter Kornbluh, eds., *Politics of Illusion: The Bay of Pigs Invasion Reexamined* (Boulder, CO: Lynne Rienner Publishers, 1998), pp. 89, 101; "Memorandum No. 1 From the Cuba Study Group to President Kennedy," June 13, 1961, *Foreign Relations of the United States, 1961–1963*, vol. 10, *Cuba, January 1961–September 1962* (Washington, DC: U.S. Government Printing Office, 1997), pp. 579.

53. Blight and Kornbluh, *Politics of Illusion*, pp. 92, 175; "Memorandum No. 1 From the Cuba Study Group to President Kennedy," pp. 580–581; "Memorandum from the Joint Chiefs of Staff to Secretary of Defense McNamara," March 10, 1961, *Foreign Relations of the United States*, pp.119–120; "Editorial Note," March 15, 1961, *Foreign Relations of the United States*, p. 160.

54. Arthur M. Schlesinger Jr., *A Thousand Days: John F. Kennedy in the White House* (Boston: Houghton Mifflin, 1965), p. 247; Theodore C. Sorensen, *Kennedy* (New York: Harper and Row, 1965), p. 291, 303.

55. Kirkpatrick, *Inspector General's Survey*, pp. 52–54.

56. Schlesinger, *A Thousand Days*, p. 247; Allen W. Dulles, *The Craft of Intelligence* (New York: Harper and Row, 1963), p. 169; Richard M. Bissell Jr., *Reflections of a Cold Warrior: From Yalta to the Bay of Pigs* (New Haven, CT: Yale University Press, 1996), p. 174. See also Jack B. Pfeiffer, *Official History of the Bay of Pigs Invasion*, vol. 5, *CIA's Internal Investigation of the Bay of Pigs*, (April 18, 1984), pp. 32–33.

57. Schlesinger, *A Thousand Days*, pp. 247–248, 250, 293.

58. Rasenberger, *Brilliant Disaster*, pp. 125, 137; Blight and Kornbluh, eds., *The Politics of Illusion*, pp. 99–100; Bissell, *Reflections of a Cold Warrior*, p. 195.

59. "Memorandum No. 1 From the Cuba Study Group to President Kennedy," pp. 583, 588. See also Schlesinger, *A Thousand Days*, pp. 247–248, 250.

60. Rasenberger, *Brilliant Disaster*, pp. 80–81, 157.

61. "Paper Prepared in the Central Intelligence Agency," April 12, 1961, *Foreign Relations of the United States, 1961–1963*, vol. 10, *Cuba, January 1961–September 1962* (Washington, DC: Government Printing Office, 1997), pp. 215–116.

62. Rasenberger, *Brilliant Disaster*, p. 299.

63. Blight and Kornbluh, *Politics of Illusion*, pp. 91–92.

64. Robert Jervis, *Perception and Misperception in International Politics* (Princeton, NJ: Princeton University Press, 1976), pp. 311–312.

65. Richard E. Neustadt and Ernest R. May, *Thinking in Time: The Uses of History for Decision-Makers* (New York: Free Press, 1986), pp. 140, 148. See also Rose McDermott, *Political Psychology in International Relations* (Ann Arbor: University of Michigan Press, 2004), pp. 171–172.

66. Schlesinger, *A Thousand Days*, pp. 246–249, 253–254, 294; Rasenberger, *Brilliant Disaster*, p. 299; Robert Dallek, *An Unfinished Life: John F. Kennedy 1917–1963* (Boston: Little, Brown, 2003), pp. 366–367; Blight and Kornbluh, *Politics of Illusion*, p.101.

67. Rasenberger, *Brilliant Disaster*, p. 137.

68. "Memorandum No. 3: Conclusions of the Cuba Study Group," June 13, 1961, *Foreign Relations of the United States, 1961–1963*, vol. 10, *Cuba, January 1961–September 1962* (Washington, DC: U.S. Government Printing Office, 1997), pp. 603–604.

69. Kirkpatrick, *Inspector General's Survey*, pp. 55–56; Rasenberger, *Brilliant Disaster*, p. 171.

70. Schlesinger, *A Thousand Days*, p. 274.
71. Rasenberger, *Brilliant Disaster*, p. 141.
72. Sorensen, *Kennedy*, pp. 301, 309.
73. Quoted in Dallek, *An Unfinished Life*, p. 361; Richard Reeves, *President Kennedy: Profile of Power* (New York: Simon & Schuster, 1993), p. 77. See also Schlesinger, *A Thousand Days*, p. 294.
74. See, e.g., Kirkpatrick, *Inspector General's Survey*; Rasenberger, *Brilliant Disaster*; Blight and Kornbluh, *Politics of Illusion*.
75. Quoted in William Westmoreland, *A Soldier Reports* (Garden City, NY: Doubleday, 1976): p. 321.
76. George Tenet, *At the Center of the Storm: My Years at the CIA* (New York: HarperCollins, 2007), p. 45; Betts, *Surprise Attack*, pp. 68–80; Chaim Herzog, *The War of Atonement: October, 1973* (Boston: Little, Brown, 1975); Avi Shlaim, "Failures in National Intelligence Estimates: The Case of the Yom Kippur War," *World Politics* 38 (April 1976): 348–380.
77. Robert Jervis, Richard Ned Lebow, and Janice Gross Stein, *Psychology and Deterrence* (Baltimore: John Hopkins University Press, 1985), pp. 19–29, chaps. 3-4.
78. Henry Kissinger, *Years of Upheaval* (Boston: Little, Brown, 1982), pp. 460, 465.
79. Janice Gross Stein, "Calculation, Miscalculation, and Conventional Deterrence II: The View from Jerusalem," in *Psychology and Deterrence,* ed. Robert Jervis, Richard N. Lebow, and Janice G. Stein (Baltimore: Johns Hopkins University Press, 1985); Janice Gross Stein, "Building Politics into Psychology: The Misperception of Threat," in *Political Psychology Classic and Contemporary Readings*, ed. Neil J. Kressel (New York: Pentagon House Publishers, 1993).
80. Uri Bar-Joseph and Arie W. Kruglanski, "Intelligence Failure and Need for Cognitive Closure: On the Psychology of the Yom Kippur Surprise," *Political Psychology* 24 (March 2003): 75–99.
81. Douglas MacEachin, *Predicting the Soviet Invasion of Afghanistan: The Intelligence Community's Record* (Washington, DC: CIA Center for the Study of Intelligence, 2002).
82. Raymond Garthoff, *Détente and Confrontation: American-Soviet Relations from Nixon to Reagan* (Washington, DC: Brookings Institution, 1985): pp. 924–965.
83. Jervis, Lebow, and Stein, *Psychology and Deterrence*, p. 19.
84. Alex Roberto Hybel, *Power over Rationality: The Bush Administration and the Gulf Crisis* (Albany: State University of New York Press, 1993), pp. 29–32, 55.
85. James A. Baker III, *The Politics of Diplomacy* (New York: Putnam, 1995), p. 274. See also Richard N. Haass, *War of Necessity, War of Choice: A Memoir of Two Iraq Wars* (New York: Simon and Schuster, 2009), p. 230. See also Hybel, *Power over Rationality*.
86. Haass, *War of Necessity*, p. 136.
87. See, e.g., William E. Odom, "How Far Can Soviet Reform Go?" *Problems of Communism* 36 (November–December 1987), p. 30.

88. Tenet, *Center of the Storm*, p. 45; Gregory F. Treverton, *Reshaping National Intelligence for an Age of Information* (New York: Cambridge University Press, 2001), pp. 4–5.

Chapter Four

1. Quoted in William Stueck, "The March to the Yalu: The Perspective from Washington," in *Child of Conflict: The Korean-American Relationship, 1943–1953*, ed. Bruce Cumings (Seattle: University of Washington Press, 1983), p. 233.
2. Harry S. Truman, *Memoirs by Harry S. Truman*, vol. 2, *Years of Trial and Hope* (Garden City, NY: Doubleday, 1956), p. 331. See also P. K. Rose, "Two Strategic Intelligence Mistakes in Korea, 1950: Perceptions and Reality," *Studies in Intelligence* (Fall–Winter 2001): 57–65; Glenn D. Paige, *The Korean Decision (June 24–30, 1950)* (New York: Free Press, 1968), pp. 71–75.
3. Paige, *Korean Decision*, p. 156.
4. Testimony of Secretary of State Dean Acheson, United States Senate, *Military Situation in the Far East, Hearings Before the Committee on Armed Services and the Committee on Foreign Relations, 82nd Congress, 1st Session, to Conduct an Inquiry into the Relief of General of the Army Douglas MacArthur from His Assignments in That Area, Part 3* (Washington, DC: U.S. Government Printing Office, 1951), June 5, 1951, p. 1991; Alexander George and Richard Smoke, *Deterrence in American Foreign Policy: Theory and Practice* (New York: Columbia University Press, 1974), pp. 166, 169.
5. George and Smoke, *Deterrence*, p. 166.
6. The evidence is vast. One example of officials' thinking is "Memorandum by the Central Intelligence Agency: Threat of Full Chinese Communist Intervention in Korea," October 12, 1950, *Foreign Relations of the United States, 1950, Korea*, vol. 7 (Washington, D.C.: Government Printing Office, 1976), pp. 933–934.
7. Melvyn P. Leffler, *A Preponderance of Power: National Security, the Truman Administration, and the Cold War* (Stanford, CA: Stanford University Press), pp. 366–367.
8. See, e.g., Testimony of Secretary of State Dean Acheson, United States Senate, *Military Situation in the Far East*, part 3, June 5, 1951, p. 1936; David Halberstam, *The Coldest Winter: America and the Korean War* (New York: Hyperion, 2007), p. 94; John Foster Dulles, "A Militarist Experiment," Department of State Bulletin, XXIII (July 10, 1050), pp. 49–50.
9. Rose, "Two Strategic Intelligence Mistakes," pp. 58–60; Harvey A. DeWeerd, "Strategic Surprise in the Korean War," *Orbis* 6 (Fall 1962): 435–452; Paige, *Korean Decision*, p. 75; George and Smoke, *Deterrence*, p. 168; Alexander Ovodenko, "(Mis)interpreting Threats: A Case Study of the Korean War," *Security Studies* 16 (April–June 2007), p. 273–276; Leffler, *Preponderance of Power*, pp. 367–370; Eliot A. Cohen "Only Half the Battle: The Chinese Intervention in Korea, 1950," *Studies*

in Intelligence (Fall 1988), pp. 56–57; George F. Kennan, *Memoirs 1925–1950* (New York: Pantheon, 1967), p. 484.

10. Matthew B. Ridgway, *The Korean War* (Garden City, NY: Doubleday, 1967), p. 11. See also George and Smoke, *Deterrence*, pp. 170–171.

11. George and Smoke, *Deterrence*, p. 168.

12. Sergei Goncharov, John W. Lewis, and Litai Xue, *Uncertain Partners: Stalin, Mao, and the Korean War* (Palo Alto, CA: Stanford University Press, 1995), pp. 131, 135, 137–151, 200; Halberstam, *Coldest Winter*, pp. 51, 92; George and Smoke, *Deterrence*, pp. 157, 168–169.

13. Paige, *Korean Decision*, p. 260; Halberstam, *Coldest Winter*, p. 94.

14. Chen Jian, *China's Road to the Korean War: The Making of the Sino-American Confrontation* (New York: Columbia University Press, 1994), pp. 85–90, 112, 155–156, 161, 171–172, 343; Goncharov, Lewis, and Xue, *Uncertain Partners*, pp. 135–148; Nikita Khrushchev, *Khrushchev Remembers: The Glasnost Tapes* (Boston: Little, Brown, 1990), pp. 144–116; Nikita Khrushchev, *Khrushchev Remembers: The Last Testament* (Boston: Little, Brown, 1974), pp. 367–371; Halberstam, *Coldest Winter*, pp. 49–51, 95; John R. Merrill, *Korea: The Peninsular Origins of the War* (Newark: Universality of Delaware Press, 1989), pp. 143-144.

15. Halberstam, *Coldest Winter*, p. 92.

16. Jian, *China's Road*, pp. 112, 134, 263, 288; Goncharov, Lewis, and Xue, *Uncertain Partners*, pp. 146, 153–154.

17. Jian, *China's Road*, pp. 161–162.

18. Peter Lowe, *The Origins of the Korean War*, 2nd ed. (New York: Longman, 1986); Robert R. Simmons, *The Strained Alliance: Peking, P'yŏngyang, Moscow and the Politics of the Korean Civil War* (New York: Free Press, 1975), pp. 110–130; Burton I. Kaufman, *The Korean War: Challenges in Crisis, Credibility, and Command* (Philadelphia: Temple University Press, 1986), pp. 32–33; Bruce Cumings, *The Origins of the Korean War*, vols. 1 and 2 (Ithaca, NY: Cornell University Press, 2004); Merrill, *Korea*.

19. Halberstam, *Coldest Winter*, p. 95.

20. See, e.g., Harry S. Truman, "Radio Report to the American People on Korea and on U.S. Policy in the Far East, April 11, 1951," *Public Papers of the Presidents of the United States: Harry S. Truman, 1951* (Washington, DC: Government Printing Office, 1965), pp. 223–224.

21. Richard K. Betts, *Surprise Attack: Lessons for Defense Planning* (Washington, DC: Brookings Institution, 1982), pp. 51–54; Ernest R. May, "The Nature of Foreign Policy: The Calculated versus the Axiomatic," *Daedalus* 91 (Fall 1962), p. 658.

22. Harry S. Truman, *Memoirs by Harry S. Truman*, vol. 1, *Year of Decisions* (Garden City, NY: Doubleday, 1955), pp. 120–121. See also Paige, *Korean Decision*, p. 114.

23. Paige, *Korean Decision*, p. 23.

24. Ernest R. May, *"Lessons" of the Past: The Use and Misuse of History in American Foreign Policy* (New York: Oxford University Press, 1973), pp. 80, 85.

25. Truman, *Memoirs*, vol. 2, p. 333. See also pp. 331, 339–340.

26. Truman, *Memoirs*, vol. 2, p. 334. See also Dean Acheson, *Present at the Creation: My Years in the State Department* (New York: Norton, 1969), pp. 405–406.

27. Truman, *Memoirs*, vol. 2, p. 337; Paige, *Korean Decision*, pp. 114, 137, 170, 174, 178, 331.

28. Quoted in Paige, *Korean Decision*, p. 331.

29. Truman, "Radio Report to the American People on Korea and on U.S. Policy in the Far East, April 11, 1951," p. 223–224.

30. Quoted in Halberstam, *Coldest Winter*, p. 93.

31. Paige, *Korean Decision*, pp. 100, 114, 124.

32. Paige, *Korean Decision*, pp. 139–140.

33. Paige, *Korean Decision*, pp. 165–166, 245–246, 249–250, 260–261.

34. George and Smoke, *Deterrence*, p. 145–146; Paige, *Korean Decision*, pp. 128; May, *"Lessons" of the Past*, pp. 52–69, 83.

35. Truman, *Memoirs*, vol. 2, pp. 331, 335–337, 339, 387, 397; Rose, "Two Strategic Intelligence Mistakes"; Paige, *Korean Decision*, pp. 109, 132–133, 171.

36. Acheson, *Present at the Creation*, p. 405. See also p. 471; Truman, *Memoirs*, vol. 2, 387.

37. Truman, *Memoirs*, vol. 2, pp. 339–341, 345–346, 378–379, 387–388, 398; Acheson, *Present at the Creation*, p. 406, 472; Paige, *Korean Decision*, pp. 134, 164, 169–171, 224, 258; Ovodenko, "(Mis)interpreting Threats," p. 275; Leffler, *Preponderance of Power*, pp. 366–367, 369, 400; Halberstam, *Coldest Winter*, pp. 92–93; Rosemary Foot, *The Wrong War: American Policy and the Dimensions of the Korean Conflict, 1950–1953* (Ithaca, NY: Cornell University Press, 1985), p. 167.

38. Truman, *Memoirs*, vol. 2, pp. 337, 339; Paige, *Korean Decision*, pp. 175–178; May, *"Lessons" of the Past*, pp. 75–78; Jian, *China's Road*, pp. 119–120.

39. George and Smoke, *Deterrence*, p. 148, 170.

40. May, *"Lessons" of the Past*, pp. 72–80, 84; Richard E. Neustadt and Ernest R. May, *Thinking in Time: The Uses of History for Decision Makers* (New York; Free Press, 1986), pp. 35–48.

41. Betts, *Surprise Attack*, p. 56.

42. DeWeerd, "Strategic Surprise"; Truman, *Memoirs*, vol. 2, p. 350; Paige, *Korean Decision*, pp. 133, 172–173; Ovodenko, "(Mis)interpreting Threats," pp. 262, 274, 276–277; Leffler, *Preponderance of Power*, p. 400; Jian, *China's Road*, pp. 170–171.

43. Truman, *Memoirs*, vol. 2, pp. 379, 387, 397, 399; Acheson, *Present at the Creation*, p. 472.

44. Truman, *Memoirs*, vol. 2, p. 399; Acheson, *Present at the Creation*, p. 482.

45. Jian, *China's Road*, p. 170.

46. John Hersey, *Aspects of the Presidency* (New Haven, CT: Ticknor and Fields, 1980), p. 28, originally published as John Hersey, "Mr. President, II—Ten O'Clock Meeting," *New Yorker*, April 14, 1951, p. 52.

47. David S. McLellan, "Dean Acheson and the Korean War," *Political Science Quarterly* 83 (March 1968), p. 36; Testimony by Secretary of Defense George Marshall, in U.S. Senate, *Military Situation in the Far East,* part 1, May 14, 1951, p. 703; Truman, "Radio Report to the American People on Korea and on U.S. Policy in the Far East, April 11, 1951," p. 223–224.

48. Woodrow J. Kuhns, *Assessing the Soviet Threat: The Early Cold War Years* (Washington, DC: Center for the Study of Intelligence, 1997), p. 450; Jian, *China's Road*, pp. 135–141, 156; Goncharov, Lewis, and Xue, *Uncertain Partners*, pp. 159–176.

49. Rose, "Two Strategic Intelligence Mistakes," p. 63.

50. Jian, *China's Road*, p. 161, chap. 7; Goncharov, Lewis, and Xue, *Uncertain Partners*, pp. 187–195; Halberstam, *Coldest Winter*, pp. 345, 361.

51. George and Smoke, *Deterrence*, p. 215.

52. Ovodenko, "(Mis)interpreting Threats"; George and Smoke, *Deterrence*, pp. 211–217, 221; McLellan, "Dean Acheson," pp. 17–21; Allen S. Whiting, *China Crosses the Yalu: The Decision to Enter the Korean War* (Santa Monica, CA: Rand, 1960), pp. 151–162, 169–171; Betts, *Surprise Attack*, p. 61; Leffler, *Preponderance of Power*, p. 378; Stueck, "March to the Yalu," p. 211; Richard Ned Lebow, *Between Peace and War: The Nature of International Crisis* (Baltimore: Johns Hopkins University Press, 1981), pp. 210–211; Tsou Tang, *America's Failure in China, 1941–50* (Chicago: University of Chicago Press, 1963), pp. 579–590; Goncharov, Lewis, and Xue *Uncertain Partners*, pp. 159, 184, 194; Jian, *China's Road*, pp. 127–128, 217–218.

53. Jian, *China's Road*, pp. 157–160, chap. 5.

54. McLellan, "Dean Acheson," pp. 36–37.

55. George and Smoke, *Deterrence*, pp. 214–218; Betts, *Surprise Attack*, p. 62; Truman, *Memoirs*, vol. 2, p. 341, 359–362; Paige, *Korean Decision*, pp. 166–167, 246–247, 251; Ovodenko, "(Mis)interpreting Threats," pp. 277–283; Leffler, *Preponderance of Power*, p. 375; Stueck, "March to the Yalu," pp. 229–230; Lebow, *Between Peace and War*, pp. 213.

56. McLellan, "Dean Acheson," pp. 21–22; George and Smoke, *Deterrence*, pp. 218.

57. Alan Whiting, *China Crosses the Yalu* (Stanford, CA: Stanford University Press, 1968), p. 169.

58. Truman, *Memoirs*, vol. 2, p. 360; Acheson, *Present at the Creation*, p. 454.

59. George and Smoke, *Deterrence*, pp. 205–206.

60. Acheson, *Present at the Creation*, p. 451; George and Smoke, *Deterrence*, pp. 215–216; Stueck, "March to the Yalu," pp. 220–231.

61. George Kennan, *Memoirs 1925–1950*, pp. 487–489; George Kennan, *Memoirs 1950–1963* (New York: Pantheon, 1969), pp. 23–24.

62. George and Smoke, *Deterrence*, pp. 191–192.

63. Testimony of Secretary of State Dean Acheson, U.S. Senate, *Military Situation in the Far East*, part 3, June 7, 1951, p. 2101. See also Foot, *Wrong War*; William

Stueck, *The Road to Confrontation: American Policy Toward China and Korea, 1947–1950* (Chapel Hill: University of North Carolina Press, 1981); Lebow, *Between Peace and War*, pp. 208–209; Jian, *China's Road*, pp. 169–170; "Memorandum by the Central Intelligence Agency: Threat of Full Chinese Communist Intervention in Korea," October 12, 1950, *Foreign Relations of the United States, 1950, Korea*, vol. 7 (Washington, DC: Government Printing Office, 1976), p. 934.

64. Truman, *Memoirs*, vol. 2, pp. 365–366; Paige, *Korean Decision*, p. 172; George and Smoke, *Deterrence*, pp. 212, 215; McLellan, "Dean Acheson," pp. 18–20; Joseph C. Goulden, *Korea: The Untold Story* (New York: McGraw-Hill, 1983), pp. 287–288; Ovodenko, "(Mis)interpreting Threats," pp. 262, 277–278; Richard E. Neustadt, *Presidential Power and the Modern Presidents* (New York: Free Press, 1990), p. 114; Testimony of Gen. Hoyt Vandenberg, U.S. Senate, *Military Situation in the Far East*, part 2, May 29, 1951, p. 1504; Stueck, "March to the Yalu," p. 211; Jian, *China's Road*, p. 170; Halberstam, *Coldest Winter*, pp. 370–372.

65. "Memorandum by the Central Intelligence Agency: Threat of Full Chinese Communist Intervention in Korea," p. 934; Jian, *China's Road*, pp. 169–170.

66. Jian, *China's Road*, p. 170.

67. DeWeerd, "Strategic Surprise," p. 436.

68. Truman, *Memoirs*, vol. 2, pp. 344, 361–363, 372–373, 373–377, 381; DeWeerd, "Strategic Surprise," pp. 436, 446–448; Acheson, *Present at the Creation*, pp. 452, 462–465; Ovodenko, "(Mis)interpreting Threats"; Kavalam M. Panikkar, *In Two Chinas: Memoirs of a Diplomat* (London: Allen and Unwin, 1955), pp. 108-111; Betts, *Surprise Attack*, pp. 57–60; Edwin P. Hoyt, *On To The Yalu* (Briarcliff Manor, NY: Stein and Day, 1984), p. 198; P. K. Rose, "Two Strategic Intelligence Mistakes"; George and Smoke, *Deterrence*, p. 200–201, 223; Stueck, "March to the Yalu," pp. 211–212, 219; Lebow, *Between Peace and War*, pp. 157, 172–174; Halberstam, *Coldest Winter*, pp. 13–15; Goncharov, Lewis, and Xue, *Uncertain Partners*, pp. 170–171, 175; Jian, *China's Road*, pp. 163–164, 169, 172, 180.

69. Rose, "Two Strategic Intelligence Mistakes"; Betts, *Surprise Attack*, pp. 58–62; Ovodenko, "(Mis)interpreting Threats"; Betts, *Surprise Attack*, pp. 56–57; George and Smoke, *Deterrence*, pp. 201, 208–217; Leffler, *Preponderance of Power*, p. 378; Eliot A. Cohen and John Gooch, *Military Misfortunes: The Anatomy of Failure in War* (New York: Free Press, 1990), p. 170; Jian, *China's Road*, p. 169; Foot, *Wrong War*, p. 80.

70. "Memorandum by the Central Intelligence Agency: Threat of Full Chinese Communist Intervention in Korea," pp. 933–934.

71. De Weerd, "Strategic Surprise," p. 451.

72. Acheson, *Present at the Creation*, p. 452. See also J. Lawton Collins, *War in Peacetime: The History and Lessons of Korea* (Boston: Houghton Mifflin, 1969), p. 173.

73. Truman, *Memoirs*, vol. 2, p. 362.

74. Truman, *Memoirs*, vol. 2, pp. 365–366; Text of conference quoted in Richard H. Rovere and Arthur M. Schlesinger Jr., *The MacArthur Controversy and*

American Foreign Policy (New York: Noonday Press of Farrar, Straus and Giroux, 1965), pp. 275-285.

75. Lebow, *Between Peace and War*, pp. 158–162; Halberstam, *Coldest Winter*, pp. 42–43.

76. Cohen and Gooch, *Military Misfortunes*, p. 173.

77. Acheson, *Present at the Creation*, pp. 464–465. See also Truman, *Memoirs*, vol. 2, p. 377; Hoyt, *On to the Yalu*, p. 264.

78. "Memorandum by the Central Intelligence Agency: National Intelligence Estimate on Chinese Communist Intervention in Korea," November 8, 1950, *Foreign Relations of the United States, 1950, Korea*, vol. 7 (Washington, DC: Government Printing Office, 1976), pp. 1101–1106.

79. Ovodenko, "(Mis)interpreting Threats," pp. 261–264; Cohen "Only Half the Battle," pp. 58–59.

80. Truman, *Memoirs*, vol. 2, p. 359.

81. Halberstam, *Coldest Winter*, pp. 324, 329, 386.

82. Truman, *Memoirs*, vol. 2, p. 360; Acheson, *Present at the Creation*, pp. 452–453.

83. George and Smoke, *Deterrence*, pp. 196–198, 202–203. See also Acheson, *Present at the Creation*, p. 454; Leffler, *Preponderance of Power*, p. 377–378.

84. Neustadt, *Presidential Power*, p. 107.

85. Truman, *Memoirs*, vol. 2, p. 362.

86. Leffler, *Preponderance of Power*, p. 379–380; Cohen and Gooch, *Military Misfortunes*, p. 175.

87. Truman, *Memoirs*, vol. 2, p. 382.

88. Lebow, *Between Peace and War*, pp. 177–183.

89. George and Smoke, *Deterrence*, pp. 223–224; Acheson, *Present at the Creation*, pp. 466, 468; Neustadt, *Presidential Power*, pp. 121–122; Leffler, *Preponderance of Strength*, p. 396.

90. Truman, *Memoirs*, vol. 2, p. 380; Acheson, *Present at the Creation*, pp. 465–466.

91. Acheson, *Present at the Creation*, p. 464.

92. Truman, *Memoirs*, vol. 2, p. 385; De Weerd, "Strategic Surprise," pp. 436, 448; Betts, *Surprise Attack*, pp. 61–62; George and Smoke, *Deterrence*, pp. 210–211, 218; Neustadt, *Presidential Power*, p. 119; Cohen, "Only Half the Battle," p. 56.

93. Truman, *Memoirs*, vol. 2, p. 381. Also see pp. 386–387; Acheson, *Present at the Creation*, p. 467.

94. See, e.g., Hoyt, *On to the Yalu*, p. 264; Rose, "Two Strategic Intelligence Mistakes"; Halberstam, *Coldest Winter*, pp. 56–57.

95. Samuel L. A. Marshall, *The River and the Gauntlet: Defeat of the Eighth Army by the Chinese Communist Forces, November, 1950, in the Battle of the Chongchon River, Korea* (New York: Morrow, 1953), p. 1.

96. Quoted in Neustadt, *Presidential Power*, p. 122.

97. McLellan, "Dean Acheson," p. 34 and fn 45. See also Leffler, *Preponderance of Power*, p. 379–380; Stueck, "March to the Yalu," pp. 202–203, 228.

98. Neustadt, *Presidential Power*, p. 114.

99. Betts, *Surprise Attack*, p. 61.

100. Acheson, *Present at the Creation*, pp. 467–468. See also Betts, *Surprise Attack*, p. 61; Neustadt, *Presidential Power*, p. 120.

101. George and Smoke, *Deterrence*, pp. 171, 191, 227; Betts, *Surprise* Attack, p. 56; Halberstam, *Coldest Winter*, p. 329.

102. See, e.g., Ronald J. Caridi, *The Korean War and American Politics: The Republican Party as a Case Study* (Philadelphia: University of Pennsylvania Press, 1968), pp. 83–84.

103. George and Smoke, *Deterrence*, pp. 211, 226–230; Neustadt, *Presidential Power*, p. 120; Leffler, *Preponderance of Power*, p. 379.

104. Acheson, *Present at the Creation*, p. 466.

105. Leffler, *Preponderance of Power*, pp. 376–377.

106. Leffler, *Preponderance of Power*, p. 396; Cohen, "Only Half the Battle," p. 57.

107. Leffler, *Preponderance of Power*, pp. 379–380, 397.

108. James I. Matray, "Truman's Plan for Victory: National Self-Determination and the Thirty-Eighth Parallel Decision in Korea," *Journal of American History*, 66 (September 1979): 314–333.

109. Robert Jervis, "Hypotheses on Misperception," *World Politics* 20 (April 1968), pp. 465–466.

110. George and Smoke, *Deterrence*, p. 208.

111. Janis, *Groupthink*.

112. Janis, *Groupthink*, pp. 3–4, 7–8, 11–12.

113. Janis, *Groupthink*, pp. 9, 13.

114. Janis, *Groupthink*, p. 10.

115. Janis, *Groupthink*, p. 71.

116. Janis, *Groupthink*, pp. 58–59.

117. Janis, *Groupthink*, p. 58.

118. Janis, *Groupthink*, p. 59.

119. Janis, *Groupthink*, p. 60. See also p. 71.

120. Kennan, *Memoirs 1925–1950*, pp. 487–489; Kennan, *Memoirs 1950–1963*, pp. 23–24.

121. "Draft Memorandum Prepared by the Policy Planning Staff," July 22, 1950, *Foreign Relations of the United States, 1950, Korea*, vol. 7 (Washington, DC: Government Printing Office, 1976), pp. 449–554. See also Leffler, *Preponderance of Power*, p. 375; Stueck, "March to the Yalu," pp. 196–200; Lowe, *Origins*, pp. 181–184.

122. See, e.g., Paige, *Korean Decision*, pp. 289, 307; Janis, *Groupthink*, pp. 49–52.

123. Janis, *Groupthink*, pp. 243–248.

124. Janis, *Groupthink*, p. 194. See also pp. 69–71.

125. Truman, *Memoirs*, vol. 2, pp. 342–343; Acheson, *Present at the Creation*, p, 412; Paige, *Korean Decision*, pp. 258–259; Janis, *Groupthink*, pp. 2194–2195.

126. Collins, *War in Peacetime*, p. 14.

127. Janis, *Groupthink*, p. 49.
128. Janis, *Groupthink*, p. 4.
129. Janis, *Groupthink*, pp. 250–259.
130. Janis, *Groupthink*, pp. 242–243.
131. Janis, *Groupthink*, pp. 243–245, 248–260.
132. Janis, *Groupthink*, p. 256.
133. Paige, *Korean Decision*, p. 233.
134. Leffler, *Preponderance of Power*, pp. 368–369.
135. Leffler, *Preponderance of Power*, pp. 377–380.
136. Janis, *Groupthink*, p. 254.
137. Paige, *Korean Decision*, pp. 136, 143, 164, 174, 179, 320.
138. Quoted in Stueck, "March to the Yalu," p. 233.

Chapter Five

1. George W. Bush, *Decision Points* (New York: Crown, 2010), p. 242. Also see pp. 268–270.
2. Bush, *Decision Points*, p. 229; Condoleezza Rice, *No Higher Honor: A Memoir of My Years in Washington* (New York: Crown, 2011), p. 198; Douglas J. Feith, *War and Decision: Inside the Pentagon at the Dawn of the War on Terrorism* (New York: Harper, 2008), pp. 238–239, 245–246, 274; George Tenet, *At the Center of the Storm: My Years at the CIA* (New York: HarperCollins, 2007), pp. 308–309, 322, 395; Ron Suskind, *The Price of Loyalty* (New York: Simon and Schuster, 2004), pp. 76, 86, 96–97; Michael R. Gordon and Bernard E. Trainor, *Cobra II: The Inside Story of the Invasion and Occupation of Iraq* (New York: Pantheon Books, 2006), pp. 14, 126; Thomas E. Ricks, *Fiasco: The American Military Adventure in Iraq* (New York: Penguin Press, 2006). pp. 42–43; Robert M. Gates, *Duty* (New York: Alfred A. Knopf, 2014), p. 93; Ron Suskind, *The One Percent Doctrine* (New York: Simon and Schuster, 2006), pp. 62, 254; and Jane Mayer, *The Dark Side: The Inside Story of How the War on Terror Turned into a War on American Ideals* (New York: Doubleday, 2008), pp. 4–5; Robert Draper, *To Start a War: How the Bush Administration Took America into Iraq* (New York: Penguin, 2020), pp. 102, 208.
3. George W. Bush, "President Bush Outlines Iraqi Threat," October 7, 2002, George W. Bush White House Archives, https://georgewbush-whitehouse.archives.gov/news/releases/2002/10/20021007-8.html,
4. Draper, *To Start a War*, p. 337.
5. Suskind, *One Percent Doctrine*, pp. 62, 254.
6. See, e.g., Karl Rove, *Courage and Consequence* (New York: Threshold Editions, 2010), p. 339.
7. Bush, *Decision Points*, pp. 242–247; Bob Woodward, *Plan of Attack* (New York: Simon and Schuster, 2004), pp. 249–250. The briefing was on what could be

declassified to explain Iraq's WMD programs to the public and covered the nature of the evidence of WMDs.

8. Dick Cheney, "Remarks by the Vice President to the Veterans of Foreign Wars 103rd National Convention," August 26, 2002, George W. Bush White House Archives, https://georgewbush-whitehouse.archives.gov/news/releases/2002/08/20020826.html.

9. Draper, *To Start a War*, p. 180.

10. Draper, *To Start a War*, p. 94.

11. Donald Rumsfeld, press conference at the Department of Defense, September 26, 2002. See U.S. Senate Select Committee on Intelligence, "Report on Whether Public Statements Regarding Iraq by U.S. Government Officials Were Substantiated by Intelligence Information together with Additional and Minority Views," 110th Congress, 2nd Session, June 2008, p. 45.

12. The text of Powell's speech can be found at https://www.washingtonpost.com/wp-srv/nation/transcripts/powelltext_020503.html

13. Bush, "President Bush Outlines Iraqi Threat."

14. George W. Bush, "President Bush Addresses the Nation," March 19, 2003. Retrieved from George W. Bush White House Archives, https://georgewbush-whitehouse.archives.gov/news/releases/2003/03/20030319-17.html

15. Melvyn P. Leffler, "The Decider: Why Bush Chose War in Iraq," *Foreign Affairs*, November/December 2020, p. 150.

16. Bush, *Decision Points*, pp. 245, 247; Donald Rumsfeld, *Known and Unknown* (New York: Penguin, 2011), pp. 432, 434.

17. See, e.g., Hans Blix, *Disarming Iraq* (New York: Pantheon Books, 2004).

18. Draper, *To Start a War*, p. 71.

19. Richard N. Haass, *War of Necessity, War of Choice: A Memoir of Two Iraq Wars* (New York: Simon and Schuster, 2009), p. 230.

20. Feith, *War and Decision*, pp. 238–239, 245–246, 273-274; Suskind, *Price of Loyalty*, pp. 76, 86, 96–97; Gordon and Trainor, *Cobra II*, pp. 14, 126; Ricks, *Fiasco*, pp. 42–43; Haass, *War of Necessity*, pp. 5–6, 212–216, 220, 231, 234, 245, 272–273; Peter Baker, *Days of Fire: Bush and Cheney in the White House* (New York: Doubleday, 2013), p. 207.

21. Rice, *No Higher Honor*, pp. 506–507.

22. Tenet, *Center of the Storm*, p. 395.

23. Tenet, *Center of the Storm*, pp. 308–309. See also p. 322.

24. Paul R. Pillar, *Intelligence and U.S. Foreign Policy: Iraq, 9/11, and Misguided Reform* (New York: Columbia University Press, 2011), p. 13.

25. George Packer, *The Assassin's Gate: American in Iraq* (New York: Farrar, Straus and Giroux, 2005); p. 45.

26. Pillar, *Intelligence and U.S. Foreign Policy*, pp. 14, 51–55; Draper, *To Start a War*, pp. 176–177.

27. Haass, *War of Necessity*, p. 5.

28. *Public Papers of the Presidents of the United States, Administration of George W. Bush, 2002*, book 1, *January 1 to June 30, 2002* (Washington, DC: Government

Printing Office, 2004), p. 556. See also Draper, *To Start a War*, pp. 51, 112–113, 180–181, 184.

29. Pillar, *Intelligence and U.S. Foreign Policy*, pp. 36, 53. See also Draper, *To Start a War*, p. 200.

30. Paul R. Pillar, "Intelligence, Policy, and the War in Iraq," *Foreign Affairs*, March/April 2006, p. 18.

31. Draper, *To Start a War*, pp. 207–208.

32. Senior Administration Official Holds Background Briefing on Weapons of Mass Destruction in Iraq, As Released by the White House, July 18, 2003, https://fas.org/irp/news/2003/07/wh071803.html; Michael Isikoff and David Corn, *Hubris: The Inside Story of Spin, Scandal, and the Selling of the Iraq War* (New York: Crown, 2006), pp. 137, 295–296. Condoleezza Rice reports that "The NSC Principals ... read the NIE from cover to cover." Rice, *No Higher Honor*, p. 198.

33. Draper, *To Start a War*, pp. 217–218. See also Pillar, *Intelligence and U.S. Foreign Policy*, p. 42.

34. See, e.g., Draper, *To Start a War*, pp. 49, 69–70, 102–103, 204–205, 209–217, 258–260, 276–283, 308, 352, 391–392.

35. Robert Jervis, *Why Intelligence Fails* (Ithaca, NY: Cornell University Press, 2010), pp. 126–128, 146–150; Draper, *To Start a War*, pp. 209–217.

36. Quoted in Draper, *To Start a War*, p. 217.

37. Richard Kerr et al., "Collection and Analysis on Iraq Issues for the US Intelligence Community," *Studies in Intelligence* 49, no. 3 (2005): pp. 47–54.

38. Kerr et al., "Collection and Analysis." See also Draper, *To Start a War*, pp. 102–103.

39. Pillar, *Intelligence and U.S. Foreign Policy*, pp. 32; Jervis, *Why Intelligence Fails*, pp. 150–155.

40. Department of Defense News Briefing, February 12, 2002, www.defense.gov/Transcripts/Transcript.aspx?TranscriptID=2636; Press Conference at NATO Headquarters, Brussels, Belgium, June 6, 2002, www.defense.gov/Transcripts/Transcript.aspx?TranscriptID=3490. See also Pillar, *Intelligence and U.S. Foreign* Policy, p. 151.

41. Rumsfeld, *Known and Unknown*, p. 433.

42. Draper, *To Start a War*, pp. 67, 244–245, 248, 252–255, 302, 305–306, 339.

43. Haass, *War of Necessity*, p. 231.

44. Pillar, "Intelligence, Policy, and the War in Iraq," p. 18; Haass, *War of Necessity*, p. 231; David L. Phillips, *Losing Iraq* (Boulder, CO: Westview, 2005), p. 64.

45. Pillar, *Intelligence and U.S. Foreign Policy*, pp. 142–147.

46. See, e.g., Peter H. Stone, "Were Qaeda-Iraq Links Exaggerated?" *National Journal*, August 9, 2003, pp. 2569–2570; Feith, *War and Decision*, p. 265; Isikoff and Corn, *Hubris*, pp. 109–114; Phillips, *Losing Iraq*, p. 61; Draper, *To Start a War*, pp. 100, 130–131, 134–135, 138–140, 147–149, 155–156, 174, 218–219, 340.

47. George W. Bush, "President Delivers 'State of the Union,'" January 28, 2003, George W. Bush White House Archives, https://georgewbush-whitehouse.archives.gov/news/releases/2003/01/20030128-19.html.

48. Pillar, "Intelligence, Policy, and the War in Iraq," p. 21.

49. Suskind, *One Percent Doctrine*, p. 23.

50. Stone, "Were Qaeda-Iraq Links Exaggerated?" pp. 2569–2570; Jervis, *Why Intelligence Fails*, p. 134.

51. Pillar, "Intelligence, Policy, and the War in Iraq," pp. 18, 21; Jervis, *Why Intelligence Fails*, p. 134.

52. Draper, *To Start a War*, p. 173.

53. Bush, *Decision Points*, pp. 242–247; Woodward, *Plan of Attack*, pp. 249–250; Draper, *To Start a War*, p. 263–266; Pillar, *Intelligence and U.S. Foreign Policy*, p. 32. The briefing was on what could be declassified to explain Iraq's WMD programs to the public and covered the nature of the evidence of WMDs. Draper, *To Start a War*, p. 269, reports that deputy national security advisor Stephen Hadley found the case regarding nuclear weapons was weak at a January 6, 2003, briefing.

54. Rice, *No Higher Honor*, p. 198, 200.

55. Draper, *To Start a War*, pp. 267–268.

56. Kevin Woods, James Lacey, and Williamson Murray, "Saddam's Delusions: The View from the Inside," *Foreign Affairs*, May/June 2006.

57. Haass, *War of Necessity*, p. 245.

58. Woods, Lacey, and Murray, "Saddam's Delusions."

59. Tenet, *Center of the Storm*, pp. 45–46, 330–332; Woods, Lacey, and Murray, "Saddam's Delusions," p. 6; Haass, *War of Necessity*, p. 230.

60. Bush, *Decision Points*, pp. 224, 242, 245; Tenet, *Center of the Storm*, pp. 45–46.

61. Bush, *Decision Points*, p. 242. See also 268–270.

62. Jervis, *Why Intelligence Fails*, pp. 145–148.

63. Jervis, *Why Intelligence Fails*, pp. 126–132, 149, 152–153; Haass, *War of Necessity*, p. 245; Pillar, *Intelligence and U.S. Foreign Policy*, p. 152–153; Draper, *To Start a War*, pp. 209–217.

64. Jervis, *Why Intelligence Fails*, p. 147.

65. See, e.g., Feith, *War and Decision*, p. 265; Isikoff and Corn, *Hubris*, pp. 109–114; Phillips, *Losing Iraq*, p. 61; Draper, *To Start a War*, pp. 100, 130–131, 134–135, 138–140, 147–149, 155–156, 174, 218–291.

66. Tenet, *Center of the Storm*, pp. 344–345.

67. Senate Select Committee on Intelligence, *Report of the Select Committee on Intelligence on Postwar Findings about Iraq's WMD Programs and Links to Terrorism and How They Compare with Prewar Assessments*, S. Report 109-331, 109th Cong., 2nd sess., September 8, 2006.

68. Jervis, *Why Intelligence Fails*, p. 134.

69. See, e.g., Pillar, *Intelligence and U.S. Foreign Policy*, pp. 150–151; Stone, "Were Qaeda-Iraq Links Exaggerated?" pp. 2569–2570.

70. See, e.g., Tenet, *Center of the Storm*, pp. 349–350. The president learned of one such effort and asked a CIA official if his people had crossed the line.

71. Select Committee on Intelligence, U.S. Senate, *Report of the Select Committee on Intelligence on Postwar Findings about Iraq's WMD Programs and Links to*

Terrorism and How They Compare with Prewar Assessments; Commission on the Intelligence Capabilities of the United States Regarding Weapons of Mass Destruction, *Report to the President of the United States* (Washington, DC: Commission on the Intelligence Capabilities of the United States, March 31, 2005). See also Jervis, *Why Intelligence Fails*, p. 133; Pillar, "Intelligence, Policy, and the War in Iraq," p. 21; Haass, *War of Necessity*, p. 231.

72. Pillar, "Intelligence, Policy, and the War in Iraq," pp. 21–23.

73. Draper, *To Start a War*, p. 338.

74. Jervis, *Why Intelligence Fails*, pp. 135–136; Pillar, "Intelligence, Policy, and the War in Iraq," pp. 21–22; Pillar, *Intelligence and U.S. Foreign Policy*, pp. 54–55.

75. Draper, *To Start a War*, pp. 155–156, 227, 258–260, 268–269, 276, 390; Jervis, *Why Intelligence Fails*, p, 127.

76. Packer, *Assassin's Gate*, p. 61.

77. Robert Jervis, "Why Intelligence and Policymakers Clash," *Political Science Quarterly* 125 (Summer 2010), p. 203; Draper, *To Start a War*, pp. 100, 134, 138–139, 153–156.

78. Pillar, "Intelligence, Policy, and the War in Iraq," p. 23; Stone, "Were Qaeda-Iraq Links Exaggerated?" pp. 2569–2570; Jervis, *Why Intelligence Fails*, pp. 150–151.

79. Tenet, *Center of the Storm*, pp. 347, 356–358, 373; James Risen, *State of War: The Secret History of the CIA and the Bush Administration* (New York: Free Press, 2006), pp. 75–76; Phillips, *Losing Iraq*, pp. 60–61, 73, chap. 7; Barton Gellman, *Angler: The Cheney Vice Presidency* (New York: Penguin Press, 2008), pp. 222–225, 247; Isikoff and Corn, *Hubris*, pp. 109–114; Feith, *War and Decision*, pp. 263–272; Draper, *To Start a War*, pp. 89, 149–154, 197; Packer, *Assassin's Gate*, pp. 65, 106–107.

80. Rice, *No Higher Honor*, pp. 105–106; Gellman, *Angler*, pp. 81–90, 135–139, 162–173, 351; James P. Pfiffner, "Policy Making in the Bush White House," *Presidential Studies Quarterly* 39 (June 2009): 363–384; Tenet, *Center of the Storm*, p. 373; Baker, *Days of Fire*, pp. 95–97, 174–175; Draper, *To Start a War*, pp. 101, 270; Mayer, *Dark Side*, p. 5.

81. Pillar, "Intelligence, Policy, and the War in Iraq," pp. 24–25.

82. Haass, *War of Necessity*, p. 235. See also Pillar, *Intelligence and U.S. Foreign Policy*, pp. 29–30.

83. Gordon and Trainor, *Cobra II*, p. 64. See also Bob Woodward, *Bush at War* (New York: Simon and Schuster, 2002), pp. 137, 217, 227–228; Rice, *No Higher Honor*, pp. 198–199 for the importance of this strategic goal. For evidence that Bush, as well as Rice and other administration supporters (e.g., the president's foreign intelligence advisory board member Phillip Zelikow), doubted that Iraq constituted an imminent threat to the United States, see Woodward, *Bush at War*, pp. 49, 350; and John Mearsheimer and Stephen Walt, "Letter," *London Review of Books* 28, no. 10 (May 25, 2006); and Ricks, *Fiasco*, p. 13, which quotes former CENTCOM Chief Gen. Anthony Zinni as saying, "We didn't see the Iraqis as a formidable force. We saw them as a decaying force."

84. Michael C. Desch, "America's Liberal Illiberalism: The Ideological Origins of Overreaction in U.S. Foreign Policy," *International Security* 32 (Winter 2007–2008), p. 38. See also Draper, *To Start a War*, pp. 338–339, 401.

85. Draper, *To Start a War*, pp. 15, 37–38.

86. Draper, *To Start a War*, pp. 99–100.

87. Project for a New American Century, *Open Letter to President Clinton*, January 26, 1998. See also Draper, *To Start a War*, pp. 15–16.

88. Ron Suskind, *The Price of Loyalty* (New York: Simon and Schuster, 2004), pp. 72–75. See also the meeting on February 1, 2001, Suskind, *Price of Loyalty*, pp. 82–86.

89. Richard A. Clarke, *Against All Enemies: Inside America's War on Terror* (New York: Free Press, 2004), pp. 30, 231–232.

90. National Commission on Terrorist Attacks on the United States, *The 9/11 Commission Report* (New York: Norton, 2004), pp. 335–336, 559 fn 63; Woodward, *Plan of Attack*, p. 25; Glenn Kessler, "U.S. Decision on Iraq Has Puzzling Past," *Washington Post*, January 12, 2003; Clarke, *Against All Enemies*, p. 30–31; Draper, *To Start a War*, pp. 16–17, 79, 88–89, 100; Packer, *Assassin's Gate*, p. 40.

91. Draper, *To Start a War*, pp. 18, 18–21, 79, 82; Packer, *Assassin's Gate*, p. 41.

92. Clarke, *Against All Enemies*, pp. 32–33. There is some reason to challenge the details of Clarke's characterization, but not the general point. See *9/11 Commission Report*, p. 559, fn 61. See also Draper, *To Start a War*, pp. 41–42.

93. Packer, *Assassin's Gate*, p. 41.

94. *9/11 Commission Report*, p. 335; Draper, *To Start a War*, p. 21.

95. Bush, *Decision Points*, p. 234; Draper, *To Start a War*, pp. 41, 46. In Rumsfeld, *Known and Unknown*, p. 425, Rumsfeld remembers being asked to do so on September 26, 2001, but there is reason to believe this date is incorrect. See Bob Woodward, "How Rumsfeld Misleads and Ducks Responsibility in His New Book," *Foreign Policy*, March 1, 2001.

96. Haass, *War of Necessity*, p. 235.

97. George W. Bush, "President Delivers State of the Union Address," January 29, 2002, George W. Bush White House Archives, https://georgewbush-whitehouse.archives.gov/news/releases/2002/01/20020129-11.html.

98. Draper, *To Start a War*, pp. 124–125.

99. Draper, *To Start a War*, pp. 51, 112–113, 180–181, 184, 225; Haass, *War of Necessity*, p. 5; *Public Papers of the Presidents of the United States, Administration of George W. Bush, 2002*, book 1, p. 556.

100. Bush, *Decision Points*, p. 239.

101. Draper, *To Start a War*, pp. 320–322, 234.

102. See, e.g., James Dobbins et al., *Occupying Iraq: A History of the Coalition Provisional Authority* (Santa Monica, CA: RAND Corporation, 2009); Nora Bensahel et al., *After Saddam: Prewar Planning and the Occupation of Iraq* (Santa Monica, CA: RAND Corporation, 2008); Ricks, *Fiasco*; Gordon and Trainor, *Cobra II*; Phillips, *Losing Iraq*; L. Paul Bremer III, *My Year in Iraq* (New York: Threshold Editions, 2006);

Seymour Hersh, *Chain of Command* (New York: HarperCollins, 2004); Gates, *Duty*, p. 115; Thomas E. Ricks, *The Gamble* (New York: Penguin Press, 2009), p. 102; Peter W. Rodman, *Presidential Command* (New York: Knopf, 2009), p. 257–258; Haass, *War of Necessity*, 231; Draper, *To Start a War*, pp. 311–312, 315–316, 354–355, 375–377, 401.

103. Draper, *To Start a War*, pp. 234–235, 401.

104. See, e.g., Draper, *To Start a War*, pp. 178–179, 191, 234, 329–330, 350.

105. Quoted in Peter Slevin and Dana Priest, "Wolfowitz Concedes Iraq Errors," *Washington Post*, July 24, 2003. See also Draper, *To Start a War*, pp. 328–329.

106. Draper, *To Start a War*, p. 330.

107. Packer, *Assassin's Gate*, pp. 114–117.

108. Haass, *War of Necessity*, pp. 254–258, 273. See also p. 215.

109. Pillar, "Intelligence, Policy, and the War in Iraq," pp. 18–19; Jervis, *Why Intelligence Fails*, p. 134; Senate Select Committee on Intelligence, *Report of the Select Committee on Intelligence on Prewar Intelligence Assessments about Postwar Iraq*, 110th Cong., 1st sess., May 31, 2007, p. 31.

110. Walter Pincus, "Ex-CIA Official Faults Use of Data on Iraq Intelligence 'Misused' to Justify War," *Washington Post*, February 10, 2006.

111. Packer, *Assassin's Gate*, p. 113.

112. Kerr et al., "Collection and Analysis," pp. 47–54; Pillar, *Intelligence and U.S. Foreign Policy*, p. 49.

113. Norah Bensahel, "Mission Not Accomplished: What Went Wrong with Iraqi Reconstruction," *Journal of Strategic Studies* 29 (June 2006): 454–462; Packer, *Assassin's Gate*, pp. 113–117, 133, 143–144, 147, 407; Draper, *To Start a War*, p. 234; Haass, *War of Necessity*, p. 237.

114. Packer, *Assassin's Gate*, p. 118. See also p. 407.

115. Packer, *Assassin's Gate*, pp. 42, 61, 100–148; Draper, *To Start a War*, pp. 234–240, 313–316, 319–331, 360–366.

116. Packer, *Assassin's Gate*, p. 129.

117. Gordon and Trainor, *Cobra II*, p. 497–498, 503–504; Packer, *Assassin's Gate*, p. 117.

118. Packer, *Assassin's Gate*, chap. 4, pp. 300, 306, 446; Phillips, *Losing Iraq*; Rodman, *Presidential Command*, p. 261.

119. Quoted in Eric Schmitt and David E. Sanger, "Aftereffects: Reconstruction Policy; Looting Disrupts Detailed U.S. Plan to Restore Iraq," *New York Times*, April 28, 2005.

120. Phillips, *Losing Iraq*, p. 156; Bush, *Decision Points*, pp. 199, 367; Packer, *Assassin's Gate*, pp. 144, 306, 326.

121. Rumsfeld, *Known and Unknown*, pp. 221, 429–430, 464, 480–481, 517, 520–521, 664–665, 667, 720; Draper, *To Start a War*, p. 166–167. See also pp. 203–203.

122. Draper, *To Start a War*, pp. 337–338.

123. Rice, *No Higher Honor*, p. 507.

124. Draper, *To Start a War*, pp. 162–168, 271–273, 338.

125. Feith, *War and Decision*, p. 433; Rumsfeld, *Known and Unknown*, pp. 515–519; Rice, *No Higher Honor*, p. 238; Bob Woodward, *State of Denial* (New York: Simon and Schuster, 2006), pp. 197–198; see also p. 442; Bob Woodward, *The War Within: A Secret White House History 2006–2008* (New York: Simon and Schuster, 2008), pp. 49–50; Tenet, *Center of the Storm*, pp. 426–428, 431, 437; Risen, *State of War*, p. 3; Michael R. Gordon, "Fateful Choice on Iraq Army Bypassed Debate," *New York Times*, March 17, 2008; Gordon and Trainor, *Cobra II*, pp. 482–483; Edmund Andrews, "Envoy's Letter Counters Bush on Dismantling of Iraqi Army," *New York Times*, September 4, 2007; Draper, *To Start a War*, pp. 364–365; Packer, *Assassin's Gate*, pp. 146, 190–196; Ricks, *Fiasco*, p. 158.

126. Mayer, *Dark Side*, pp. 34, 41–43, 52, 55, 64, 68–70, 80–89, 123–124, 186–188, 220–221, 234–236, 265, 268–269.

127. Bush, *Decision Points*, pp. 258–260.

128. Rumsfeld, *Known and Unknown*, pp. 515–519.

129. Lady Gwendolen Cecil, *Life of Robert, Marquis of Salisbury*, vol. 2 (London: Hodder and Stoughton, 1921), p. 145.

130. For incentives for leaders to persevere in flayed policies, see George Downs and David Rocke, *Optimal Imperfection? Domestic Uncertainty and Institutions in International Relations* (Princeton, NJ: Princeton University Press, 1995), chap. 3; Hein Goemans, *War and Punishment: The Causes of War Termination and the First World War* (Princeton, NJ: Princeton University Press, 2000).

131. Quoted in Todd Purdum, "Prisoner of Conscience," *Vanity Fair*, February 2007, p. 14.

132. Woodward, *Plan of Attack*, pp. 415–416.

133. Quoted in Woodward, *State of Denial*, 325–326. See also p. 371; Bush, *Decision Points*, pp. 199, 367; and Matt Latimer, *Speech-less: Tales of a White House Survivor* (New York; Crown, 2009), p. 184.

134. Pillar, "Intelligence, Policy, and the War in Iraq," pp. 24-25; Woodward, *Plan of Attack*, p. 139; Woodward, *War Within*, 106–107; Woodward, *State of Denial*, p. 260; Packer, *Assassin's Gate*, p. 392.

135. Bush, *Decision Points*, p. 393; Scott McClellan, *What Happened: Inside the Bush White House and Washington's Culture of Deception* (New York: Public Affairs, 2008), pp. 207–209; Haass, *War of Necessity*, p. 236.

136. Stephen Skowronek, "Leadership by Definition: First Term Reflections on George W. Bush's Political Stance," *Perspectives on Politics* 3 (December 2005), pp. 820, 823.

137. Suskind, *One Percent Doctrine*, p. 308.

138. Gates, *Duty*, pp. 115–116; Rodman, *Presidential Command*, p. 257–258; Woodward, *Plan of Attack*, pp. 415–416; Woodward, *State of Denial*, p. 455; Draper, *To Start a War*, pp. 372–374, 377, 387–394.

139. Gordon and Trainor, *Cobra II*, p. 497.

140. Bush, *Decision Points*, pp. 258–259, 268.

141. Baker, *Days of Fire*, p. 334.

142. Bush, *Decision Points*, p. 268. See also Draper, *To Start a War*, p. 393.

143. Bush, *Decision Points*, pp. 258–259, 393. Bush also argued that if he had acted sooner on the surge, it would have created a rift that war critics in Congress would have exploited to cut off funding and prevent the surge from succeeding. It seems a stretch, however, to argue for the continuation of a failed policy because a better policy may not receive support.

144. David Priess, *The President's Book of Secrets* (New York: Public Affairs, 2016), pp. 267–269.

145. Bush, *Decision Points*, pp. 371, 378. See also Rumsfeld, *Known and Unknown*, p. 694; Rice, *No Higher Honor*, p. 506; Draper, *To Start a War*, p. 400.

146. Woodward, *Bush at War*, pp. 136–137, 145, 168, 342. See also Suskind, *Price of Loyalty*, pp. 165–166.

147. Gates, *Duty*, p. 94; Woodward, *War Within*, 431, 433; Suskind, *Price of Loyalty*, pp. 165–166; McClellan, *What Happened*, pp. 127, 145, 203, 208; Suskind, *One Percent Doctrine*, p. 308. But see Rove, *Courage and Consequence*, pp. 124; Haass, *War of Necessity*, p. 236.

148. A number of Bush's close associates thought the president asked probing questions. See Karen Hughes, *Ten Minutes from Normal* (New York: Viking, 2004), pp. 93, 282; Rove, *Courage and Consequence*, pp. 124, 168, 171; Rumsfeld, *Known and Unknown*, pp. 319, 694; Robert Gates, who joined the administration at the end of 2006, provides a more mixed view. See Gates, *Duty*, p. 94.

149. See Suskind, *Price of Loyalty*, pp. 57–60, 107–109, 126, 148–149, 153, 170–171, 295–306; McClellan, *What Happened*, pp. 127, 145, 203, 208; Tenet, *Center of the Storm*, p. 308–309, 322.

150. Clarke, *Against All Enemies*, pp. 243–244; McClellan, *What Happened*, pp. 145; Suskind, *One Percent Doctrine*, p. 79; Tenet, *Center of the Storm*, p. 308–309, 322; and Pillar, *Intelligence and U.S. Foreign Policy*, p. 13.

151. See *9/11 Commission Report*, pp. 260–262; Woodward, *Plan of Attack*, p. 80.

152. Woodward, *Plan of Attack*, p. 295; Ricks, *Fiasco*, p. 42.

153. Rumsfeld, *Known and Unknown*, p. 456; Woodward, *State of Denial*, pp. 226, 237, 336–337, 419; Woodward, *Plan of Attack*, pp. 80, 149, 151; Isikoff and Corn, *Hubris*, p. 357; Suskind, *Price of Loyalty*, pp. 57–60, 107–109, 126, 144–149, 153, 170–171, 295–306; Woodward, *War Within*, p. 106.

154. Isikoff and Corn, *Hubris*, p. 310.

155. Packer, *Assassin's Gate*, p. 145; Draper, *To Start a War*, pp. 324, 366–367. When Garner told Rumsfeld about Bremer's mistakes, the secretary of defense replied that it was too late to change policy.

156. Rumsfeld, *Known and Unknown*, p. 456; Woodward, *Plan of Attack*, p. 251–252, 272, 416–417; Woodward, *State of Denial*, p. 90; Woodward, *War Within*, 28.

157. Bush, *Decision Points*, p. 251.

158. Woodward, *Plan of Attack*, p. 272; Woodward, *State of Denial*, p. 90.

159. Bush, *Decision Points*, p. 251.

160. Catherine Lutz, "US and Coalition Casualties in Iraq and Afghanistan," Watson Institute for International Studies, Brown University, February 21, 2013; Draper, *To Start a War*, p. 402.

161. "How Common Is PTSD in Veterans?" National Center for PTSD, Department of Veterans Affairs, https://www.ptsd.va.gov/understand/common/common_veterans.asp.

162. Lutz, "US and Coalition Casualties."

163. Amy Hagopian et al., "Mortality in Iraq Associated with 2003–2011 War and Occupation: Findings from a National Cluster Sample Survey by the University of Iraq Collaborative Mortality Study," *PLOS Medicine*, October 15, 2013.

164. Haass, *War of Necessity*,, pp. 5–6, 212–216, 220, 234, 257–258, 272; Woodward, *War Within*, pp. 28, 50; Isikoff and Corn, *Hubris*, p. 310; Ivo Daalder and I. M. Destler, "In the Shadow of the Oval Office," *Foreign Affairs*, January/February 2009, pp. 125–126; Rumsfeld, *Known and Unknown*, pp. 318–327, 329, 323, 456–457, 485, 491–492, 494, 498, 510–511, 517–519, 523, 525, 602; Feith, *War and Decision*, pp. 143–144, 245, 250, 273, 283–284, 439; Tenet, *Center of the Storm*, p. 308; Suskind, *One Percent Doctrine*, pp. 111, 224; Woodward, *State of Denial*, pp. 109, 190–191, 241, 249, 267, 379–381, 404, 408, 455; and Suskind, *Price of Loyalty*, pp. 121, 125–126, 144–149, 156, 273; Gellman, *Angler*, chaps. 11–12, pp. 81–90, 135–139, 162–173, 320, 323, 340–342, 351; Draper, *To Start a War*, pp. 73–76, 81, 84–87, 117–123; Risen, *State of War*, pp. 63–66; Stephen Benedict Dyson, "What Really Happened in Planning for Postwar Iraq?" *Political Science Quarterly* 128, no. 3 (2013): 465; Mayer, *Dark Side*, pp. 186–188; Rodman, *Presidential Command*, pp. 249–251, 256, 262–271; Packer, *Assassin's Gate*, pp. 112–113.

165. Bush, *Decision Points*, p. 82; Rumsfeld, *Known and Unknown*, p. 82.

166. Bush, *Decision Points*, p. 268.

Chapter Six

1. Barbara W. Tuchman, *The March of Folly: From Troy to Vietnam* (New York: Ballantine Books, 1984), p. 384.

2. Robert Jervis, *Perception and Misperception in International Politics* (Princeton, NJ: Princeton University Press, 1976), p. 410.

3. See, e.g., Richard E. Neustadt and Ernest R. May, *Thinking in Time: The Uses of History for Decision Makers* (New York: Free Press, 1986), p. 9; Donald Rumsfeld, *Known and Unknown* (New York: Penguin, 2011), pp, 20, 221, 665, 667; Richard N. Haass, *War of Necessity, War of Choice: A Memoir of Two Iraq Wars* (New York: Simon and Schuster, 2009), pp. 272–273.

4. Neustadt and May, *Thinking in Time*, chap. 3.

5. Jervis, *Perception and Misperception*, chap. 12, is especially good in discussing the need to examine premises and the challenges of doing so. See also

Robert Jervis, *Why Intelligence Fails* (Ithaca, NY: Cornell University Press, 2010), pp. 131–132.

6. Tuchman, *March of Folly*, p. 319.

7. Arie W. Kruglanski, "Lay Epistemo-logic—Process and Contents: Another Look at Attribution Theory," *Psychological Review* 87, no. 1, (1980): 7-87; Ziva Kunda, *Social Cognition: Making Sense of People* (Cambridge, MA: MIT Press, 1999), pp. 224–225, 235–239. See also Leon Festinger, *Conflict, Decision, and Dissonance* (Palo Alto, CA: Stanford University Press, 1964).

8. Leon Festinger, *A Theory of Cognitive Dissonance* (Stanford, CA: Stanford University Press, 1957).

9. George P. Shultz, *Turmoil and Triumph* (New York: Scribner's, 1933), pp. 263, 819.

10. Lyn Nofziger, *Nofziger* (Washington, DC: Regnery, 1992), p. 45. Also see p. 285.

11. On this process, see Charles Taber, "Information Processing and Public Opinion," in *The Oxford Handbook of Political Psychology*, ed. David O. Sears, Leonie Huddy, and Robert Jervis (New York: Oxford University Press, 2003), pp. 433–76; and Milton Lodge and Charles Taber, "Implicit Affect for Political Candidates, Parties, and Issues: An Experimental Test of the Hot Cognition Hypothesis," *Political Psychology* 26 (December 2005): 455–482; Charles Taber, Milton Lodge, and Jill Glather, "The Motivated Construction of Political Judgments," in *Citizens and Politics: Perspectives from Political Psychology*, ed. James Kuklinski (New York: Cambridge University Press, 2001), pp. 198–226.

12. See Jervis, *Perception and Misperception*, chap. 4 for an excellent overview.

13. Kunda, *Social Cognition*, p. 224.

14. See Paul R. Pillar, *Intelligence and U.S. Foreign Policy: Iraq, 9/11, and Misguided Reform* (New York: Columbia University Press, 2011), pp. 170-171.

15. Kunda, *Social Cognition*, p. 235.

16. See Jervis, *Why Intelligence Fails*, pp. 24–25; Jervis, *Perception and Misperception*, pp. 213–315.

17. Jervis, *Perception and Misperception*, p. 292–295. See pages 291–297 for a discussion of mechanisms for attitude preservation.

18. Jervis, *Why Intelligence Fails*, pp. 151–152.

19. H. R. Haldeman, *The Ends of Power* (New York: Times Books, 1978), p. 34.

20. Shultz, *Turmoil and Triumph*, pp. 263, 1133.

21. See Jervis, *Why Intelligence Fails*, chap. 10 for an argument that wishful thinking is not pervasive in decision making.

22. See, e.g., Gordon M. Goldstein, *Lessons in Disaster: McGeorge Bundy and the Path to War in Vietnam* (New York: Holt, 2008), pp. 172–173, 179–180, 186, 188–190, 215, 226.

23. See, e.g., James Thomson, "How Could Vietnam Happen?" *Atlantic Monthly* (April 1968): 47–53. See also Jervis, *Why Intelligence Fails*, chap. 10.

24. See Ernest R. May, *"Lessons" of the Past: The Use and Misuse of History in American Foreign Policy* (New York: Oxford University Press, 1973); Jervis,

Perception and Misperception, chap. 6; Yuen Foong Khong, *Analogies at War: Korean, Munich, Dien Bien Phu and the Vietnam Decisions of 1965* (Princeton, NJ: Princeton University Press, 1992); Yaacov Y. I. Vertzberger, *The World in Their Minds: Information Processing, Cognition, and Perception in Foreign Policy Decision-Making* (Palo Alto, CA: Stanford University Press, 1990); Jack S. Levy, "Learning and Foreign Policy: Sweeping a Conceptual Minefield," *International Organization* 48 (Spring 1994): 279–312; Neustadt and May, *Thinking in Time*.

25. Amos Tversky and Daniel Kahneman, "Judgment under Uncertainty: Heuristics and Biases," *Science* 185 (September 1974): 1124–1131; Khong, *Analogies at War*, pp. 11–14, 36–37.

26. Mark Schlesinger and Richard R. Lau, "The Meaning and Measure of Policy Metaphors," *American Political Science Review* 94 (September 2000): 611–626.

27. Jervis, *Perception and Misperception*, p. 220.

28. A. J. P. Taylor, *From Napoleon to Lenin* (New York: Harper and Row, 1966), p. 64.

29. Khong, *Analogies at War*, pp. 8–9, 14, 36–37, 217, 229; May, *"Lessons" of the Past*; Stanley Hoffmann, *Gulliver's Troubles, or the Setting of American Foreign Policy* (New York: McGraw-Hill, 1968); Abraham Lowenthal, *The Dominican Intervention* (Cambridge, MA: Harvard University Press, 1972), pp. 153–162; Deborah Welch Larson, *Origins of Containment: A Psychological Explanation* (Princeton, NJ: Princeton University Press, 1985), pp. 332–339; and Yaacov Vertzberger, "Foreign Policy Decisionmakers as Practical-Intuitive Historians: Applied History and Its Shortcomings," *International Studies Quarterly* 30 (June 1986): 223–247.

30. Jervis, *Perception and Misperception*, chap. 6.

31. Jervis, *Perception and Misperception*, pp. 220, 226, 280–282.

32. Khong, *Analogies at War*, pp. 10–11, 14, 20–22, 14, 37–40, 223–225, 256.

33. Jervis, *Perception and Misperception*, chap. 11.

34. Jack S. Levy, "Political Psychology and Foreign Policy," in *The Oxford Handbook of Political Psychology*, ed. David O. Sears, Leonie Huddy, and Robert Jervis (New York: Oxford University Press, 2003), pp. 265–266.

Index

Abelson, Robert P., 110
Achen, Christopher, 111
Acheson, Dean, 18, 52, 55, 60, 65–67, 69–70, 74, 76–77, 116, 128, 130–34
affective consistency. *See* motivated reasoning
Afghanistan, Soviet invasion of, U.S. premises regarding likelihood of, 53
African embassy attacks, 79
Ahern, Thomas, Jr., 122
al-Qaeda, 83, 85, 87, 89, 91, 98–99
analogy: Crimean War as, 42; domino theory as, 17–23, 106; Ethiopia, Mussolini invasion of, as, 58–59; France in Indochina as, 17–18, 27; German strategy in World War I as, 44; Greece, Communist threat to, as, 59; Korean War as, 2–14, 16–17, 30, 34, 106; "loss" of China as, 26–30; Manchuria, Japanese invasion of, as, 58–59; misuse of, 17–23, 26–30, 42–43, 106–7; Munich Agreement as, 12–13, 16–17, 59, 106–7; power of, 106–7; risks of, 106–7; Russian civil war as, 42; Russian mobilization in World War I as, 43; use of in decision making, Austria, Hitler and, 58; utility of, 106–7
Andrews, Edmund, 142
Arab-Israeli 1973 War, U.S. and Israeli premises regarding likelihood of, 52–53. *See also* motivated reasoning
Army War College, 94
Australia, 20, 47
Austria, Hitler and, as analogy, 58

Bacon, Francis, 5, 111
Baker, James A., III, 53, 127

Baker, Peter, 136, 139, 143
Ball, George, 17, 34, 116, 118–19, 121–22
Bar-Joseph, Uri, 127
Bartels, Larry, 111
Bartsch, William H., 125
Bay of Pigs invasion, 50–52, 104–5; consequences of, 52; premises regarding, x, 9, 50–52; wishful thinking about, 104–5. *See also* motivated reasoning
Bazerman, Max, 110
Bensahel, Norah, 140–41
Berlin Airlift, 55, 59–60
Berman, Larry, 120
Beschloss, Michael, 114
Betts, Richard, 36, 45, 61, 114–15, 119–24, 127, 129–34
bin Laden, Osama, 80
Bissell, Richard M., Jr., 50–51, 126
Blainey, Geoffrey, 124
Blight, James D., 113–16, 118–23, 125–27
Bonaparte, Napoleon, 40
bounded rationality, biasing information processing, 3, 108; reasons for, 2–3
Bradley, Omar, 70, 76
Braybrooke, David, 109
Brehm, Jack, 110
Bremer, L. Paul, III, 98–99, 140, 143
Brereton, Lewis, 49
Brigham, Robert K., 113–16, 118–23
Bundy, McGeorge, 17, 22, 24, 32, 34, 116, 119
Bundy, William, 29, 116
Bureau of Intelligence and Research, U.S. Department of State, 81
Burke, John P., 120–21

Burma, 18, 20
Burton, John, 125, 129
Bush, George H. W., 53, 91
Bush, George W., 135–37, 140, 142; and Iraq, invasion of, 79–90, 100; and Iraq, post-invasion, 79–100

Cambodia, 15, 20–23
Cann, Damon, 110
Cardona, José Miró, 51
Caridi, Ronald J., 134
Caro, Robert A., 120
Castro, Fidel, 50–52
Cecil, Gwendolen, 142
Center for Strategic and International Studies, 94
Central Intelligence Agency (CIA): and Bay of Pigs invasion, 50–51, 126; and Cuban Missile Crisis, 37–38, 127; and Iraq War, xi, 79–83, 85–92, 99–100, 138; and Korean War, 55–56, 66, 75, 128, 132–33; and Soviet invasion of Afghanistan, 53, 81; and Vietnam War, 14–16, 21–23, 25, 117–18, 122, 126
Chamberlain, Neville, 12
Chanda, Nayan, 115
Cheney, Richard, 79–80, 84, 91, 94, 99, 136
China: and Korean War, 55, 57, 59–74, 107; and Vietnam War, 12, 14–16, 20, 22–26, 30–31, 35, 106
Choi, Jong Kun, 112
Churchill, Winston, 48, 125
Clarke, Richard, 91, 140, 143
Clifford, Clark, 17, 116
Clinton, William J., 54, 91
cognitive closure, 5, 53. *See also* motivated reasoning
cognitive consistency, need for, 2–3. *See also* motivated reasoning
cognitive miser. *See* bounded rationality
Cohen, Arthur, 110
Cohen, Eliot A., 128, 132–33
Cohen, Warren I., 114
Cohen, William, 81
Collins, J. Lawton, 75, 132, 134
communism, containment of, 55. *See also* Korean War, Chinese intervention in; Korean War, June 1950 attack; Vietnam War
communism as an international conspiracy, as premise. *See* Korean War, Chinese intervention in; Korean War, June 1950 attack; Vietnam War
confirmation bias. *See* motivated reasoning
Congress (U.S.), impact on premises, 107–8
Connaughton, Richard, 125
Cooper, Chester, 117
Corn, David, 137–39, 143–45
Council on Foreign Relations, xi, 28, 94
Crimean War, as analogy, 42
Cuban Missile Crisis, U.S. premises underlying, 37–38. *See also* motivated reasoning
Cumings, Bruce, 128–29

Daalder, Ivo, 144
Dallek, Robert, 126–27
Dawes, Robyn M., 110
Dean, Andrea M., 118
Dearlove, Richard, 89
decision makers: characteristics of, 5–7, 55–56; encourage supportive information, 4, 97–100; resistance to change, 3–6. *See also* Afghanistan; Arab-Israeli 1973 War; Bay of Pigs invasion; bounded rationality; Cuban Missile Crisis; embargo, 1806–1814; French military planning in World War I; German military planning in World War I; Gorbachev, Mikhail; groupthink; India; Iran; Iraq, invasion of; Iraq, post-invasion; Korean War, Chinese intervention in; Korean War, June 1950 attack; Kuwait, Iraq invasion of; motivated reasoning; Norway, German invasion of; Operation Barbarossa; Pearl Harbor, Japanese attack on; Philippines, Japanese 1941 attack on; premises; Tet Offensive; Vietnam War
decision making, 1–9; accuracy goals and, 102–3; debate, utility of, 105; defensive avoidance and, 4, 104; devil's advocate and, 105; impossibility inference and, 36; influences on, 6–7, 101; information, ambiguity of, 10, 36, 46, 54, 103–4; information, discrediting sources of, 104; low self-esteem and, 76–77; problem definition and, x, 1–2, 8–9, 101–2; requirements for rational, 2; stress, avoidance and, 4, 76–77, 104; studying, ix–x, 1–9; understanding, lack of, ix, 7;

INDEX

149

wishful thinking and, 4, 32, 104–5. *See also* Afghanistan; Arab-Israeli 1973 War; Bay of Pigs invasion; bounded rationality; Cuban Missile Crisis; embargo, 1806–1814; French military planning in World War I; German military planning in World War I; Gorbachev, Mikhail; groupthink; India; Iran; Iraq, invasion of; Iraq, post-invasion; Korean War, Chinese intervention in; Korean War, June 1950 attack; Kuwait, Iraq invasion of; motivated reasoning; Norway, German invasion of; Operation Barbarossa; Pearl Harbor, Japanese attack on; Philippines, Japanese 1941 attack on; premises; Tet Offensive; Vietnam War

Defense, U.S. Department of: and Iraq War, 85, 87, 91–96, 98; and Korean War, 30, 55, 60; and Vietnam War, 30. *See also* Cohen, William; Marshall, George; McNamara, Robert; Rumsfeld, Donald

defensive avoidance, 4, 104. *See also* motivated reasoning

Deibel, Terry L., 118
de Rivera, Joseph, 112
Desch, Michael C., 140
Destler, I. M., 144
de Vreese, Claes H., 110
De Weerd, Harvey A., 132–33
Dien Bien Phu, 19
disconfirmation bias. *See* motivated reasoning
dissonance reduction. *See* motivated reasoning
Dobbins, James, 140
Dobbs, Michael, 123
domino theory, 17–23
Downs, George, 142
Draper, Robert, 135–44
Druckman, James N., 110
Duelfer, Charles, 83
Dulles, Allen W., 126
Dulles, John Foster, 128
Dutch East Indies, 48
Dyson, Stephen Benedict, 144

Edwards, George C., III, 112, 120
Eisenhower, Dwight D.: and Hungarian uprising, 27; and Vietnam, 14, 16, 19–20, 27–28, 30, 117

Ellsberg, Daniel, 27, 120
embargo, 1806–1814, 38–40; costs of, 39–40; premises underlying, x, 9, 38–40, 101. *See also* motivated reasoning
Ethiopia, Mussolini invasion of, as analogy, 58–59
Evans, Richard J., 124
experts, outside, impact on premises, 108

Fein, Jordan, 110
Feith, Douglas, 89, 91, 135–39, 142, 144
Ferrell, Robert H., 117
Festinger, Leon, 110, 145
Fiske, Susan, 109
Foot, Rosemary, 130–32
Ford, Harold P., 114–15, 118, 122
Forest Service, U.S., 4
Formosa. *See* Taiwan
Franks, Tommy, 94
French military planning in World War I, 41; premises underlying, xi, 8–9, 41. *See also* motivated reasoning
Fulbright, William J., 28, 104

Gaddis, John Lewis, 118
Gallatin, Albert, 39
Garner, Jay, 95, 99, 143
Garthoff, Raymond, 127
Gates, Robert M., 135, 141–43
Gelb, Leslie H., 114–15, 119–22
Gellman, Barton, 139, 144
General Agreement on Trade and Tariffs, 56
Geneva Accords, 14, 16
George, Alexander, 7, 62, 64, 72, 112–13, 128–34
German military planning in World War I, premises underlying, 41–42. *See also* motivated reasoning
Gerow, Leonard T., 48
Gilovich, Thomas, 110
Glather, Jill, 111, 145
Goemans, Hein, 142
Goering, Hermann, 37
Goethe, Johann Wolfgang von, 1
Goldstein, Gordon M., 118, 120–22, 125, 145
Goncharov, Sergei, 129, 131–32
Gooch, John, 132–33
Gorbachev, Mikhail, 26; U.S. premises regarding restructuring, 54. *See also* motivated reasoning

Gordon, John, 125
Gordon, Michael, 90, 135–36, 139–42
Gorodetsky, Gabriel, 124
Goulden, Joseph C., 132
Graff, Henry F., 121
Great Britain, 18, 38–40, 42, 89
Greece: Communist threat to as analogy, 59; and Truman Doctrine, 18
Greenstein, Fred I., 120–21
Griffin, Dale, 110
groupthink, 7, 72–77
Gulf of Tonkin incident, 29
Gulf War, 34, 53, 79

Haass, Richard, 81–82, 90, 93
Hadley, Stephen, 92, 94, 97–98, 138
Hagopian, Amy, 144
Halberstam, David, 128–33
Haldeman, H. R., 104, 145
Hamill, Ruth, 111
Haney, Patrick J., 112
Hanson, Victor Davis, 123
Hastie, Reid, 110
Helms, Richard, 25, 118
Herek, Gregory, 112
Herring, George C., 13, 15–16, 35, 114–15, 118–23
Herrmann, Richard K., 112
Hersey, John, 62, 130
Herzog, Chaim, 127
Hess, Rudolph, 42
history, decision maker ignorance of, 107
Hitler, Adolf, 12, 42–44, 58–59, 106
HMS *Leopard*, 39
Ho Chi Minh, 17–18
Hoffmann, Stanley, 146
Holsti, Ole, 112
House International Relations Committee (U.S.), 95
Hoyt, Edwin P., 132–33
Hughes, Karen, 143
Humphrey, Hubert H., 28, 120
Hungarian 1956 uprising, 27
Hunt, Michael H., 115
Huntley, Chet, 20, 117
Hussein, Saddam, xi, 53, 78–93, 95, 97, 100, 106–7
Huth, Paul, 112
Hybel, Alex Roberto, 127

impossibility, inference of, 36. *See also* motivated reasoning
India, 18–20, 65–66; U.S. premises regarding likelihood of testing nuclear weapons, 54
Indochina, 15, 17–19
Indonesia, 19–21
information, ambiguity of, 10, 36, 46, 54, 103–4. *See also* Iraq, invasion of; Pearl Harbor, Japanese attack on
information, discrediting sources of, 104
International Monetary Fund, 56
Iran, overthrow of Shah, U.S. premises regarding likelihood of, 53. *See also* motivated reasoning
Iran-Contra affair, wishful thinking about, 104
Iraq, 34
Iraq, invasion of, ix, 34, 79–90; analysis and debate, lack of, 81–85; assumed need for, x, 9, 79–90, 101; costs of, 100; decision-making process and, x, 81–90, 98–100; intelligence agencies and, 79–90; misinterpreting Saddam Hussein, 85–87, 107; pandering to leaders and, 88–89; politicization of intelligence about, 87–90; premises underlying, 8, 79–81; premises underlying, failure to evaluate, 79–90, 100; risk aversion of leaders and, 79–81, 106. *See also* motivated reasoning
Iraq, post-invasion, 90–100, 104–5; analysis, lack of, about, 93–100; costs of, 100; dissent about, discouraging, 97–100; intelligence agencies and, 91–94, 99–100; intuition, reliance on, and, 98–100; outside experts, role of, 108; planning, lack of, for, 94–98; premises underlying, 90–93, 98; premises underlying, inability to evaluate in face of failure, 96–100, 108; reevaluation of premises, 98; strength, perceived need to show and, 97; underestimating problems with, x, 9, 90–100, 102, 107; wishful thinking about, 104–5. *See also* motivated reasoning
Isikoff, Michael, 137–39, 143–44

Janis, Irving, 4, 72–77, 111–12, 124, 134–35
Japan, 16, 19, 55, 60; attack on Pearl Harbor, 44–48, 107; attack on Philippines, 48–50, 107; invasion of Manchuria as analogy, 58–59; and Korean War, 71

Jefferson, Thomas, embargo of 1806–1814, x, 9, 38–40, 102
Jervis, Robert, 37, 101, 106, 109–12, 123–24, 126–27, 134, 137
Jian, Chen, 64, 129–32
Joffre, Joseph, 41
Johnson, Lyndon B., and Vietnam, 11–18, 21–31, 32–34, 104; as decision maker, 29–30, 33; domestic concerns and, 26–30. *See also* Vietnam War
Joint Chiefs of Staff: and Bay of Pigs invasion, 50; and Korean War, 70, 75; and Vietnam War, 19–20, 22, 30–32, 34
Jost, John T., 110

Kahan, Dan M., 111
Kahin, George McT., 113, 115, 118–21
Kahneman, Daniel, 5, 109–10, 112, 146
Karnow, Stanley, 115
Kaufman, Burton I., 129
Kay, David, 99
Kearns, Doris, 113–15, 117, 120–22
Kennan, George F., 64, 74, 129, 131, 134
Kennedy, John F., 7, 10, 18, 112; and Bay of Pigs invasion, x, 50–52, 104–5; and Vietnam, 20, 22, 26–27, 30, 34
Kennedy, Robert, 104
Kent, Sherman, 123
Kerr, Richard, 83, 137, 141
Kertzer, Joshua, 6, 12
Kessler, Glenn, 140
Khmer Rouge, 15
Khobar Towers bombing, 79
Khong, Yuen Foong, 113–16, 118, 120–22, 146
Khrushchev, Nikita, 13, 129. *See also* Cuban Missile Crisis
Kim Il-Sung, 56
Kimmel, Husband, 45–47
Kirkpatrick, Lyman, 125–27
Kissinger, Henry, 53, 127
Knobloch-Westerwick, Silvia, 110
Knorr, Klaus, 123
Korean War, Chinese intervention in, 66–77; analogies, use of, in, 58–59; decision makers, characteristics of, 55–56, 74–77; dismissing warnings of, 64, 66–70; groupthink and decisions about, 72–77; leeway in responding to, 60–61; maintaining credibility, 60–61, 105–6; misinterpreting Stalin and Mao about, 57, 62–64, 107; public opinion about U.S. response, 68, 71; reexamining premises about, obstacles to, 70–72; underestimating capabilities of China and, 107; underestimating likelihood of, ix–x, 9, 55–77; U.S. premises regarding, 61–77; warnings of, 64–66. *See also* motivated reasoning
Korean War, June 1950 attack, 55–61; containing communism and, 59–61; decision makers, characteristics of, 55–56, 74–77; misinterpreting Stalin and, 57, 62, 107; resisting aggression and, 58–59, 105–6; U.S. premises regarding probability of, 56–58, 101; U.S. premises underlying response to, 58–61. *See also* motivated reasoning
Kornbluh, Peter, 125–27
Kruglanski, Arie W., 127, 145
Kucsova, Simona, 110
Kuhns, Woodrow J., 131
Kunda, Ziva, 111–12, 123, 145
Kuwait, Iraq invasion of, 34; U.S. premises regarding, 53

Lacey, James, 138
Laos, 11, 20–23, 27
Larson, Deborah Welch, 146
Latimer, Matt, 142
Lau, Richard, 112, 146
Lebow, Richard Ned, 127–33
Leeper, Thomas J., 110
Leeson, Peter T., 118
Leffler, Melvyn P., 128, 130–36
Leites, Nathan, 7, 112
Lemnitzer, Lyman, 20, 117
Lepper, Mark R., 111
Levy, Jack S., 111, 116, 146
Lewis, John W., 115, 119, 129, 131–32
Lindblom, Charles, 109
Lodge, Milton, 110–12, 145
Logevall, Fredrik, 29, 33, 114, 118–22
Lomperis, Timothy, 115
Lord, Charles, 111
Lowe, Peter, 129, 134
Lowenthal, Abraham, 146
Lutz, Catherine, 144

MacArthur, Douglas: and fall of Philippines, 1941, 48–50; and Korean War, 59, 63–71, 73–75, 77

MacEachin, Douglas, 127
Madison, James, and embargo, 1806–1814, 38–40
Malacca Straits, 47
Malaya, 48
Malone, Dumas, 123
Manchuria: Japanese invasion of, as analogy, 58–59; Korean War and, 63–66
Mann, Leon, 4, 111
Mansfield, Mike, 28
Mao Zedong, 25, 60, 62–63, 66, 69, 107
March, James G., 109
Marshall, George, 48, 50, 56, 67, 76, 131
Marshall, Samuel L., 133
Marshall Plan, 56
Matray, James I., 134
May, Ernest, 26–27, 32, 51, 58, 60, 109, 113, 120, 126, 129–30, 144, 146
Mayer, Jane, 135, 139, 142, 144
Mayer, Kenneth R., 112
Mayhew, David, 8, 113
McCarthy, Joseph, 77
McClellan, Scott, 142–43
McCone, John, 38, 117, 119
McDermott, Rose, 126
McLellan, David S., 131
McMaster, H. R., 29–31, 116–23
McNamara, Robert, 9, 15, 21–23, 25, 32, 34, 101, 113–16, 118–23
McNaughton, John, 24–25, 119
Mearsheimer, John, 139
media, impact on premises, 107
Merrill, John R., 129–30
Messimy, Adolphe, 41
Michel, Victor-Constant, 41
Mitchell, John, 104
Molotov-Ribbentrop Pact, 42
Moreman, Tim, 125
Mortensen, Daniel R., 125
Morton, Louis, 125
Mothes, Cornelia, 110
motivated reasoning, x, 2–6, 101–8; and Afghanistan, Soviet invasion of, 53; and Arab-Israeli 1973 War, 52–53; and Bay of Pigs invasion, 50–52; cognitive closure and, 5, 53; Cuban Missile Crisis, 37; defensive avoidance and, 4, 104; and embargo, 1806–1814, 38–40; and French military planning in World War I, 41–42; and German military planning in World War I, 41–42; and Gorbachev, Mikhail, 54; and India, 54; inference of impossibility and, 36; and Iran, 53; and Iraq, invasion of, 79–90, 100; and Iraq, post-invasion, 90–100; and Korean War, Chinese intervention in, 66–77; and Korean War, June 1950 attack, 55–61; and Kuwait, Iraq invasion of, 34; and Norway, German invasion of, 38; and Operation Barbarossa, 42–44; and Pearl Harbor, Japanese attack on, 44–48; and Philippines, Japanese 1941 attack on, 48–50; and Tet Offensive, 52; and Vietnam War, 10–35
Munich Agreement as analogy, 12–13, 16–17, 59, 106
Murphy, David E., 124
Murray, Williamson, 138
Mussolini, Benito, 58–59

National Commission on Terrorist Attacks on the United States, 140
National Defense University Institute for National Strategic Studies, 94
National Security Council, 18–19, 22, 24, 55, 60, 91–92, 97, 99, 116–19, 121, 137
Neustadt, Richard, 32, 51, 68, 109, 120, 122, 126, 130, 132–34, 144, 146
New Zealand, 20, 47
Nicholas II (tsar), 43
Nilsson, Nils J., 109
Nisbett, Richard E., 110
Nixon, Richard, 104
Nofziger, Lyn, 103, 145
Norway, German invasion of, British premises regarding likelihood of, 38. *See also* motivated reasoning

Odom, William, 127
Office for Reconstruction and Humanitarian Assistance for Iraq, 95
Okinawa, 20
operational code, 7
Operation Barbarossa, 42–44; consequences of, 42; Soviet premises regarding, xi, 9, 42–44; use of analogies by Soviets, 43–44
Operation Rolling Thunder, 11, 31
Ovodenko, Alexander, 128, 130–33

Packer, George, 82, 94, 136, 139–44
Paige, Glenn, 58, 76, 116, 128–32, 134–35

Palmer, Bruce J., 123
Panikkar, Kavalam M., 132
Patty, John W., 112
Pearl Harbor, Japanese attack on, 44–48; consequences of, 47; underestimating capabilities of Japan and, 45, 107; U.S. premises regarding likelihood of, ix, 9, 45–48, 101. *See also* motivated reasoning
Pfeiffer, Jack B., 126
Pfiffner, James P., 139
Philip II (king of Spain), 2
Philippines, 20, 47
Philippines, Japanese 1941 attack on, 48–50; consequences of, 49; U.S. premises regarding likelihood of, 48–50, 101. *See also* motivated reasoning
Pillar, Paul, 82, 90, 116, 118, 122–23, 136–39, 141–43, 145
Pincus, Walter, 141
Pleshakov, Constantine, 124
Polavin, Nick, 110
Powell, Colin, 80, 84, 86, 88–89, 91, 96, 100, 136
Prague Spring, 27
Prange, Gordon W., 124–25
premises: as agents of change, 107–8; change, resistance to, 3–6, 101–5; change in nature of, 108; as constraints on change, 103–5; decision making, impact on, x, 1–9, 101–2; domestic policy, impact on, 102; history, misreading of, and, 105–6; nature of, 108; pandering to leaders' views, 6; problem definition, impact on, x, 1–2, 8–9, 101–2; reexamining, necessity of, 102–5; reexamining, obstacles to, 2–6, 70–72, 103–5; sources of, 105–7; study of, ix–x, 6–9; substance of, 1; underpinnings of, psychological, 2–6. *See also* Afghanistan; Arab-Israeli 1973 War; Bay of Pigs invasion; Cuban Missile Crisis; embargo, 1806–1814; French military planning in World War I; German military planning in World War I; Gorbachev, Mikhail; India; Iran; Iraq, invasion of; Iraq, post-invasion; Korean War, Chinese intervention in; Korean War, June 1950 attack; Kuwait, Iraq invasion of; motivated reasoning; Norway, German invasion of; Operation Barbarossa; Pearl Harbor, Japanese attack on; Philippines, Japanese 1941 attack on; Tet Offensive; Vietnam War
Press, Daryl G., 25
Priess, David, 143
Priest, Dana, 141
prior attitude effect. *See* motivated reasoning
public opinion, impact on premises, 107
Purdum, Todd, 142

Quezon, Manuel, 49

Radford, Arthur, 19, 117
RAND, 94
Ransom, Harry H., 123, 125
Rasenberger, Jim, 125–27
Reagan, Ronald, 103–4
Redlawsk, David A., 110–11
Reeves, Richard, 127
Renshon, Jonathan, 110
Rice, Condoleezza, 79, 81–82, 85, 88, 91, 94, 96, 135–39, 141–43
Ricks, Thomas E., 135–36, 139–43
Ridgway, Matthew B., 57, 129
Risen, James, 139, 142, 144
Roberts, Geoffrey, 124
Rocke, David, 142
Rodman, Peter W., 141–42, 144
Roosevelt, Franklin D., 12
Rose, P. K., 62, 128, 132
Ross, Lee, 110–11
Rove, Karl, 135, 143
Rovere, Richard H., 132
Rumsfeld, Donald, 80, 84, 91–92, 94–96, 101, 136–37, 140–44
Rusk, Dean: and Korean War, 18, 59, 116; and Vietnam War, 13, 18, 22, 24, 34, 116, 119
Russell, Richard, 28
Russian civil war as analogy, 42

Sadat, Anwar, 53
Salisbury, Lord (Robert Gascoyne-Cecil, 3rd Marquess of Salisbury), 96
Sanger, David E., 119
satisficing. *See* bounded rationality
Schandler, Herbert Y., 113–16, 119, 121–22
Schell, Jonathan, 118
Schelling, Thomas, 31, 121
Schiff, Ashley, 111

Schlesinger, Arthur M., Jr., 126–27, 132
Schlesinger, Mark, 146
Schlieffen Plan, 41
Schmitt, Eric, 141
Senate Foreign Relations Committee (U.S.), 28, 104
Senate Select Committee on Intelligence (U.S.), 88, 136, 138, 141
Service, Robert, 124
Sheehan, Neil, 115–16, 118–19, 122
Shinseki, Eric, 93
Shlaim, Ari, 127
Shultz, George P., 145
Silberman-Robb commission, 88
Simmons, Robert R., 129
Simon, Herbert A., 109
Singapore, 21; British premises regarding, 48; 1941 surprise attack on, 47–48
Skowronek, Stephen, 142
Slevin, Peter, 141
Slothuus, Rune, 110
Smoke, Richard, 62, 64, 72, 128–34
Sorensen, Theodore, 112, 126–27
South Korea, 55–77
Soviet Union, 13, 129; and Cuban Missile Crisis, 37–38, 52; and invasion of Afghanistan, 53; and Korean War, 56–65, 67–68, 71, 73; and Operation Barbarossa, xi, 9, 42–44; and pressure on Turkey, 18; and Vietnam War, 11–16, 24–26, 30–31, 35
Speer, Albert, 123
Stalin, Joseph: and Korean War, 57, 62, 107; and Operation Barbarossa, 42–44
Stanley, Matthew, 110
State, U.S. Department of, 18, 60; and Iraq War, 81–82, 90, 94, 96; and Korean War, 65, 116, 128; and Vietnam War, 18. *See also* Acheson, Dean; Powell, Colin; Rice, Condoleezza; Rusk, Dean
Stein, Janice Gross, 112, 127
Stimson, Henry, 36, 47
Stone, Peter, 137–39
stress, avoidance of in decision making, 4, 76–77, 104
Stueck, William, 128, 131–35
Summers, Harry G., Jr., 113, 123
surprise attacks, psychological basis for, 36–37. *See also* Afghanistan, Soviet invasion of; Arab-Israeli 1973 War; Korean War,

Chinese intervention in; Korean War, June 1950 attack; Kuwait, Iraq invasion of; Norway, German invasion of; Operation Barbarossa; Pearl Harbor, Japanese attack on; Philippines, Japanese 1941 attack on
Suskind, Ron, 135–36, 138, 140, 142–44

Taber, Charles S., 110–12, 145
Taiwan, 20, 63
Tang, Tsou, 131
Tatu, Michael, 115
Taylor, A. J. P., 106, 146
Taylor, Maxwell, 21
Taylor, Shelley E., 109
Tenet, George, 81, 85, 88–89, 100, 127–28, 135–36, 138–39, 142–44
Tetlock, Philip, 6, 112
Tet Offensive, U.S. premises regarding probability of, 52. *See also* motivated reasoning
Thailand, 18, 20, 46, 48
Thomson, James C., 114
Thórisdóttir, Hulda, 110
Trainor, Bernard, 90, 135–36, 139–42
Treverton, Gregory F., 128
Truman, Harry S.: as decision-maker, 56, 58–59, 61, 69, 74–77; and Korea, 55–77
Truman Doctrine, 18, 55, 60
Tuchman, Barbara, 2, 101–2, 109, 122, 124, 144–45
Tucker, Nancy Bernkopf, 114
Turkey, Truman Doctrine and, 18
Turley, William, 115
Tversky, Amos, 109–10, 146
Twomey, Steve, 124

United Nations, 56–57, 61, 74, 80
U.S. Institute of Peace, 94
USS *Chesapeake*, 39
USS *Cole* bombing, 70

VanDeMark, Brian, 119, 121
Vandenberg, Hoyt, 132
Vertzberger, Yaacov Y. I., 146
Viet Cong, 17, 22, 31
Viet Minh, 18–19
Vietnam War, ix–x; analogies, use of, and, 12–13, 16–18, 26–30, 34; assuming problem, x, 9–35, 101; civil war, views of,

16–17; Communist conspiracy, view of, and, 11, 13–23, 30–31, 33, 107; containing communism and, 13–14, 16–27, 33, 35; costs of, 11; deceiving public about, 29–30; decision-making process and, ix, 29–30, 33; domestic concern about, 26–30; domino theory and, 17–23; escalation of, 27, 31–32, 105, 107; failure to question premises underlying, 11–35, 108; fear of "losing" Vietnam and, 26–30; fear of provoking China and USSR and, 30–31, 33, 35, 106; Great Society and, 27–28; leeway in decision making about, 27–29; maintaining credibility and, 23–26, 105–6; outside experts, role of, 108; premises, impact of, on decisions, 32–35; premises underlying, 11–35; public opinion about, 28–29; resisting aggression and, 12–13, 23, 105–6; role of nationalism in, 14–17, 107; underestimating problems and, 33–35, 102, 107; wishful thinking about, 32, 105. *See also* motivated reasoning

Walker, Stephen G., 112, 113
Walt, Stephen, 139
War of 1812, 40
Watergate, 104
Wayne, Stephen J., 112
Westmoreland, William, 28, 120, 127
Whiting, Alan, 131
wishful thinking, 4, 32, 104–5. *See also* motivated reasoning
Wohlstetter, Roberta, 45–46, 48, 124–25
Wolfowitz, Paul, 91, 93
Wood, Gordon, 40, 123
Woods, Kevin, 138
Woodward, Bob, 97, 135, 138–40, 142–44
World Bank, 56
World Trade Organization, 56
World War I. *See* French military planning in World War I; German military planning in World War I
World War II. *See* Pearl Harbor, Japanese attack on; Philippines, Japanese 1941 attack on

Xue, Litai, 129, 131–32

Zaller, John R., 111
Zelikow, Phillip, 139
Zhou Enlai, 65–66
Zhukov, Georgi, 44
Zinni, Anthony, 139

Milton Keynes UK
Ingram Content Group UK Ltd.
UKHW042326091023
430247UK00003B/24